Christian Theology
A Case Method Approach

Christian Theology

A Case Method Approach

Editors
Robert A. Evans, Thomas D. Parker

Consulting Editors
Keith R. Bridston, John B. Cobb, Jr.,
Gordon D. Kaufman

Wipf & Stock
PUBLISHERS
Eugene, Oregon

Wipf and Stock Publishers
199 W 8th Ave, Suite 3
Eugene, OR 97401

Christian Theology
A Case Method Approach
Edited by Evans, Robert A. and Parker, Thomas D.

ISBN: 1-57910-842-3
Publication date 12/21/2001
Previously published by Harper and Row, 1976

To the Fellows and Staff of
the Case Study Institute 1971–1976

Contents

Preface

KEITH R. BRIDSTON

In *Two Modes of Thought: My Encounters with Science and Education* James Bryant Conant asserts: "To me . . . Langdell is to be placed among the great American inventors of the nineteenth century" (New York: Simon and Schuster, 1964, p. 45). Conant is referring to Christopher Columbus Langdell. He was appointed by President Charles W. Eliot of Harvard as the first Dean of the Law School in 1870. Conant says: "His invention was a pedagogic tool, not a material object to be sure. Yet . . . it became as revolutionary in its impact on the United States as, say, the McCormick reaper" (p. 33).

Langdell, whom President Eliot counted "a man of genius," introduced the case method into legal education. His principle was simple: "Law, considered as a science, consists of certain principles or doctrines. To have such a mastery of these as to be able to apply them with constant facility and certainty to the ever-tangled skein of human affairs, is what constitutes a true lawyer; and hence to acquire that mastery should be the business of every earnest student of the law" (from *A Selection of Cases on the Law of Contracts: With References and Citations Prepared for Use as a Textbook in Harvard Law School* [Boston: Little, Brown, 1871], quoted in Conant, p. 33). In order to attain mastery of these principles and doctrines of the law Langdell argues his new pedagogic method: since each doc-

---

KEITH R. BRIDSTON is Professor of Systematic Theology, Pacific Lutheran Seminary and was the founding Director of the CSI. He was educated at Yale University and Yale Divinity School, receiving his Ph.D. from the University of Edinburgh. His publications include being an editor of *Casebook on Church and Society* and author of *Mission, Myth and Reality*, and *Church Politics*. He is an ordained Lutheran pastor.

trine "has arrived at its present state by slow degrees . . . [and] is a growth, extending in many cases through the centuries . . . this growth is to be traced in the main through a series of cases; and much the shortest and the best if not the only way of mastering the doctrines effectually is by studying the cases in which it is embodied" (p. 46–47).

Professor Joseph Redlich, an eminent Austrian professor of law, in a report for the Carnegie Foundation for the Advancement of Teaching in 1913 on the method said: "Langdell's method created an extraordinary change, as it were at a single stroke. . . . The case method is an entirely original creation of the Americans in the realm of law. . . . It is indeed particularly noteworthy that this new creation of instruction in the common law sprang from the thought of a single man, Christopher Columbus Langdell, who, as the originator of this method, became the reformer of the Harvard Law School, and in this way of American university law schools in general" ("The Case Method in American Law Schools," bulletin no. 8; quoted in Conant, pp. 48–49).

The new method was not to be adopted without considerable resistance, even within Dean Langdell's own faculty. A new law school was organized as a direct protest to it. And it was not until 1890 that another institution, the Columbia Law School, adopted the case method. However, by 1908 when the Graduate School of Business Administration was organized at Harvard, the method had seemed to prove itself sufficiently for the new business school to take it over as the main pedagogic principle for its own program.

Almost sixty years later in 1967 the Episcopal Theological School in Cambridge celebrated its centennial year with a series of occasions to assess the present and look forward to the future. Under the administration of former Dean John B. Coburn and coordinated by Professor Owen C. Thomas, one of these events was a convocation of representatives of various professional schools to discuss the whole area of professional education in the twentieth century, the results of which were later published by the American Association of Theological Schools as a special edition of its journal *Theological Education* (Spring 1974). During the meeting I made a presentation of a case method for teaching theology which I had begun to use when I first began to teach in Indonesia in 1952 and later, in 1963 at the Pacific

Lutheran Theological Seminary with the collaboration of Rev. Otto Bremer, a Harvard Business School M.B.A., refined for my courses in systematic theology using essentially the HBS model. The reactions were mixed. Of course, the empirical-inductive method was not completely unfamiliar to the theological seminary world. The Clinical Pastoral Education movement with its clinical verbatims, the "contextual" approach of Professor Joseph Fletcher at ETS including the use of cases in the area of ethics, the field education and internship programs all reflected a case method philosophy. Only one book, however, dealt directly with the case method for theological teaching and referred to the Harvard model: Professor Wesner Fallaw's *The Case Method in Pastoral and Lay Education* published in 1963 (Philadelphia: Westminster Press).

In any event, the case method had not been employed in the three "classical" disciplines of Bible, history, and theology. One who challenged my approach was Professor Gordon Kaufman of the Harvard Divinity School. He doubted, he said, its applicability to such an abstract field as metaphysics, for example. This provoked an interesting discussion, including a supportive statement from Professor Harold Berman of the Harvard Law School asserting that the whole Bible might be considered a grand "case book."

When Walter D. Wagoner was Associate Dean of the Graduate Theological Union in Berkeley, we discussed the possibility of obtaining a grant to investigate the utility of the case method for theological teaching. It was not, however, until he became Director of the Boston Theological Institute that the actual proposal was formulated. He and Yorke Allen, Jr. of the Sealantic Fund, Inc. (both of whom participated in the ETS meeting) convened a small group, including representatives from the Harvard Business School, to consider a project. Eventually, underwritten by a generous grant from the Sealantic Fund and sponsored by the BTI and the American Association of Theological Schools, the Case Study Institute was launched in 1971, with myself as Director, Ms. Ann Meyers, formerly a researcher at HBS, as Associate Director, and Professor Fred K. Foulkes of HBS as Advisor. A major component in its program was a summer workshop conducted in collaboration with Harvard Business School staff to introduce theological teachers to the case method and train them in case writing and case teaching. Over 150 theological professors from the

United States and Canada representing almost every discipline will have graduated as Fellows of the CSI by the summer of 1976.

Professor Harold Berman, who served as a member of our advisory committee, was not entirely in agreement with the extent to which the Case Study Institute reflected the Harvard Business School system as its basic method model. On his insistence and under his guidance I attended classes and consulted with faculty members and students at the Harvard Law School. It was an illuminating experience and it bore out Professor Berman's contention that in some ways the legal model had peculiar affinities with theology insofar as both were bound to deal with cases involving history and tradition, precedent and authorities. The advisory committee's discussion of the report of my observations sparked Gordon Kaufman's interest—he was then a member of the committee. In a memo of March 5, 1973 he wrote: "I am really rather excited about the idea, which came out of the . . . discussion the other day, of how case method might be used for teaching theoretical concepts, i.e. by setting out a case then giving a series of analyses (or 'opinions') on it from different theological perspectives, which would show the way in which each of these perspectives deals with the relevant issues in the case. For the first time I am able to see a possibility of utilizing case method for complex theological issues, and I would like to see further discussion of this possibility developed. . . . It seems to me the objective of such preliminary discussion should be the development of a conception of a case book in theology which would directly implement this approach to the teaching of theology."

It was not until over a year later, after I had returned to Berkeley, that I was able to convene the small group he suggested. Supported by a grant through Dr. Jesse Ziegler of the Association of Theological Schools, Gordon Kaufman, Professor Robert Evans of McCormick Theological Seminary in Chicago, Professor John Cobb of Claremont, and I met at Claremont to discuss the project. The consensus corresponded fairly closely to the original proposal. Fortunately, Professor Evans would be at Harvard on his sabbatical and very generously agreed, together with his colleague Professor Thomas Parker of McCormick, to take on the formidable task of soliciting, collecting, and editing the material. Such is the genesis of this *Christian Theology: A Case Method Approach.*

Herbert Butterfield noted in his *Origins of Modern Science* (New York: Free Press, 1965) that intellectual and conceptual breakthroughs often seem deceptively simple when viewed retrospectively, from the other side of the divide. That is one reason for laying out some of the historical developments which led to the production of this book. The experimentation with case method in theology, particularly as that has been articulated through the Case Study Institute, has been a collegial adventure. But it is also true that certain individuals have been particularly instrumental in the success of the endeavor: Yorke Allen, Jr., Dr. Jesse Ziegler and the staff of the ATS, Dr. Walter D. Wagoner, under whose household umbrella of the BTI the Case Study Institute flourished, and Senior Associate Dean George F. F. Lombard of the Harvard Business School, who unfailingly supported, along with many of his colleagues, the fledgling enterprise. We are also particularly grateful for the financial support for this particular project provided by the curricular development program of the Association of Theological Schools and to Robert Lynn and the Lilly Endowment, Inc. for both encouragement and a special grant to make this project possible.

Christian Theology
A Case Method Approach

An Introduction for Students of Christian Theology

ROBERT A. EVANS

The nine cases contained in this work represent a variety of issues which call for a response: hunger and faith, language and commitment, doubt and death. A significant factor common to the cases is that each describes an actual slice of human life in the world. None of the cases is an imaginative illustration designed to undergird a point about to be or already made by an instructor in theology. Each case has been field researched and incorporates the actions, statements, and expressed feelings of the participants in these human dramas. The authors are trained case writers who seek not to interpose their own judgments and convictions into the situation. Though the cases are usually disguised in order to respect and protect the privacy of the persons and institutions involved, the participants, whenever possible, have approved and released their own cases.

However, a case, at least as it is employed in this book, is not simply a case history or a verbatim that includes either the entire range of background data or all the comments made on a given occasion. The selection of information focuses on specific issues or problems that require a response or a decision on the part of one or more participants in the case. Each of these cases is judged to reflect

---

ROBERT ALLEN EVANS is Professor of Philosophy of Religion and Applied Christianity, McCormick Theological Seminary, Chicago and Associate Director of the CSI Summer Workshop. He studied at Yale University, University of Edinburgh, the University of Basel and received his Ph.D. from Union Theological Seminary, New York. He is the author of *Intelligible and Responsible Talk About God, Belief and the Counter Culture*, and editor of *The Future of Philosophical Theology*. He is an ordained Presbyterian minister.

issues of sufficient human significance to merit analytic scrutiny and a quest for creative alternatives. Each case poses a problem with substantive ambiguity so that men and women of intelligence and sensitivity would genuinely disagree about what ought to be done. The case itself does not supply an answer or solution to the dilemma. Rather, the case focuses on a decision point—a decision concerning action and/or understanding. Both types of cases, for action or reflection, demand a response and seek to place the responsibility for that decision not only on the characters in the case, but also upon the participants studying the case. What stand would we take in a similar situation, and what reasons would we give for our decision? The focus in the case method is toward owning one's decisions and developing intelligible rationale for one's stance. For a moment the student is urged to suspend disbelief and be drawn into these segments of human life in the world.

The claim for credibility made possible by the insistence on authentic cases informs the vision which has motivated this particular work. The editors see their primary goal in bridging two gaps in theological education: (1) that between theory and practice, and (2) that between learned theology and owned or internalized theology. The need for this "bridging" is demonstrated in numerous situations in the parish, pastorate, and seminary.

The gap between theory and practice is illustrated in the persistent suspicion that the study of Christian doctrines and symbols, whether drawn from Scripture, tradition or experience, has little or no relation to the practice of ministry by clergy or laity. The creeds of the Church and the writings of theologians are often cited as prime examples of theological reflection which fail to illumine or inform concrete situations. It is the experience and consequent conviction of the editors that laypersons, pastors, and theological students alike are frequently surprised and excited with the connection between doctrine and experience, between articles of the creed and their regular routine, between theory and practice which emerge through an encounter with the case method approach to Christian theology.

Perhaps the potential for the case method is best documented through a means consistent with the approach by including brief excerpts from three occasions when a case employed in this book was taught in a parish, a continuing education program for pastors, and a seminary class. These "cases on cases" provide a paradigm of the problems, promises, and need for a case method approach.

"The unwillingness to deal with my own death, to put any concrete meaning to Christian hope in a life after death, never really came home to me until this discussion about the Grahams." So a father confessed to the assembled group of fifty parents and high school young people during a feedback session on their hour-long discussion of the case "Dance of Life." "What amazes me," he continued, "is that my daughter Susan seems to understand better than I do Mr. Graham's anger with God and yet his trust in his daughter's decision to go off the dialysis machine and give up her present life. Does that mean Susan's Christian faith is stronger than mine? Or that she is just more naive?"

Susan's father never received an answer to his question because an officer of the youth group broke into the discussion. " 'Dance of Death' would be a good title for our discussion this evening. We were half way through the hour before we took Sara's faith seriously. We danced around her death the way we dance around our own. I hear a number of us asking for a follow-up on this case, one that doesn't leave us hanging, but that identifies some resources of theology—resources of grace for the Grahams, the Church, and for ourselves."

Before the case teacher called for an adjournment of the discussion to the lounge, another student got in a parting shot: "I didn't think it was such a hot idea to invite our parents to join us in the discussion of cases like those we used on our spring retreat. But this discussion was better than I thought it would be. My parents were more understanding of Sara's sister Tracy in her reluctance to let Sara die than I would have imagined. Also, my Mom seems like a better theologian than my Dad. Anyway, if this is what theology can be, maybe it has a chance even in *our* church."

The week of continuing education for the twenty pastors of the regional conference was drawing to a close as one member of the group, experimenting with a newly acquired skill, taught his colleagues the case, "Give Us This Day Our Daily Bread." The case concentrates on Senator Berg seeking the advice of members of his house church on his vote for pending U.S. legislation for foreign aid through food distribution. Berg's basic choice was between a limited "triage" strategy for distributing food to the world's hungry versus legislation which allotted the aid on humanitarian grounds alone. The case had come to be affectionately nicknamed by the pastors:

"Berg on Bread." In the midst of the discussion one of the participants interrupted the flow of exchanges. She declared, "It is difficult for me to continue analyzing Berg's Christian responsibility and how he is informed on either option by Scripture and tradition, when what is tearing me up is a basic theological contradiction in *my* ministry to the poor in this city. Is it *possible* to follow the radical demands of Christ for obedience when you are in a position of power? The cunning of strategy, sometimes called stewardship, undercuts faith as radical trust. I am caught in a crisis of faith as much as Berg is, and the theologians at our denominational seminary are often no help at all."

"We have been struggling to apply directly simplistic concepts of 'obedience' and 'love' to international relations and urban problems on hunger," another pastor retorted. "The demand of Christ is to use theology to appropriate the Word, not simply transpose it. Theologians, including professors, pastors and people, have had a failure not only of nerve but of creativity, both of which are the gifts of the Spirit. We have not sought to explicate faith in relation to the human situation, but only profess it and confess it. The creed has lost its cutting edge."

Students filed out of the final session of the team-taught ecumenical seminar, "Nature of the Church: A Catholic-Protestant Dialogue," and headed for the apartment of their Jesuit professor for supper and an agape service. A Presbyterian student commented on the afternoon's case, a forerunner of "Proclaim the Good News," as they walked along. "The pastor in that case had no clear understanding of his ecclesiology. He couldn't implement mission priorities because he didn't have a clue how mission or sacraments fit together with the nature and purpose of the Church. And to be honest, I may have been in the same boat as that pastor had we not analyzed a case like this and shown concretely how our understanding of the Church would inform the options available to the pastor or the lay elder in this situation. Our analysis forced me either to abandon doctrine altogether or connect doctrine with practice. My Presbytery would be unable to live with the first alternative and I am now unwilling to settle for anything but the second."

A fellow student from the Roman Catholic diocesan seminary insisted, "At the beginning of the term I would have said a dispute between a pastor and a layperson over the conditions under which the Eucharist is served could easily be resolved along lines of authority. Now I am not so sure; there are more fundamental issues at stake. Perhaps our "Presbyterian Prof" was right about this church when he jokingly entitled this case "The Last Supper." My consideration of the pastor's problem with the Eucharist which failed to be a means of grace has given me a fresh appreciation for the sacramental richness of my own tradition." He pulled out the liturgy for the agape service, prepared by a joint committee of students representing the seminaries participating in the course, and said, "Initially I rebelled because it didn't seem possible for us to celebrate the Eucharist at the end of the course as *one* in the body of Christ. Though I still have some questions, I am now more comfortable with the agape service. I need to be clearer about the implications of joint celebration of the sacrament for both of our communions."

As a result of the case method, a group of parents and young people in a suburban congregation came to see the Apostles' Creed confession of the "life everlasting" as a relevant means for their understanding of life and death. A group of pastors, some of whom admitted that for them disciplined theological reflection was dormant, discovered that the initial declaration of the Creed, "I believe," held promise and power that *might* speak to their own crises of faith. They asked one another, "Is faith primarily radical trust or active response?" A group of seminarians realized that clarity as well as conviction about the doctrine of "the holy catholic church," in the language of the Creed, could radically affct the form and style of their own ministry even when unacknowledged. In each of these instances the case method became at least a starting point for spanning the apparent chasm between theory and practice in theology.

Another dimension of the vision for this project is to overcome the gap between learned and owned or internalized theology. In seminary tests and papers, ordination examinations and pastors' evaluations, even in parish study groups on Church pronouncements or encyclicals and books in contemporary theology the emphasis tends to be on the acquaintance and mastery of ideas and data, on *learned* theology. The primary criterion in each of these endeavors seems to be the accuracy with which one can grasp and articulate the theological insights of scripture, Church tradition, or leading contemporary theologians. Unfortunately, one often feels theologically competent if he or she cites and persuasively interprets the words of an authoritative theologian. However, it is difficult to tell whether one has made a decision and taken a stand so that theology becomes not only learned but also *owned*. Because this "owning" is hard to evaluate objectively, it is often neglected.

"Readiness for ministry," at any level of theological education, from seminary to church officer training, is frequently measured by articulated knowledge or demonstrable skills rather than the capacity to internalize and apply theological insights. Granted, the ability to take responsibility for one's faith commitments and understand critically and creatively the implications for ministry in word and deed has never been declared unimportant. However, this ability has been very difficult to discern in a classroom setting. No method seemed to be available that both reflected this priority for internalized, critical, theological reflection and at the same time provided a means to facilitate this very capacity or skill.

Initial experience with the case approach suggests that this may be a method many students and teachers of Christian theology can employ creatively in the "gap-spanning" quest. The three field-testing examples seem to confirm this hope. A father in the church sponsored, cross-generational case discussion moves from a nonthreatening discussion of Sara's death and the Christian meaning of "life after death" to a declaration about an unwillingness to deal with his own death or the impact of Christian hope on his life. A pastor interrupts the debate on Senator Berg's vote on food legislation to expose her own crisis of faith concerning the radical demand of Christ for obedience in her own ministry. Finally, the conflict over the celebration of the Eucharist becomes the occasion for a Protestant theological student to own a doctrine of the Church and struggle with its implications while a Roman Catholic colleague reconsiders his support of a joint celebration of the communion in an ecumenical setting.

Encounters such as these, representative of many other experiences of employing the case method, suggest that learned theology may be in the process of becoming an owned theology. With the case method as a catalyst, the distance between theory and practice may be shortened. It is too early to make a final evaluation of this experiment in theological education. The editors of this volume have sought to address both the promise and the problems discovered by those already involved in this method of teaching.

A short sketch of the distinctive factors involved in this project, i.e. a case method approach to the discipline of systematic theology, Christian doctrine or dogmatics, may supplement Professor Bridston's informative Preface on the genesis of the method and provide a helpful preamble to outlining the goals of this work.

An Experiment in Theological Education in Progress

This book contains not only the nine cases but also over thirty theological "briefs" or commentaries on the cases, prepared by distinguished theologians representing a wide variety of perspectives on Christian theology. It is the linking of the briefs with the cases which marks the distinctive component in this particular presentation of Christian theology. To understand more fully the unique dimension of this experiment in theological education one may need some clues as to how these cases could be studied and what role a critical examination of the briefs may play.

The primary pedagogical model (or in light of the work on adult education by scholars such as Malcolm Knowles, one could say *andragogical* model) for this project was not that of the Harvard Business School but of the Harvard Law School which had also pioneered in the use of the case method. It was believed that use of the legal model might compensate for one of the initial criticisms of the case method, namely, the lack of depth reflection from a theological perspective on a concrete human situation. Thus legal opinions offered in a court of law provided the original analogy for supplementing each theological case with several briefs prepared by different theologians. This new approach sought to combine the original advantage of an experientially based situation or case with the added dimension of critical reflection from a variety of perspectives.

Since the theological brief was an original experiment in the teaching of theology, since many of the respondents were not trained in the case method, and no one had previously written this particular type of brief, some guidelines were given to each theologian invited to respond to a case:

> A theological brief may be compared to a brief a lawyer might write or an opinion a judge might render concerning a case being tried in a court of law. It discerns salient issues raised by the case in relation to a particular article of faith, discusses them, and gives an opinion which helps foster an understanding of the case and form judgments about the issues raised. The purpose of such a brief is to enlarge understanding of both the article of belief and the way it informs thought and action in a life setting.
>
> A theological brief should indicate which decisions have theological

implications in relation to the article of faith being discussed, and (if possible) argue for a particular resolution of the problem. The "decision points" are more prominent in some cases than others, but all cases involve decisions made in the light of persons' understandings of themselves and their world which are theological at the root.

It is the hope of the editors that each student will also be in the process of formulating his or her own brief informed by one's own theological convictions. Thus the summary of advice given to the authors of the briefs contained in this work constitutes applicable guidelines for a student to facilitate theologizing. It would be helpful for a reader to outline a tentative brief of his or her own *before* reading the contributions of the responding theologians.

The briefs which follow each case were not intended to stand as unchallengeable authorities on the theological issues raised in the case or on the article of faith which they seek to address in the Creed. Nor are the briefs *necessarily* representative of a particular perspective on the Christian theology associated with a denomination, tradition, or position, although this was one goal of the initial invitations. Due to the freedom of the authors and prior commitments of some theologians which made them unable to participate in spite of their interest in the project, not all issues are covered in a strictly representative manner, and certainly no issue is dealt with in an exhaustive way. Rather, each brief is a thoughtful and sensitive response to a concrete human situation in light of a specific section of the Creed and rooted in the convictions of the responding theologian.

Since the invited theologians themselves often engage in constructive disagreement, both about the crucial issues raised by the cases and the decision or action which appears most prudent, the student of theology should feel liberated from any intimidation by the representative theologians. Each reader should be critical of the briefs in her or his own preparation and discussion of the case. The test of both the briefs one reads and the brief being developed by the student will be the clarity, logical consistency, and faithfulness to the Christian tradition reflected in one's own theological thinking. One's theologizing should be shaped and tested in a critical dialogue with the briefs.

One significant goal of this project was to provide a book which could be used as a supplementary text for theological seminaries on an ecumenical basis. Representatives from Conservative-Evangelical, Roman Catholic and Orthodox, and Liberal Protestant traditions were invited to prepare briefs. The book not only seeks to introduce a new pedagogical method for theology but encourages constructive dialogue between different theological perspectives. However, the text was designed to be *supplementary*, since many schools prefer a primary text that represents a position in concert with their tradition. It is our hope that this book eventually may also be employed to provide a common theological ground for future ecumenical and interconfessional dialogue among clergy, lay people, and seminarians. Students may be exposed to some representatives of other theological positions, not through the filter of their own professors, but directly as these representatives address themselves to a concrete human situation.

As a supplementary text this book does not pretend to fill the role of the sole or primary text for an introductory course in theology. It is not simply introductory, however, since the briefs, while seeking to avoid unnecessary technical language, often assume definitions of basic theological terms and acquaintance with fundamental doctrines and positions which must be supplied by a more comprehensive and systematic text or by the theological instructor. The best use of this text requires strong companions in the form of solid theological reference books and competent teachers.

This experiment in theological education is also more than introductory because the briefs are often only suggestive of a more developed and more clearly articulated view by the author of the brief. Thus each author was asked to submit a short list of annotated readings, including at least one work by him or herself, so students could pursue theological perspectives that interested or challenged them. This book seeks to be an experience and encounter with cases and briefs that will provoke creative and critical theological reflection on the part of the reader.

Although the work originated in the quest for a rich and responsible addition to a seminary or divinity school curriculum, it is clearly not limited to that field. As experience with the method and the "cases on cases" evidence, the book and certainly the case method approach appear applicable in college, university, and even high school courses in religion, in continuing education for pastors (particularly the in-service Doctor of Ministry programs), and in parish Christian education programs. The cases can be discussed at various levels of sophistication and application, from graduate school to youth groups. Some local pastors during field testing used the briefs as a resource to enrich their own theological reflection as case teachers but initially employed only the cases as the focus for discussion within the local church. Then reference was made to the availability of the briefs for those who wished to pursue their own theologizing further.

A discussion on teaching and learning by the case method is offered in an appendix which lists additional resources. Seminary students or pastors who are exposed to *Christian Theology: A Case Method Approach* encounter not only a method to increase their own theological capacity, but also a possible tool to employ in the forms of ministry for which they may be preparing.

Such a wide-ranging ecumenical and educational experiment as this seemed to argue for the establishment of a National Advisory Council composed of theologians associated with the major theological traditions and yet a group small enough in number to meet on a regional basis. This council was formed to assist in the selection of cases, contributors, and the briefs to be employed, as well as to provide advice, support, and critique to the editors. The names of the members of the National Advisory Council who gave their time and wisdom to this project are recognized in a list following the Introduction.

Some of the contributors to this volume share reservations and honest doubts whether the case method deserves the enthusiastic response that it has received by some members of the discipline or even whether it holds the promise proposed in this Introduction. Yet these theologians generously contributed their time, energy, and wisdom to the project in order that both the promises and problems of the method might be subjected to further and more comprehensive exploration in the seminary and the Church. The use of the case method for teaching theology is still experimental. The editors will welcome the suggestions, criticism, and revisions that students or teachers of theology wish to offer. A symbol that this experiment in theological education is in process and that the editors and Advisory Council seek your critique and suggestions is indicated by the response form included in this work. If further editions are warranted, it is our intent to supplement and revise both cases and briefs to be more serviceable to the needs of those teaching and learning to theologize.

Assumptions, Goals, and Limitations of the Theological Case Method

As noted in the Preface, cases have been employed in theological education prior to the explorations of the Case Study Institute, notably in the area of Christian ethics and practical theology. The distinctive dimension of the case method as it is utilized in this project is not only the use of the brief but also a particular style of case writing and case teaching. The field of Christian ethics has long used examples or cases in point. When such cases were taught as genuinely open-ended and not primarily as a means to authenticate or illustrate an ethical insight, principle, or methodology, and when the material was drawn from documented encounters, then we have a forerunner of the theological case method.

Another distinguishing factor is the characteristic decision-orientation of this case method, requiring some issue-focused selection of material, in contrast to the complete record of the verbatim so effectively used in practical theology, especially pastoral counseling. When this material was edited, so as to highlight a particular choice or turning point which demanded a response from counselor or client, then we had an illustration of and resource for the case approach as refined in what has been called the HBS (Harvard Business School) model. The cases in this book embody these distinctive features of case writing as adopted and developed by the Case Study Institute (CSI).

Although there is no canonized model for case writing or teaching among the graduates of the CSI workshops, there are some teaching assumptions and goals, as well as a declaration of limitations which might be helpful aids to the student of theological cases who may one day employ the method as a teaching tool.

1. Assumptions

A completed theological case could be compared to a well-written but condensed mystery story. All the appropriate clues are present. There is no hidden information known only to the teacher of the case. The only limitation on information is the same human one operating for the actual participants in the case. The aim of the case-oriented teaching style, which is one of the most distinctive elements in this approach, is to foster and facilitate the student's analytic and creative skills in the area of theological reflection. Accomplishment of this goal is based not only on skill and sensitivity of the case teacher, but on certain working assumptions about the pedagogical style as related to theology:

A. Skill-facilitating. The initial assumption is that the case method actually does facilitate analytical and creative theological skills. Many teaching methods demonstrate or point to the skills or capacities that one is to learn. The case method assumes that a person will actually grow and develop in his or her ability to analyze carefully and to create perceptive, imaginative alternatives for the participants in the case and for oneself. This working assumption has been confirmed by students and teachers who have experimented with theological cases. The accompanying implication discovered in this skill development is that both analysis and creativity are dependent upon and enriched by others. Perhaps this is best illustrated by the experience of many case teachers who find that a case they teach regularly is constantly changing and coming alive in new ways through the insights and perspectives of different students. So the teaching plan or note employed by most case instructors always demands revision as the instructor draws on and incorporates the theological discernment of students as well as his or her own research and reflection. What the Christian tradition has often called the community of faith appears for many to be an important resource in finding authentic, humane, and imaginative alternatives in a case situation.

B. Self-involving and Affirming. The second working assumption is that the case discussion, more than many other methods, will rely on the resources of the student in analyzing the problem, selecting a creative alternative, and developing a theological rationale for the form of action or understanding that he or she comes to own. Experience in seminaries and churches with the case method approach (comparing it to the use of role-playing, learning games, simulation) affirms the working assumption that this is one of the most self-involving pedagogical styles presently available in theological education. Participants find themselves drawn into a discussion of the case precisely because it seems to make contact with similar elements in their own experience. Also a case provides a nonthreatening point of entry into controversial discussion since one begins by sharing views about Sara Graham or Senator Berg and what she or he ought to do. After one is involved in the case discussion, a shift frequently occurs and participants share their own judgments and convictions. The responsibility for a decision frequently becomes an element of such involvement.

Another side of this working assumption shared by many case teachers and students is that a genuine trust is communicated, not only for the mutual contributions of student and teacher, but also for the personhood of others as they participate in this dialogical form of education. The case approach to teaching tends to confirm in a pedagogical style the biblical affirmation of creatures made in the image of God. Some theological traditions would also profess that this milieu of trust opens both student and instructor to the possibility of becoming resources of the Holy Spirit for one another. A type of self-affirmation can take place through the support and critique which emerge from the instructor as well as from the students' reciprocal responsiveness to judgments, insights, and feelings. From a cross-generational discussion in a suburban church to a seminary classroom setting, the case method assumes the mutual respect and critical appreciation of one another's humanity. This method bears the promise and potential of a self-involving and self-affirming reciprocal process which may call participants to be accountable to one another, to the richness of their theological traditions, and ultimately to the Christian God confessed in the Creed.

2. Goals

Whether or not they are specifically articulated, most educational experiments have both learning and teaching goals for what they hope to see occur in students. Each instructor will have his or her specific goals for using the method, depending on the particular context of the course of study. However, some advocates of the case approach to Christian theology have expressed goals which seek to aid theological reflection for ministry. Students are invited to share in and take responsibility for these educational expectations.

A. Wisdom. This term has a rich and multifaceted meaning in the Old and New Testaments as well as in the philosophical tradition, but a common goal for those seeking wisdom seems to be integration—the integration of knowledge, discernment, and action. The model employed here seeks a "bringing together" of the resources of the biblical and theological traditions with actual decision about, and understanding of, the reality of human life in the world. Cases function in at least two ways in relation to wisdom. First, they function as "catalysts" for theological thinking by posing the concrete issues in such a penetrating and demanding form that students often return to the biblical and theological resources with a new vitality and commitment. Cases that raise the issue of christology frequently motivate students to seek, on their own initiative, exegetical aids on the Gospel of John and historical or theological commentaries on the christological councils. Theological briefs contribute to this quest for wisdom by providing illustrations of the integrative process in theological reflection.

Second, for those seeking wisdom, the case may also function as an evaluative instrument in testing the degree to which integration has progressed. The earlier example of the seminary class on ecclesiology may illustrate the opportunity to test the degree of integration that has occurred. In this instance, each student had at some point summarized major learnings by sharing with the class an analysis of a new case in light of his or her own ecclesiology. The class evaluation session included specific recommendations for action with a defense of these alternatives on biblical and theological grounds.

If a student is consistently unable to make the connection between a doctrine of the Church and actual alternatives of understanding and action in ministry, then it seems appropriate to assume that the student has failed in at least one task of theological education. In such a case the instructor might also question the adequacy of the educational method employed. The aim to move toward wisdom in a sense of integration is one of the goals of this project as the theological briefs add both a catalytic and evaluative factor to the discussion.

B. Maturity. From Paul's first letter to the Corinthians (the second and third chapters) down through the generations of the community of faith. Christians have sought not only wisdom, especially the wisdom of God, but also maturity. It is, according to Paul, among the mature that one may impart wisdom. One dimension of Christian maturity is the ability to make decisions guided by faith and to take responsibility for the consequences of those decisions within the community of faith and beyond it. Preliminary data seems to affirm that the case method both forces and facilitates this theological "owning" process. It encourages participants to be more critical of their own theological assumptions and more open to hearing with critical appreciation the position taken by others from a different theological perspective. The cases and the briefs seem to test the adequacy of theological theories and doctrinal interpretations against experience. The method encourages interconfessional and interdisciplinary dialogue as one seeks Christion understanding that is mature enough to comprehend the theological pluralism in our midst and demanding enough to insist that one's own position be clearly articulated and tested in the community of interpretation that is constituted by the wider Christian Church.

C. Skill. No methodology or instructor can guarantee what will happen to a student or to the educational process as it develops. These are always unknown elements. Yet most teachers certainly expect more than exposure to ideas and methods. They expect a capacity or skill to develop. According to an address to the American Academy of Religion 1975 by Professor Thor Hall, reporting on a comprehensive survey being conducted on the discipline of systematic theology, there is a need for theology to recover its credibility. Perhaps part of the "credibility gap" results from the lack of attention given to developing and evaluating the analytical, critical, and creative capacities and skills of theological reflection. One facet of the task of the theological student and teacher is to develop discernment. The case method becomes a measure of and means to the goals of wisdom, maturity, and skill.

3. Limitations

Investment in any experiment in theological education involves commitment to and advocacy of the promise of the project. However, one cannot ignore the problems that also exist or one is no longer conducting an experiment. The editors of this text, with other professors and pastors, have been struggling to employ and improve the case method for teaching theology in seminary and parish for the last five years. Lest one give the impression that the case method is the panacea for teaching theology, we must identify some limitations of the method, as seen by those developing the approach, particularly since this project was in part conceived to address these limitations.

A. Lacks Depth. The case method may lack the dimension of critical depth in the teaching of theology when employed exclusively. Some courses in given institutions, such as the Harvard Business School, use the case method almost exclusively. It is often assumed by representatives of these institutions that the student will acquire on his or her own initiative and time the information or skills needed to address the cases. This philosophy tends to favor a pragmatic stress on the decision-making skill of the future professional. The focus is on a style of leadership, approach to decision making, and criteria for evaluation that are perhaps appropriate for the business executive or consultant but not appropriate for the pastor and theologian. The biblical and theological tradition plays a normative role in theological education. Therefore, the exclusive use of the case method in theology may lack critical depth in addressing specific issues and problems and gives insufficient attention to the resources of theology as they inform the discussion and decisions that surround a case.

In view of this limitation, the use of cases needs to be coordinated in some way with the study of the Bible and historic and contemporary resources of the Church, to name only some possible sources. The situations of case teaching cited in the Introduction and the problems evident there may illustrate this point. In the first "case on cases" the officer of the youth group is clear that the group should not be left hanging following this catalytic use of the case, "Dance of Life." His plea is to identify and further explore the resources of theology and the Church available not only hypothetically to the individuals in the case but actually to the participants in the case discussion. In reality this discussion was followed with a series of sessions on biblical and theological insights on death with appropriate study and a final case to assess what learnings may have occurred. In the second illustration alternatives and illumination, provided by additional theological and scientific perspectives, were pursued by the pastors' regional conference in a subsequent study. Consequently, these pastors came to aid one another in theological reflection more effectively than the house church members appeared to help. Senator Berg. Third, a seminarian in the ecclesiology seminar has recovered an appreciation for the sacramental tradition from which he came. However, that was a consequence of the catalytic and evaluative power of the case which motivated him to reexamine his own tradition from the creeds and councils to Küng and Dulles.

Krister Stendahl, speaking as a professor of New Testament, made this point in a different way when he addressed the CSI Summer Workshop in 1973. He noted that the first "case book" of the early Church was the Bible, particularly the Pauline epistles. Paul did not write general theology to a general reader; he drew on the resources of his theological experience and tradition to address and illumine particular problems for a particular group of people. A significant danger of the case method is that one may get so absorbed in the variety of issues posed and so excited about the degree of involvement in a case, that the level of focused reflection and thus of genuinely new insights, sometimes described as a dimension of revelation, may be overlooked and/or underestimated. If the method is going to have a dimension of critical depth, it demands students who will assume responsibility to probe and investigate materials beyond the case.

The means selected in this project to relate theological resources and insights to a case is through a legal rather than managerial model. The added component in the exploration of the use of case method in theology is the theological brief. The task of the brief is to apply directly the resources available to theology, from the perspective of the theologian writing the brief, the problem or issue described. This provides theological resources which the teacher and student can use in understanding the situation. Student and teacher must build on these resources if the limitation of critical depth is to be overcome.

B. Hides Assumptions. The method may hide implicit value judgments. Unless the case teacher is skilled and very self-conscious about the method, it bears the potential of being manipulative. This controlling may be less evident because the method tends to affirm student involvement and contribution as well as focus on the concerns, interests, and insights of the class. However, the case teacher and students often have basic theological assumptions and criteria operating that influence their recommendations. Instructors and students experienced in the method urge that ways be sought to make these assumptions explicit either through an introductory lecture by the instructor or opportunities for students and instructor to share during the case discussion. The point can be illustrated by a discussion with one of the instructors at Harvard Business School when one editor was inquiring about the criteria employed for evaluating a proposed program to solve a dilemma in a business case. The response was that there were no predetermined criteria for an acceptable solution apart from the content and boundaries of the particular case. The editor's experience in the Harvard Business School sessions, however, has not confirmed this instructor's claim. Rather, there appeared to be an assumed business "trinity" which was implicitly operative in almost every business case this editor observed: profitability, efficiency, and growth. This is not necessarily objectionable if these criteria are surfaced and critically examined. If not, the case study method has the potential of being a much more subtle and powerful form of indoctrination than lecture and discussion methods.

For the method to be an effective instrument in preparation for ministry, care must be taken by both student and instructor to examine the presuppositions involved in the analysis of a case. Case teaching experience suggests that at least a working definition of what is meant by terms such as *life after death*, *responsibility*, and *evangelism* is crucial in guarding against implicit value judgments that shape one's learning through a case. A list of suggested questions to consider while studying a case or a small study group that meets prior to the general discussion are two possible ways to offset this limitation. The theological briefs in this volume also seek to expose some of these implicit value judgments in order that they may be critically and appreciatively considered. The limitations of implicit value judgments (not unique to the case method) can never be completely overcome, but they may be modified through the process of self-conscious and consistent exposure. This discussion of limitations and efforts toward compensation brings us to a brief description of the plan of this edition.

Theology and the Creed

As the idea of this book developed in the initial consultations, several alternatives appeared as a means to shape the project. Three basic criteria of theological accountability emerged: (1) faithfulness to the biblical witness; (2) responsibility to the diversity of theological traditions represented by the respondents; and (3) commitment to the importance of mature theological reflection for ministry. The project was originally described as "Systematic Theology and the Case-Study Method." Some members of the National Advisory Council argued that "systematic theology" had a prescriptive rather than a descriptive connotation among some of the institutions and churches that might seek to apply this approach to the teaching of theology. "Christian Theology: A Case Method Approach" appears more adequately to reflect the original intent of the project.

No single agreed-upon definition for theology seemed possible for this project, or, indeed, for any other project of comparable scope. This is due to the variety of starting points and resources that might be argued as appropriate for Christian theology. The sources for Christian theology and their relative authority has been vigorously debated in the history of theology up to the present time. The author of a theological brief may emerge with different recommendations partially because he or she draws upon one of the traditional sources of theology such as the Bible, revelation, tradition, experience, or reason. Another author may base judgments on a combination of sources or on other resources altogether. Clear criteria and the relative degree of authority cannot be assigned in advance; rather, these become factors in theological reflection.

However, some working assumptions do need to be articulated, both in order to be explicit, rather than covert, and to be self-critical. To recognize the historic pluralism of theological positions does not condemn one to saying nothing about the nature of the theological task; after all, every responsible position tries to do justice to several basic structural elements. Disciplined reflection, some understanding of human life in the world, and an affirmation of Christian faith in God shape this enterprise. It is hard to imagine a Christian theology which takes another faith as its normative perspective, fails to take account of the phenomena of human life in the world, or disdains disciplined reflection. The way in which these primary elements are understood varies greatly; this is the seed of our theological diversity and dialogue. These are issues to be illumined in the discussion of cases and briefs, under the guidance of the case teacher representing a particular theological tradition. They are not issues to be decided beforehand by the coordinators of the project.

Long ago Calvin noted that the Bible could be likened to a pair of spectacles. Wearing them the believer could form correct judgments about the relation of God and humankind, for example. Perhaps theology functions in an analogous way in this project so that disciplined reflection like that contained in the briefs will function as spectacles through which one views the issues raised in the discussion of the case. The actual cases have a crucial role as the focus for disciplined reflection and discussion. If the theologian devotes most of his or her time to examining the spectacles of faith, the materials that make up the lenses, or how they are ground, then one is not likely to see much else very clearly. And if one is as nearsighted as some of us, he or she is liable to fall down. Also if there are no spectacles for those who hope for better vision or if the prescription is not adjusted periodically, then the reality of the world is blurred or out of focus. However, if theology is one of the aids provided for looking at the reality of human life in the world from the standpoint of Christian faith in God, then student and teacher alike may on occasion see more clearly, more sharply, with the eyes of faith through the spectacles of theology.

The cases in this book involve persons related to the community of faith reflecting on a problem or issue posed by the reality of human life in the world. The cases also tend to concentrate on decisions posed for individuals. This is partially the result of actual data for cases presently available. This fact was also influenced by the primary audience originally projected for the book, members of the seminary and the Church community. However, the content of these nine cases should not imply that all the editors or the contributors think theology is limited to the Church or to what one editor called "Christian folk thinking." Even the working outline of theology given in the Introduction suggests a broader understanding. Nor should the immediate focus on the individual presuppose a privatization of experience. The decisions initially posed to individuals have communal and sometimes cosmic dimensions as some respondents have argued in their briefs and thus have criticized the selection of cases. The cases selected for this volume were never intended to be exhaustive of the doctrinal issues in the creed. Rather, they were chosen on the basis of actual case material available and because they functioned as stimulating points of entry for theological discussion of a particular theme. It would perhaps have been more helpful to have several cases for each section, but every experiment has practical limitations.

Members of the advisory council selected the Apostles' Creed as an organizing principle for the topics to be discussed. This format is not intended to prescribe belief but to describe it. The Apostles' Creed served in the earlier Church to identify key issues or articles of Christian belief that were thought to be faithful to the biblical witness; it was concise enough to function as a basic outline for Christian confession. Since the Creed was selected primarily for thematic rather than doctrinal reasons, no hidden bias for a confessional approach to Christian theology is implied. Some traditions represented by respondents and students do not accept a normative role for any creed, and none is intended. The advisory council debated the use of this creed as opposed to some others. The Apostles' Creed was ultimately chosen because of its historic link with the ancient Church, its relative simplicity and conciseness in identifying articles of belief, and its widespread use in worship and study in local congregations. It also represents the traditional order of theological *loci* and so provides a link to the works of theologians in the past.

The Creed was divided into nine sections for the purposes of study. As an introduction to each of these sections, Editor Thomas D. Parker provides a short sketch of biblical and historical background for the development of various articles, noting an ecumenical consensus or a divergence where one exists. Following this same thematic division of the Creed, several authors were commissioned to prepare cases. Field research, interviews, numerous revisions of cases through consultation with case participants, other case writers and theologians, and a final authorization from the case participants resulted in the nine cases contained in this volume. The National Advisory Council, meeting on a regional basis, made recommendations concerning those theologians to be invited to prepare briefs. Approximately 60 percent of our invitations were accepted with many scholars declining the invitation due to other commitments, but expressing interest in and support for the project. Not all cases originally commissioned nor the first draft of most briefs invited are employed in the finished work. This is one of the consequences of an experimental procedure.

In conclusion, the editors would like to declare their indebtedness to those who helped in numerous ways to prepare the manuscript for publication: Shirley Dudley, Sylvia Gill, Dianne Strickert, and the editorial staff of Harper & Row. The project is offered to students and teachers of theology for their use, critique, and improvement.

The National Advisory Council

The Apostles' Creed

I believe in God the Father Almighty, Maker of Heaven and earth,

And in Jesus Christ his only Son our Lord; who was conceived by the Holy Spirit, born of the Virgin Mary, suffered under Pontius Pilate, was crucified, dead, and buried; he descended into hell; the third day he rose again from the dead; he ascended into heaven, and sits on the right hand of God the Father Almighty; from there he shall come to judge the living and the dead.

I believe in the Holy Spirit; the holy catholic church; the communion of saints; the forgiveness of sins; the resurrection of the body; and the life everlasting.

Amen.

Although not written by the apostles, the Creed uses ancient formulas throughout. The form in which it now appears stems from about 700 A.D. Its predecessors include the interrogatory creed of Hippolytus (c. 215), the creed submitted by Marcellus to Julius I (340) and the creed mentioned by Rufinus (c. 404), based on the usage of the church at Aquileia. There are many variants of the basic creedal form. Our present Apostles' Creed is the successor of a creed used at Rome, and while not as universal as the Creed of Nicea (325; revised at Constantinople in 381) is simpler and more widely used in the Western churches.

1

"I Believe In"

Theological Introduction

THOMAS D. PARKER

Credo is the first word in the Apostles' Creed. It sets the tone for everything which follows: faith in the one God, Father, Son and Spirit, faith which believes the Church and confesses forgiveness of sins and good hope for humankind.

The "I" (the subject who believes) is a universal "I," the believer as believer, whatever her or his particular character or circumstances. As such, the creed could be said by any Christian as a profession of personal faith at baptism or as a confession of faith by the community of faith during public worship. The Niceno-Constantinopolitan Creed (381) substitutes "we" for the "I" of the Apostles' Creed because its primary use was liturgical and educational, rather than as a personal statement at baptism.

"I believe in . . ." is a response to the gospel. In the New Testament there are several kinds of *credo* statements. Sometimes the word faith is used in an absolute sense, without any object, as when Jesus confirms that the works of the Kingdom take place "according to

---

THOMAS D. PARKER is Professor of Systematic Theology at McCormick Theological Seminary, Chicago, and a Fellow of the CSI. He studied at Los Angeles State College, San Francisco Theological Seminary, the University of Munich, and Princeton Theological Seminary where he received his Ph.D. He is the author of scholarly articles. He is an ordained Presbyterian minister.

your faith" (Mark 5:34, et al.). Other times a *credo* statement has some specific content, as the confession of Peter (Mark 8:29). In the Johannine and Pauline literature faith is a personal response: recognition of Jesus as the Christ and trust in the work of God accomplished in him (cf. Rom. 10:9, John 3:16, 14:1).

Faith has both an objective and a subjective reference. It involves recognizing something presented and responding positively to it. Faith is an "assurance" and "conviction" about something which transcends ordinary knowledge (Heb. 11:1–3, 6; 1:1–2). During the long course of Christian thinking about faith, these two references have been explored at length. Subsequent confessions have included chapters on revelation and authority on the one hand (objective faith) and chapters on the nature of faith and its relation to works of love on the other (subjective faith). The former treat the "what" in which I believe, the latter the "I" who believes.

In both Roman Catholic and Protestant statements faith receives what is given by revelation, guaranteed by authority, and offered for belief with a promise of blessing attached. There are many questions to be dealt with, of course, such as whether the contents of revelation are also reasonable, where authority is located, and the measure of personal responsibility for assent to the truths of faith. In general, statements of belief are thought to be consistent with reason, although not derived from autonomous rational processes. God has added positive witness to natural reason and insured that we encounter it by enshrining it in Scripture and proclamation faithful to Scripture. For some, this is guaranteed by the teaching office of the Church, and for others by the inward persuasion of the Spirit. Most would agree in addition that our destiny is determined by what is declared to us as the truth about God and God's will for humankind.

The faith which receives revelation modifies human existence; it is not just an intellectual exercise. A confessional statement of this principle is found in the Lutheran Augsburg Confession (1530):

> Whoever knows that in Christ he has a gracious God, truly knows God, calls upon him, and is not, like the heathen, without God. . . . Therefore . . . the Scriptures speak of faith but do not mean by it such knowledge as the devil and ungodly men possess. . . . When through faith the Holy Spirit is given, the heart is moved to do good works.

Here faith is an orientation of the self which makes everything new, a conviction which transforms the life of the one convinced. As with the objective side of faith, treatments of the subjective side move into disputed questions. Some Christian communions place more stress on the intellect, and therefore on the rational capacity of will and the need for spiritual aid and support to believe. In the nineteenth century an interpretation of faith in terms of fundamental disposition (feeling) developed and became very influential among some Christians.

As the theological tradition concerning faith grew, the original biblical and liturgical statements were set into highly detailed texts to be used for tests of orthodoxy and standards for teaching. "Whoever would be saved," the Athanasian Creed (5th or 6th c.) runs, "must, above all, keep the Catholic faith." In addition later statements often specified certain acts to be Christian responses to various social and political issues. Faith in this expanded sense includes not only personal trust and acceptance of the Christian message, but also specific actions which express that commitment as well.

Some churches, reacting to this use of theology as a test for belief or morale, are self-consciously noncreedal. While Christian belief is assumed, no particular formal statements are demanded even of the clergy. Even in churches maintaining a strong confessional position, the latitude of interpretation varies widely, as does the way the relation between the historical contents of faith and the personal-communal appropriation of faith is understood. Some of the most significant divergencies among Christian communities in our time stem from the way the meaning of faith is differently understood.

Give Us This Day Our Daily Bread

In the judgment of Senator Berg (D-Ala.) sharply differing responses to human extremity loomed behind the dry prose of the bills now before the committee. The conditions addressed were the same to be sure. Witness after witness, thirty-four in all, had profiled a grim consensus: a continuing population explosion until at least the year 2000, declining food production and natural resources, sharply rising costs for energy and critical technology, and a virtually nonexistent international strategy. Senator Berg's conclusion was as clear and certain to him as any piece of history could be: even doing its best the world community in the next decade would experience the death of millions from starvation and from malnutrition-related diseases. The question was how to respond. And on that the bills differed markedly.

By actual count thirteen bills on food aid had been submitted. A number were identical, however, so the content shook down effectively into only two distinct proposals for legislative deliberation. The first as summarized by the Bill Status Center of the Congress read as follows:

This case was prepared by Professor Larry L. Rasmussen of Wesley Theological Seminary as a basis for class discussion rather than to illustrate either effective or ineffective handling of the situation.

LARRY L. RASMUSSEN is Professor of Christian Social Ethics at Wesley Theological Seminary, Washington, D.C. and a Fellow of the CSI. He studied at St. Olaf College, Luther Theological Seminary, and received his Th.D. from Union Theological Seminary (New York). He is the author of *Dietrich Bonhoeffer: Reality and Resistance* and coauthor of *Bible and Ethics in the Christian Life*. He is a member of the American Lutheran Church.

Re: S. 455 S. 697 S. 2429 S. 2677 S. 3173 S. 6453
S. 6744 S. 7224 S. 7227 S. 8145.
Bills to prohibit, except in cases of extreme emergency, assistance under the Agricultural Trade Development and Assistance Act of 1954* to any country which does not make reasonable and productive efforts, especially with regard to family planning, designed to alleviate the causes of the need for assistance provided under such Act.

The Bill Status Center reported the second set of bills as follows:

Re: S. 610 S. 3033 S. 3121.
Bills to amend the Agricultural Trade Development and Assistance Act of 1954 to provide the United States with flexibility to carry out the national interest or humanitarian objectives of that Act.

The committee staff itself summarized the various amendments of the second set as falling into two categories: (1) amendments providing mechanisms that would have the effect of increasing by approximately 20–25 percent the U.S. food available for concessional sales and donations; (2) amendments providing stipulations that no less than 30 percent of the food aid in any given year be allocated on humanitarian grounds alone.

In addition to the bills already submitted for committee endorsement, witnesses representing an alliance of U.S. voluntary relief agencies informed the committee of a proposal for which they were presently seeking congressional sponsorship in the form of legislation. The proposal read as follows:

For each of the fiscal years 1977–80 the Food for Peace Program shall provide commodities and revenues in an amount equal to not less than 1.5% of the U.S. Gross National Product for the respective year.† These commodities and revenues shall be used for short-term relief of, and long-term solution to, world hunger, malnutrition, and their related causes and manifestations. Disposition of commodities and revenues shall be made on the basis of need alone, without respect to race, creed,

* The Agricultural Trade Development and Assistance Act, Public Law 480, is more commonly known as the Food for Peace Program. It consists of Title I "Concessional Sales" and Title II "Donations."

† Total foreign aid including food aid comprised 0.21% of the U.S. GNP in 1974.

color, nationality, or political persuasion. Recipients will be selected in accord with the United Nations' determination of Most Affected Nations.

In the senator's interpretation the first set of bills, with the stipulation of population policy, could be understood as approaching the course advocated by some of the witnesses, a course known as "food triage."* No matter how desperate the conditions, the U.S. would grant food aid only to viable nations willing to make an effective move toward bringing population under control.

Initially the senator found the population stipulation and all talk of "food triage" repugnant—and certainly unthinkable as national policy. Yet, he reflected, in the face of genuine triage conditions might it not in fact be the necessary course of hardheaded, but genuinely compassionate, responsibility? The witnesses had been compelling in their argument that wherever population is out of control and resources in critically short supply, food only feeds the next famine and aid only multiplies the human tragedy. In any case, the senator thought, the most moral outcome was surely the policy that produced the most humane conditions for the largest portion of the human family over the long term.

Still, the senator mused, there was something so utterly, intrinsically right about the second set of bills—and the relief agencies' proposal—in their unqualified response to sheer human need, whatever the outcome. And they weren't oblivious to long-range outcome. It was just that they didn't make probable success, or effectiveness, or viability, or anything else a condition for relief.

These preoccupying thoughts soon became the center of conversa-

* "Food Triage" was described to the committee as a policy analogous to medical aid triage. The latter was used in the Allied tents during World War I to determine priority in the treatment of the wounded. Three groups were designated: (1) those likely to die regardless of what was done; (2) those likely to live even without treatment; (3) those who might survive if attended immediately. With limited supplies, facilities and personnel, the third group was the only one treated. Triage meant, then, the determination of who it was that received limited critical resources when demand exceeded all available supply. In the case of the first set of bills, the stipulation on population control was a way, its supporters argued, of moving an overpopulated nation in dire need of food away from the certain fate of the first group to that of the third, and eventually the second.

tion as the senator hosted the regular Wednesday gathering of the "house church" to which the Bergs belonged. The debate over the amendments had pushed up against issues that were at the core of the faith, or so it seemed to the senator. Didn't the gospel mean taking no thought for the morrow, responding without qualification or delay to stark human need? And to those in gravest need first, without expectation of return? Didn't it mean faith as simple trust, doing what one must do as a Christian and leaving the course of history, the long-term, in God's hands? Or did the gospel mean sitting down and counting the costs, keeping watch on the common good and trying to do what could be done to make history come out right? Didn't it mean faith as stewardship, ourselves as God's agents bearing responsibility for the direction and outcome of events? Wasn't the Kingdom to be "built," at least in some measure?

Of course, the senator noted in passing, the decision on the proposed bills involved considerably more than the answers to these questions. There were other factors besides personal religious convictions. Still, wasn't there a meaning at the heart of the faith that at least set the terms of responsibility here? The query passed unanswered as the group closed with a silent sharing of bread and wine and with the Lord's Prayer: ". . . Give us this day our daily bread. And forgive us our trespasses as we forgive . . ."

As best the legislative assistant could judge, Senator Berg's vote might well be the tie-breaker as the committee decided which bill—S. 455 or S. 610—would be placed before the full Senate. No clear mandate had come from the Alabama constituency; very little mail had been received on this issue. It probably mattered little, however, as the senator could not help but feel this was one of those issues on which the citizenry expected less a reflection of its thinking than a direction for it. It was a time to lead.

At ten o'clock the Senate Select Committee on Nutrition and Human Needs convened. The roll call began immediately. "Senator Berg."

Theological Briefs

JACQUES ELLUL

The case proposed is characteristic of the numerous questions that present themselves to the Christian in real life and which remain by necessity without a satisfactory answer. It is impossible to find a Christian answer, since both options are after all equally valid, without counting the one that would say that since God accomplishes all things, we can "limit" ourselves—if we really believe—to praying without doing anything more, for God to give to everyone his daily bread. But the very fact that there is no satisfying Christian solution should make us understand certain aspects of faith.

1. To begin with, the revelation of God in Jesus Christ is not a means of resolving problems present in our societies. This revelation is a question asked about our lives and not an answer to our questions. It is even more impossible to draw from it a general system of answers. This has been attempted since the third century in "Christendom" and always results in failure. "Christianity" as an intellectual, philosophical, economic, etc., system can pretend to offer solutions, but there is then no more authentic faithfulness to revelation. There are no "Christian politics," nor is there a "Christian economic system." Nevertheless, to the extent that faith is faith in Jesus Christ *incarnate*, this faith must transfer itself to the social, political, and

---

Brief is translated by Elvire Hilgert, Assistant Librarian, McCormick Theological Seminary.

JACQUES ELLUL is Professor of Law and Government, University of Bordeaux and widely read lay theologian of the Reformed Church of France. He was educated at the University of Bordeaux where he received his doctorate in law. Among his publications in English translation are *The Technological Society*, *Violence: Reflections from a Christian Perspective*, and *Presence of the Kingdom*.

economic planes, but it is we, each one with his own specific options, who must find our own answer: one is concerned with the incarnation of one's faith, therefore with a work, and as such with expressing one's liberty in Christ. There is no objectively Christian work; one cannot refer accomplishments back to God. To say "I believe" involves at the same time committing oneself to some realization of faith. However for each of our works we must implore the forgiveness and the grace of God, even if we are convinced this work is just.

2. There is evidently opposition between the "I believe" which in the singular is a personal commitment of the individual and an expression of that which is deepest in the individual, and the establishment of a law which has a general character valid for all and implies a collective commitment. The difficulty here stems from the fact that Christians can propose a law, the contents of which in their eyes conforms to the Bible or to Christian morality, but this law must be observed and applied by people who are not Christian, who therefore do not have the same motives for accepting one particular attitude. There can be no legislation and no morality directly inspired from faith in the God of Jesus Christ, because the conduct this implies presupposes exactly this faith. Otherwise, if we are looking for a rule of conduct that would be acceptable to all, Christians and non-Christians, we are obliged to say that this rule of conduct is no more Christian than anything else. It can be very interesting, just, useful, effective, etc., but it does not express faith. Therefore, if Christians by the means of witness (or even of martyrdom) should proclaim the love of God in Jesus Christ, they do not have (contrary to what, unfortunately, the Church has done for centuries) the right to implore by constraint a certain type of morality or style of life upon people who are not Christians.

3. This appears all the more clearly if we take with complete seriousness the demand made by faith to be for others what God has been for us in Jesus Christ. In the case of assistance to one's neighbor (specifically collective assistance), this must express the love of Jesus Christ, to love as Jesus Christ loves us. Consequently, we are talking about the complete commitment of oneself, expressed by this assistance which will therefore be as limitless as the action of the "Good Samaritan"—assistance without conditions, without reservations, and expecting no gratitude. (The action of God in Jesus Christ is free,

expresses grace, and takes place without man's having to fulfill any conditions.) This assistance presumes that there is no domination over others, no pressure. This assistance must not be a means of exercising power over or guidance toward those one helps. Christian love implies no superiority. The common attitude during the nineteenth century of the Christians who gave to oblige people to come to church, or to convince them of the superiority of Christianity, is unacceptable. Finally, this assistance presumes total absence of judgment of others.

However, if we take all these presuppositions seriously, it will mean that the project of assistance to the Third World will have to be based on complete abnegation, the forgetting of personal interests (even legitimate ones), free giving, and Non-Power.* Can we, as Christians, require that non-Christians have this same attitude? Can we, if we have enough influence, impose upon them this kind of conduct? It would show a lack of love toward them. What is more, such conduct presumes great risk. What we call "the risk of faith" is not only intellectual and spiritual, it is also very concretely the risk of losing one's life (that is to say all that makes it possible to live, on the material level). Can we therefore ask a collective group without faith (and no collective group, not even the Church, has faith!) to assume such a risk? So that there is for the Christian no possibility to mitigate the radical requirement of faith. One cannot seek a midpoint, a solution in the middle, etc.

4. Can one say under these conditions that there is nothing Christians should do on the social or collective level? Of course not! But Christians (i.e., those who confess authentically, "I believe," and not those who are only listed on church rolls), belong to a society in which are represented all tendencies: ideological, political, etc. These Christians represent in society one of the streams that runs through it. For non-Christians this would be a current qualified as "political." However, Christians must bear witness to something else: they must

* There is here an essential distinction between Non-Power and Powerlessness. Non-Power is on the part of one who can do something, but who voluntarily decides not to do it, of one who has the power to decide not to exercise that power. Example: at the time of his arrest, Jesus said, "If I wished it, twelve legions of angels would come to fight for me." But he decides not to do it. The choice of Non-Power is symbolized by the Christmas Birth.

present the absolute demands made by faith with regard to each question that arises. They do not exercise power (and do not have to think they ought to), but they must introduce an element of intransigence, of radicalism in each discussion. For example, in the debate about aid to the Third World it is evident that for a Christian the percentage of 1.5 of the gross national product is not enough. In the same way, real assistance should come from an economic reconversion of developed countries and a reduction in the consumption of unnecessary products, such as a reduction in waste. In other words, Christians need not choose between two or three "reasonable" solutions. Christians must present the radical demands of faith, must take a prophetic stance in debate in such a way as to lead gradually public opinion to a deeper and more serious consciousness, which will allow then for the elaboration of a more effective system of assistance. It is not at the level of laws, but at that of the elaboration of opinion that Christians must act. But while doing this, one must remember that faith is not an opinion, where one might be concerned about winning a debate through argument; faith concerns itself with winning through witnessing.

5. The last point one should comment on is the question of the "building of the Kingdom of God." It is true that the Christian cannot limit him or herself to immediate assistance, without preoccupying him or herself with the future. The Christian must remember that this future of potential, radical starvation is foreseeable sociologically only if the individual does not act. (For example, my expectations or those at M.I.T. are probable only if no intervention of liberty takes place.) The Christian must constantly call upon persons to act without becoming discouraged and to make their own history. But planning and long-term forecasting are not the same as "building the Kingdom of God": This latter is the work of God alone who makes use, when and how He wants to, of our works. Through our works, in fact, we put at the disposal of God materials so that *He* performs the miracle of the Kingdom of Heaven (just as the loaves and fishes were brought to Jesus in the account of the multiplication of loaves). Our efforts to build the future are therefore not a coming of the Kingdom of God (which would be the result of historical evolution), but are only the most reasonable choice so that the history of man could continue, and that is all. Therefore, in each case we may have

to make decisions differing in nature, but each time these will express the reality that faith is a renewed decision.

If I were in Senator Berg's situation (but I am not!), I would answer under my own name supporting unconditional assistance without discrimination. But at that moment, to the extent to which such assistance would involve far-reaching consequences, I would be engaged in a much larger movement, which I would probably have to begin myself. In fact, it is not possible to visualize, given this option, assistance that would merely be "charitable," allowing populations to avoid just barely starving to death. There would have to be the possibility for these peoples to improve their own situation themselves. This is only possible if two conditions exist: first of all, *political nonintervention* within these people, the willingness to let them take their own destiny into their own hands, and to provide them simply with the necessary means without influencing them (accepting inevitable wastefulness and political orientations which do not please us); secondly, an *economic reconversion of the United States*, to produce fewer products that raise the standard of living within the country itself and more products needed by the Third World. I have absolutely no illusions, however, about the success of such a project. It is a very long-term task to bring about a psychological reconversion first of all of a way of thinking. I believe that in the United States, this could be built upon a renewal of the proclamation of the gospel.

Selected Bibliography

Dietrich Bonhoeffer, *Ethics* (New York: The Macmillan Co., 1962). One of the first studies attempting to base ethical decision upon the tension between the radicality of faith and the contingency of the situation as it exists. Turns ethics in a new direction.

Jacques Ellul, *Ethics of Freedom* (Grand Rapids: Wm. B. Eerdmans Publishing Co., 1976). Tries to show how Christian liberty can be the foundation of a kind of ethics, which then presupposes a re-examination of all "constructed" ethics.

Paul Ramsey, *Basic Christian Ethics* (New York: Charles Scribner's Sons, 1950). This may not be one of the most important books on ethics, but it is illustrative of the conflict between traditional and newer interpretations concerning a "lived" decision.

SCHUBERT M. OGDEN

The case before us effectively raises a question about the meaning of Christian faith that many persons today no doubt take to be important. This is the question whether such faith is to be understood as essentially passive to God's activity, and thus as the "simple trust" that is content to leave the long-term course of history in his hands; or whether faith is more appropriately understood as essentially active, in that it is believers themselves who as "God's agents" bear responsibility for the direction and outcome of historical events. Of course, one might be inclined to reply that the alternative as thus formulated is false, because Christian faith is rightly understood only as somehow essentially both—passive response to the activity of God *and* active working together with him for the liberation of the world. But the task then is to make clear exactly how and why it is both; and to do this we need to approach an answer to our question by way of some more basic considerations as to the nature of Christian faith.

Whatever else it may be or involve, Christian faith is faith in God. As such it is an understanding of oneself as a human being in the world in relation to the encompassing mystery of our existence—namely, *that* understanding according to which this final mystery itself is understood to be the boundless love whose gift and demand to humankind are decisively revealed in Jesus Christ through the witness of the Christian church. In other words, the question of faith necessarily presupposed by the Christian witness and by faith in the God whom it attests is, at bottom, the universally human question of the true understanding of our existence. To ask this "existential" question of truth, as every human being does and must simply by existing as human, is at least implicitly to ask the question of faith in God to which the Christian witness claims to represent the decisive answer.

SCHUBERT M. OGDEN is Professor of Theology and the Director of the Graduate Program in Religion, Perkins School of Theology, Southern Methodist University. He was educated at Ohio Wesleyan University, John Hopkins Univerversity, and received his Ph.D. from the University of Chicago. He is the editor and translator of *Existence and Faith: Shorter Writings of Rudolf Bultmann*, and the author of *Christ Without Myth* and *The Reality of God*. He is an ordained Methodist minister.

Because, however, Christian faith exists at all only as an *understanding* of one's existence, it is always *belief that* God is, as well as *belief in* God, as the Christian witness attests him; and, to the extent that the understanding of faith becomes explicit, the belief that God is must be explicated in the form of certain propositions that faith as such holds to be true. Even so, Christian faith is never a merely theoretical matter of holding certain propositions—even the most orthodox propositions—to be true, nor is it ever simply the belief *that* God is of which such propositions are the more or less adequate explication. On the contrary, Christian faith is always the eminently practical matter of belief *in* God as he is decisively revealed through the church's witness to Jesus; and this means that it goes beyond the mere belief that God is by being a certain way of existing in the world in relation to God as the ultimate mystery of our existence that Jesus reveals as all-embracing love.

But exactly what way of existing is the way of Christian faith? The answer, I submit, is that it is the way which involves both *trust* in God's love as the only ultimate ground of the being and meaning of all things and *loyalty* to the cause of God's love as the only cause to which we should finally be committed. And this, of course, is why Christian faith by its very nature involves both a passive and an active moment—both trusting acceptance of the *gift* of God's love, without which neither we nor the world would either be at all or have any final meaning, and loyal obedience to the *demand* of God's love that we shall love both ourselves and all our fellow creatures in our returning love for God. This, at any rate, is the understanding of faith implied by Paul when he describes the "new creation" that is Christian existence as "faith working through love" (Gal. 5:6; cf. 2 Cor. 5:17 and Gal. 6:15). For the love of one's neighbor as oneself that Paul affirms to be "the fulfilling of the law" (Rom. 13:10) is the active moment of faith itself as the fidelity to God's cause that is grounded in confidence in his love.

The alternative as formulated *is* false, then, insofar as Christian faith itself and by its very nature is loyalty to God's cause to create and redeem man and the world, as well as trust in his love as the sole ultimate ground of all things. But, more than that, there neither is nor can be any rivalry or conflict between the activity of God in which faith trusts and the activity of believers themselves insofar as they are loyal to God's cause. As often as Christians may have spoken and acted as though God and his creatures are rivals—as though God can or does do what creatures alone can do, or *vice versa*—the whole meaning of Christian faith demands the contrary conclusion. For, in creating the world, and preeminently in creating man and woman, God creates free beings who both are and, in the case of human beings, are called to be cocreators with him in the ongoing work of creation. Therefore, God's activity as Creator neither does nor can do what his creatures can and should do for themselves and one another but, precisely as the activity of his love, restricts itself to establishing and maintaining the necessary conditions of the possibility of their own creative activity. Likewise, in redeeming the world and human beings from their bondage to decay by embracing all things into his own everlasting life, God does nothing that any creature does or even can do for itself or its fellow creatures. Indeed, the only thing that conflicts with God's activity as Redeemer—and even that he lovingly suffers—is the sinful striving of human beings somehow to redeem themselves; and, so far from being a proper human activity, such striving is the very thing that keeps our activity from being truly human by so binding us to ourselves and the world that we are not really free to act for them.

There is no question, then, of Christian faith's leaving even the long-term course of history in God's hands, if that means declining the responsibility for the direction and outcome of events that human beings are created and called to assume. What faith trustingly looks to God to do is not what men and women can and loyally must do themselves if it is to be done at all but only what God alone can and does do so that faith working through love is possible and the labor of faith is not in vain. In this trust in God's creative and redemptive activity, the Christian can and, in loyalty, should assume responsibility to work together with God for the world's liberation—for the freedom of all creatures from every evil and injustice that oppresses them, and that means for the freedom of all human beings from the evils of hunger and starvation and from the structures of injustice of which they are the effects.

This is not to say, however, that Christian faith as such would dictate support for one instead of the other of the two kinds of legislation discussed in the case. Granted that the Christian can rightly pray, "Give us this day our daily bread," only by assuming, not declining, responsibility to see that every human being is adequately fed, there is more than one way of assuming this responsibility. As a matter of fact, the act of sincerely and reflectively praying this petition is itself a way of being thus responsible. For Christian prayer is not a way of instructing God but a way of instructing ourselves and our fellowmen—a means of grace by which we and they may become more fully conscious of the gift and demand of God's love in its meaning for our lives. Thus, in becoming more conscious of our common human need for daily bread and of the responsibility God lays upon each of us to meet this need, we are already acting in an important way to assume that responsibility.

Somewhat similarly, the act of supporting a bill that would make U.S. food aid available on humanitarian grounds alone and without conditions could be a way of raising the national consciousness of the demand of God that the need of every human being for daily bread be met. Not unlike the act of the conscientious objector who bears witness to peace by refusing to bear arms, such an act, regardless of its other consequences, could bear witness to love as the only finally adequate response to men's need for food. And yet the faith that works through love cannot be indifferent to consequences, nor can it ignore the conditions under which love must always realize such good as is then and there possible. Consequently, another way of assuming responsibility for human hunger could be to recognize that conditions are such as to make some form of "food triage" imperative, and thus to support the other kind of bill that would make U.S. aid conditional on the population policies and actions of any country receiving it.

The essential point, in any case, is that Christian faith as such cannot save us as believers from the kind of agonizing decisions with which Senator Berg was confronted. For faith itself is one thing, what faith demands of us here and now in the way of specific words and deeds, something else. The only thing we can be sure of is that faith always demands our loyalty to God's cause that the whole world shall be free and that we can always so trust in his limitless love as to learn from every need that confronts us what he would have us do.

SELECTED BIBLIOGRAPHY

Rudolf Bultmann and Arthur Weiser, "Πιστεύω κτλ.," *Theological Dictionary of the New Testament*, ed. Gerhard Friedrich (Grand Rapids: Wm. B. Eerdmans Publishing Co., 1968), vol. 6, pp. 174–228. This definitive article on "faith" in the New Testament lays the exegetical foundations for any adequate theological interpretation of the concept.

Gerhard Ebeling, *The Nature of Faith* (Philadelphia: Muhlenberg Press, 1961). By explicating "the essence of Christian faith" in its several aspects, Ebeling provides, *in nuce*, a complete systematic theology.

H. Richard Niebuhr, *Radical Monotheism and Western Culture* (New York: Harper & Bros., 1960). Niebuhr's analysis of faith as both "trust" and "loyalty" and his interpretation of "faith in gods and in God" are classics of twentieth-century Protestant theology.

Schubert M. Ogden, *The Reality of God and Other Essays* (New York: Harper & Row, 1966). The title essay develops an argument for "the reality of God" by way of an argument for "the reality of faith."

HEINRICH OTT

1. Senator Berg understands the decision with which he is involved as a politician to be a decision of faith. He discusses it with fellow believers. He views it in the light of the message of the Gosepel. He experiences it in the perspective of the Eucharist. Secular decision has become for him a question of faith. Now this is in harmony with the nature of faith. Faith toward God in Christ is not something outside and alongside our daily decisions and our normal life. It is not just a religious feeling or experience, or even an acceptance of statements of belief as being true. In short, faith is not something that allows itself

---

Brief is translated by Dr. Earle Hilgert, Professor of Bibliography, McCormick Theological Seminary.

HEINRICH OTT is Professor of Systematic Theology, University of Basel. He studied at the University of Marburg and the University of Basel where he received his D.Theol. His publications in English translation include *Theology and Preaching*, *God*, and *Reality and Faith: The Theological Legacy of Dietrich Bonhoeffer*. He is an ordained pastor of the Reformed Church in Switzerland.

to be defined and considered in isolation from our daily, decision-fraught existence. Rather, faith is fulfilled in and through our concrete life as active persons, with all its decisions and attitudes. The Apostle Paul's contrast of a life on the basis of faith and a life on the basis of the works of the law means that the grounds on which persons live are different (trust in God or trust in self!). This contradicts in no way the basic fact that faith is never real and effective except in human action.

Certainly the decision with which Senator Berg sees himself confronted as a Christian is an important one. Such decisions, in which it is possible to exercise leadership and also to set standards for others, at best come infrequently in the life of a Christian. But other decisions of lesser scope (how we relate to our fellowmen, what we make of our own lives) in principle have the same structure. They too should be viewed by Christians in the light of the Gospel.

2. What decision should Senator Berg make? Before I set down the basis of my personal position as a theologian, in order to avoid misunderstanding it is important to note one specification. From a theological point of view, there is no *one* right solution to the problem so that one might say every other solution rests on unbelief or hypocrisy. Rather, often (though not *always*!) in analogous situations Christians can reach differing decisions with integrity and faith. Here the word of the Apostle applies: "Who are you to pass judgment on the servant of another? It is before his own master that he stands or falls" (Rom. 14:4 RSV). God alone is judge of the consciences of his servants. This is the reason that theological considerations concerning the practical authentication of faith in concrete situations of living and deciding have nothing to do with legal casuistry. The case study also makes this plain, in that both options, as the senator ponders them, appear to be tenable for a Christian.

Therefore in what follows, I can only set forth how I would decide if I were in the senator's place, and offer the reasons that I would give for my decision, reasons drawn from the nature of faith.

3. First of all, we must call to mind here some of the essential characteristics of faith. Faith is a decision, a venture. According to Hebrews 11:1, it is "being convinced" of the unseen, of the invisible reality of God, which indeed cannot be demonstrated conclusively. Only with an existential commitment of one's whole person, which actually en-

compasses and determines one's whole life, can one be aware of this unseen reality and ground oneself in it. This is why in the New Testament faith is called *pistis*, trust: it is a decision of fundamental trust.

Of course, such a decision is by no means purely arbitrary. It does not take risks blindly. Rather, faith is also a perception. It is at once decision and perception. When a person dares to live on the basis of the unseen, to draw strength and standards not from the visible world, but from the invisible reality of God, to focus on a word of promise (the Gospel of Christ), then he or she achieves a new perception. This provides no new information concerning things, but is, as it were, a new vision of reality as a whole. The entire horizon of one's understanding of the world, of his or her experience of the world, is changed. Perception of God in faith does not consist of receiving additional information about God in the way that one can become better informed regarding any particular being in the world. Such a concept would "objectify" God to the status of a being in the world along with other beings; God would be an object along with other objects, no longer the transcendent Creator of the world. The perception of God in faith consists rather in our seeing the whole world and our own lives differently in the light of God.

At the same time, this change in our understanding and experience of the world does not happen at one stroke and once for all; it must authenticate itself ever anew, step by step in individual decisions—as, for instance, in the political decision of Senator Berg. The faith that is oriented toward the invisible God and his promise is always threatened by a purely secular point of view, which orients itself exclusively toward visible data and subjective assessment.

4. We must also be clear, however, that the believer, with trust in the invisible God, must live at the same time in the world of visible facts. One cannot simply ignore or negate rational assessment in dealing with that which is seen. For instance, intentionally to refuse to consult a physician in a case of serious illness, in order to rely instead on the miraculous power of God to heal, is to pervert faith and make it superstition. Faith, in its subjective decision and authentication does not exclude the use of reason, but includes it.

Rational assessment has only an ancillary, instrumental function in a person's dealing with the reality that surrounds him or her. Only seldom and in narrow areas of reality does such assessment go forward smoothly and unequivocally. Most of the "cases" we encounter remain doubtful and their outcome cannot be forecast with certainty. The stream of ultimately unfathomable reality is very much broader than that narrow rivulet of reality concerning which we can calculate with mathematical certainty. One has only to think of the unfathomableness of man, of the fact that he is not at his own disposal.

In every doubtful case (and such constitute not the narrow border but the broad midsection of the reality that is relevant for us!) reason must be consulted. For example, even in doubtful cases a physician will offer diagnosis and prognosis. Reason, however, is not self-sufficient; it requires a superordinate orientation; it craves, so to speak, a "higher reason."

We must agree that the case with which Senator Berg is faced is an equivocal one. In spite of the knowledge of all the experts, the course of history and the development of the world situation in coming decades cannot be predicted with certainty. Too many social and political (in short, human) imponderables are involved.

5. It is a fact of experience that reason craves a superordinate orientation. Everyday we experience the unexpected, the unfathomableness and frustration of life. One possible superordinate orientation of reason (or a "higher reason") is faith in the reality of the invisible God who has manifested himself in Jesus Christ.

With this we return to our thesis: the perception of God in faith is a new seeing, a new perceiving of reality as a whole "in the light of God." But what does this mean in concrete terms? The vision of reality by faith sees all reality "in the hands of God," and this means that for believers all reality has, so to speak, a broad margin of hope, of a future not yet come, of that which is not fixed. But hope is also directed toward a final goal, toward a final fulfillment, a final meaning. To the eyes of faith the rolls of reality are not yet sealed. This applies to the world as a whole as well as to the fate of individuals and groups. Everything is still open, open to the final determination, open, in the words of Jesus, to the Kingdom of God.

Faith's vision of the world does not consist in that which is thoroughly reckonable on the one hand, and that which is blind, meaningless, and based in chance on the other. Rather, we have only that abiding openness of reality as a whole to its ultimate future, fulfilled in meaning. And it is just this view of faith that can be authenticated in the decisions of life. For this reason I propose that Senator Berg should vote in favor of Law S. 610, which anticipates giving help without preconditions to starving peoples. By this means he will bear a witness of faith, love, and hope in an equivocal situation, and in so doing will provide a superordinate orientation for the rational deliberations that must be engaged in as the law is put into effect.

In closing I would like to point out that faith, love, and hope (cf. 1 Cor. 13) are not three different attitudes; rather, they constitute one single whole. Our case shows this clearly: the witness of faith *consists* in a decision of love on the one hand (a decision in favor of concrete persons), and of hope on the other (in that we give our decision of love a chance because we know reality is in the hand of God).

SELECTED BIBLIOGRAPHY

Gerhard Ebeling, *God and Word* (Philadelphia: Fortress Press, 1957). Faith is a "Word-event."

Heinrich Ott, *God* (Richmond: John Knox Press, 1975). Faith is a personal act of trust in a personal God.

Paul Schütz, *Wie ist Glaube möglich?* (Hamburg: Furche Verlag, 1974). Faith is the risk of freedom which goes beyond all rational systems.

PAUL PEACHEY

Why should Senator Berg have thought that his "house church" could help him reach a decision on the food bill in the first place? Certainly world food supply and "triage" are technical questions

PAUL PEACHEY is Associate Professor and past Chairman of the Department of Sociology, The Catholic University of America. He has studied at Eastern Mennonite College, University of Pennsylvania, and received his Ph.D. from the University of Zurich. He is the author of *The Church in the City* and *Who is My Neighbor?* and the editor of *Biblical Realism Confronts the Nation*. He has been executive secretary of the Church Peace Mission and taken on assignments from the Mennonite Central Committee.

which must be handled by experts, and by public officials with political experience. Furthermore, neither the churches nor the biblical sources speak unambiguously, even on moral questions. To be sure, the particular petition here before us, "Give us this day our daily bread," is a phrase of extraordinary moral and spiritual power. But by no means can it be taken as a summation of the biblical word. Indeed there are other utterances with which it stands in apparent contradiction. An important example is the charge said to have been given to our first parents: "Be fruitful, multiply, fill the earth and subdue it."

Paradoxically, the latter statement, though older, appears more contemporary in spirit. It sketches a breathtaking scenario—men and women placed in charge of the earth and its resources. "Man makes himself!" modern social and behavioral thinkers like to say. Yet in subsequent writings, notably in the New Testament, that early heroic vision seemingly falls into eclipse. The doers and the shakers, the builders of cities and empires, are suspect. In their place the servant figure or the desert hermit is often idealized. The petitioner in the prayer of the Lord seems more in keeping with this latter ideal—humble, obsequious, waiting to be fed rather than sallying forth to make the earth do his bidding. Nietzsche, the nineteenth-century critic of the faith, seemingly caught this incongruity in his denunciation of Christianity as "slave morality." One can understand how in a subsistence economy, where people are subject to the vagaries of famine and catastrophe, one can only hope and pray. But how is twentieth-century man to draw inspiration from such an ethos? Surely another theological idiom must be found!

The Bill S. 455 fits into a world where man makes himself. The tools now exist to close the gap between resources and want. If meanwhile there must be want, even starvation, let it at least be purposeful! To bring population growth within the bounds of available food resources is not only rational, but in the end, compassionate as well. To feed surplus population today in the name of compassion may condemn the many who will be born as a result to greater suffering a decade or two later. Indeed, one can argue the principle of good stewardship. Resources in any case are finite. "Triage" may be the most responsible way to manage them.

Why, then, did the voluntary agencies, among them presumably church organizations, advocate S. 610, a bill which appeared indifferent to such considerations? Were the agencies themselves a vested interest? Perhaps. But that may be too simple an answer. Furthermore, Senator Berg is himself pulled in that direction as well. The matter thus demands further reflection. Is there something amiss with the "triage" argument? Is it the premise or the logic that is flawed?

It takes little effort, of course, to discover serious difficulties with the triage thesis. Our century has been cursed with man-made catastrophes which were produced by triagelike policies, by regimes or revolutionaries ready to sacrifice those now living in the name of the happiness of the unborn. War, revolution, genocide, deportation, forced modernization and more—all have been justified by the claim that present sacrifice will preempt infinitely greater suffering in the future. To be sure, noble sentiments and ideals may at times have been involved, or, on the other hand, tragedy and "inevitability." Important moral distinctions would always be needed in a case by case evaluation. But the record stands as a clear warning: beware when the seekers or wielders of power sacrifice persons now living for some vague and future state which is surrounded by ambiguities and contingencies!

But obviously even so sobering an historical record affords no clear guide in the determination of Senate food policies. Taking responsibility for the consequences of our action, and hence calculation, surely belongs to responsible moral conduct. Firmer ground for decision must surely be sought. In these few paragraphs it would be presumptuous to expect such a ground to be adequately laid. Nonetheless, an examination of the seeming contradiction between the human posture sketched in Genesis 1 and that which appears in the petition for daily bread in the prayer of the Lord, may provide some important clues. When we view these two statements side by side, is the *mastery* motif in the former implicit as well in the *submission* motif of the latter, and vice versa, or are the two motifs incommensurable?

Some critics of the impact of Western civilization on the balance of nature and the earth's resources blame the biblical tradition for inculcating a rapacious character, the outlook expressed most eloquently in the Genesis text. Hence the exploitative outlook which does not hesitate to rape the earth for the gratification of a single generation!

Not only technological rape, but aggression, war, imperialism, and the like reached unprecedented scope under those societies most intensively under biblical tutelage. Some Christians have taken the opposite position. Western civilization, they say, has reached its superior achievements by virtue of the Christian faith. These achievements testify to the truth and virtue of that faith. Though each of these claims may seek to prove too much, it would be hard to deny that the biblical materials have been a ferment in Western history, whether or not they were properly assimilated.

Jesus, of course, at various points in his life and teaching appealed to the "beginning" as he called men and women to renewal and liberation. In fact he insisted that his was a work of fulfillment rather than of supplanting. But does he endorse the Genesis mandate? Does it enjoy priority among his concerns? Does he in the end play "grace" against "nature," if the use of this ancient pair of concepts is permitted? The question is acute, since *renunciation* rather than *control* appears to be his preoccupation. Certainly the bulldozer operator, clearing a jungle for the arts of gardening, may also pray, "Give us this day our daily bread." Yet we would forgive him if he turned to Genesis 1 for biblical inspiration rather than to Matthew 6.

In the end we must take seriously Jesus' own claim that he comes to fulfill, not to abrogate. Renunciation and humility, trust and moderation, then are qualities which temper our exercise of dominion in the earth. Jesus mercilessly exposed the rationalizations and pretensions that circle like vultures around social positions of high esteem. Advocates of "triage" who might argue, "Let's not feed those who do not contribute to the solution of the problem of want as we see it," would hardly have fared kindly in Jesus' scrutiny. This is not to say that long-range planning or population control as such would stand under his condemnation. But he does provide basic models of responsibility and obedience. More decisively than any other, Jesus is able to defer immediate rewards for remote ends. But he does what is required of him here and now, entrusting the future with its contingencies to the Father who controls it. Release from a mistaken notion of responsibility for that indeterminate future is an aspect of the freedom which Jesus proclaimed. Undoubtedly his ability to trust the Father with regard to future contingencies was an important source of personal power and humility in Jesus. Freed from such anxieties he had the resources to act responsibly in the here and now. "Sufficient unto the day is the evil thereof."

For which bill should the senator have voted? If the alternatives were in fact as stark as they appear in the account, one can hope that the argument of the voluntary agencies won out. Fortunately, however, the tasks of feeding the hungry and of addressing questions of population policy need not be mutually exclusive. But here the question of the senator's "house church," and of the worshiping congregation to which it may have belonged, appears more critical. Is that church a center of committed inquiry within which the bases emerge on which not only a congressman but all members reach responsible decisions? Is it a context within which the amazing tensions of biblical faith generate responsible Christian obedience? Is it a community which lives and acts in the spirit of the petition for daily bread, because it is freed from disbelieving anxieties concerning the uncontrollable future?

Selected Bibliography

Hendrikus Berkhof, *Christ the Meaning of History* (Richmond: John Knox Press, 1966). Berkhof sums up critically the christological discussion of recent decades. The treatment is helpful as background in efforts to understand God's rule as Creator and Savior.

Oscar Cullmann, *Salvation in History* (New York: Harper & Row, 1967). Cullmann revitalized eschatological thought in recent decades by locating Christian existence in an *already/not yet* tension. This study, coming late in his career, benefits from the criticism which his work elicited, and his own maturity.

H. I. Marrou, *Time and Timeliness* (New York: Sheed & Ward, 1969). Brief historical "homilies" by the distinguished patristic scholar at the Sorbonne, a Roman Catholic. Several brief essays bear rather directly on the present topic.

Jürgen Moltmann, *The Gospel of Liberation* (Waco, Texas: Word Books, 1973). The theologian "of hope" leaves the lecture hall for the pulpit, and the result is many vibrant lines, which may well sustain the likes of Senator Berg.

2

"God the Father Almighty"

Theological Introduction

THOMAS D. PARKER

The first article of the Creed names God according to ancient Christian usage. Jesus is reported to have used the name *father* for God in his own prayers, in his parables and in his teaching about prayer. The Lord's Prayer, itself an adaptation of a Jewish table blessing, addresses "our Father in heaven," and the first Christians regularly prayed, "Abba, Father." To confess faith in God as "father" draws on the most intimate sources of the life of faith, where expression pours forth prior to any doctrinal or creedal formula.

There is a long tradition of confessing God as father to his people, to all humankind and even to all creatures. In the Hebrew Scriptures the designation is very common, along with "lord" and "king," although God was also likened to a mother, a husband, or some nurturing animal as well. The term *father* indicated superiority in dignity and power, but also nurturing and caring. For the New Testament, God was first of all "Father of our Lord Jesus Christ," and then father of us all. For both Testaments the One from whom all things flow and on which they depend for life and breath is the One to whom all are related most intimately, i.e., as father. In cultures where the father occupied the central position of authority, such identification expressed the most significant relation conceivable. In our time many do not find the term so helpful in clearly expressing their living faith.

Yet God was believed to be not just father *per se,* but the Father Almighty or All-governing (*pantokrator*). The adjective indicated the singularity of the One who is Father, an absolute superiority in dignity and power, really incomparable to any merely earthly fathers. God is the Father "from whom the whole family in heaven and earth is named" (Eph. 3:15). In the Nicene Creed the unity of God and God's transcendence as all-governing has the effect of heightening those traditional meanings of *father* which stress origin, authority, power over life and death, and the like. The effect of such theological language is to affirm some qualities in God while at the same time denying literal, finite meanings of those qualities.

From earliest days, Christian thinkers were acutely aware of the necessity and inadequacy of their formulations with respect to the One God. On the one hand, God was confessed to be beyond all human thought, an ineffable mystery to be adored and contemplated by the soul without words. On the other, the One God was revealed through the Word incarnate in Jesus Christ and in the words of the prophets and apostles about him. To fail to attribute love, mercy, and justice to God was to fail to take this revelation seriously. But to fail to see the utter impossibility of any words adequately to define who and what God is was blasphemy. "From everlasting to everlasting thou art God" forever distinguishes the idols of our imagination, always easy to describe, from the One God, Creator, Lord, and Redeemer.

Official theological statements expanding the first article exhibit the ambiguity of language about God. The statement of the Fourth Lateran Council (1215) may stand for many others:

> We firmly believe and confess without qualification that there is only one true God, eternal, immense, unchangeable, incomprehensible, omnipotent, and indescribable, the Father, Son, and Holy Spirit; . . . they are all one substance, equally great, equally all-powerful, equally eternal; they are the one and only principle of all things.

In other documents, words like wise, holy, free, loving, gracious, just, long-suffering, and forgiving are used to ascribe various attributes to God at the same time that God's incomprehensible and eternal transcendence over anything we might otherwise call wise, holy, etc. is asserted. God is compared and contrasted with creatures by saying what God is not (e.g., not finite, infinite) or what God is in absolute measure (e.g., most wise). The use of any such terms is, of course, a major theological problem. Classical theology often resolved this problem by the notion that any language about God was based on that of which God is the cause in creatures (e.g., wisdom).

The distinctive mark of Christian faith in God, however, is not which of the several ways of speaking about God in relation to creatures it finds most adequate, but its trinitarian view. With the exception of some noncreedal churches, almost all Christian churches are trinitarian in some form or other. In this context "God is Father" does not refer directly to God's relation to us, but to the relation of the "persons" of the Trinity. Father is one of three *hypostases* ("persons") in the one essence of God. Thus God as Father is eternally generating God as Word or Son and is the fountain of the Trinity from whom the Spirit eternally proceeds.

In the period of intense theological reflection on the persons of the Trinity, it was often acknowledged (e.g., by Gregory of Nazianzus) that terms like *father, generate, proceed* and the like indicated real distinctions in God without being strictly metaphorical. In this discussion "God the Father" became a structural concept rather than one whose content is shaped by the content of human parenting. The importance of the term *father* is that it relates the biblical symbols to theological reflection about God entailed by Christian belief.

From Exodus to Exile

Anna Holmes had come a long way in her spiritual struggle, but she wondered whether her journey meant involvement with the church and whether the church were open enough for her to take the next step. She was contemplating whether or not to seek standing in her former denomination as a candidate for ordination.

Her Background

Anna came from an upper-middle-class family in central Massachusetts. She had attended and loved church as she grew up, but she said, "By the middle of my high school years, I experienced the Church as oppressive to women, as a place to preach war, criticize alcoholics, and relate socially."

"I had experiential, emotional, and moral reasons for leaving the Church, so I became a Unitarian—in part to find a unifying principle and in part to find room to think. It was in that state of mind, really seeking, that I came to Harvard in 1971."

This case was prepared by Professor Meredith B. Handspicker of Andover Newton Theological School as a basis for class discussion rather than to illustrate effective or ineffective handling of the situation.

MEREDITH B. HANDSPICKER is Professor of Practical Theology, Andover Newton Theological School and Director of the CSI Summer Workshop. He was educated at Bates College, Yale Divinity School, and received his Ph.D. from Yale University. He is the author of numerous scholarly articles and cases and is a contributor to *Casebook in Church and Society*. He is an ordained minister of the United Church of Christ.

Harvard Experience

Anna felt encouraged when she arrived at Harvard Divinity School by the number of woman students with whom she could associate. In the fall soon after she entered, the Boston Theological Institute's Women's Coalition and the NOW Task Force on Women and Religion sponsored a talk by Betty Farians, the Director of the Women's Coalition. "It was a catalytic event," Anna said. "It inspired us women to organize and get ourselves together.

"Shortly after that, Mary Daly told several of us that she had been invited to preach in Harvard Memorial Church.* I think it was the first time a woman had been asked to preach there. At any rate, Mary wanted to plan that event with other women so that it would be a political event.

"We had several meetings together, and she shared her perspective and wisdom with us. We encouraged her to do what her instincts indicated. Finally, we agreed that we would make some kind of political statement out of it by inviting women who knew what was at stake to come and participate.

"At our second meeting Mary shared her desire to make it an Exodus time: a time to talk about the sexist history and dimensions of the church in its language, theology, and structure; and a time for us to make an Exodus from the church."

The Sermon

"Mary's sermon first recapitulated much of what she had written in *The Church and the Second Sex*, and then outlined positions she later elaborated in *Beyond God the Father*. She ended with a call, God's call to us, to make our Exodus from the patriarchal and sexist church; she walked down from the pulpit, and about fifty of us walked together out of the sanctuary.

"The news media were there, and it was an exciting moment. For me it symbolized the Exodus I had made myself five years earlier. But more importantly it marked the real firming up of my feminist consciousness *and* the beginning of new theological insight."

---

* Dr. Mary Daly, Associate Professor of Theology at Boston College, preached at the church on Nov. 14, 1971.

Theological Development

"Mary gave me just what I needed: the conceptual tools to engage in an acute criticism of Christianity, tools which really rang true to me in a number of ways. What this really means, and too few people realize this, is that I was using Christian symbols and concepts to criticize and recreate my own tradition.

"What was happening to me was an enormous and extraordinary conversion. My coming into consciousness as a feminist corresponded directly with my coming into a new deep connectedness with God."

During this time, Anna was working with New Community Projects, a countercultural organization encouraging the formation of new communities. For her this fit with what she called "my fantasy about what the early Church was like—small communities experiencing transformation."

Her experience of conversion continued through hospital chaplaincy training during the summer of 1972. In the Intensive Care Unit Anna prayed with people, and she observed, "I couldn't exactly pray to the Goddess of all wonder and life.

"I found myself praying to the Creator God, the Advocate God, the Sustainer, Redeemer, Judge, Comforter and Companion God. All my words were like a process at work in me and not something I decided to do—it was really like the Holy Spirit charging around in Anna Holmes.

"In addition, as a result of the hospital experience, I found myself taking Jesus very seriously as a healer. He was a healer and I wanted to be one too. He was also a teacher and a politico for me. And in my teaching and work in a church I encouraged others to discover how they could heal each other, teach each other, and work together politically."

Exile

"About this time I began to feel that perhaps I had not really made an exodus, but was in exile. I began to find trinitarian language useful theologically; it rang true to much of my experience and helped me make sense out of my life.

"I remembered a professor from Trinity College of Hartford whom

I'd worked with in summer school in Rome a number of years ago. He said, 'Anna, the Trinity is God trying to help us understand God.' This began to make real sense to me.

"In Jesus, God came to us as a person, to make God real to us. And yet that person, really to be of impact, had to be removed from presence in the world; God's continual reminder of that presence is the power and force of the Holy Spirit.

"I'm a confessed, and excited, trinitarian. I work with the doctrine of the Trinity in unusual ways—I can and sometimes do speak of God the Father, but never limit myself to that one image, and intentionally encourage the use of other images.

"What Mary Daly did for me, really, was enable me to reappropriate my tradition at a deeper, richer, and more critical level. She has incredible insight and sensitivity into the tradition, and for me her thought has turned exodus into feminist exile."

The Next Step

"I think now I'm ready to cast my lot with the wandering people of God—and to say that the Church is my place of exile. But I'm not sure. I have to ask myself, 'Anna, are you kidding yourself? Are you really a Christian?' And I wonder about the church. Will it be open to me, accept me and my call, and let me work in new ways with other people?"

Appendix

Mary Daly, a Professor at Boston College, has become one of the most outspoken ideologists of the women's liberation movement from the philosophical perspective. In her own words, "The women's revolution, insofar as it is true to its own essential dynamics, is an ontological, spiritual revolution, pointing beyond the idolatries of sexist society and sparking creative action in and toward transcendence." (*Beyond God the Father: Toward a Philosophy of Women's Liberation* [Boston: Beacon Press, 1973] p. 6) She does not see this a limiting concern to women alone, however, for "The becoming of woman implies universal human becoming. It has everything to do with the search for ultimate meaning and reality, which some would call God." (*Beyond God the Father*, p. 6)

While Daly is aware that few theologians ascribe "maleness" to God, she calls attention to the way the *images* of faith still operate to sustain male dominance. "The biblical and popular image of God as a great patriarch in heaven, rewarding and punishing according to his mysterious and seemingly arbitrary will, has dominated the imaginations of millions for thousands of years. . . . If God in 'his' heaven is a father ruling 'his' people, then it is in the 'nature' of things and according to divine plan and the order of the universe that society be male-dominated." (*Beyond God the Father*, p. 13)

Theological Briefs

THOMAS J. J. ALTIZER

It has been well said that there is only one theological problem for the Christian today and that is the problem of God, and only one theological answer and that is the answer of Christ. Of course, Spirit may well be an essential mediating category in this correlation. But if we know Spirit religiously or "spiritually," we certainly do not yet know Spirit theologically, and there lies the heart of our problem. Perhaps it is true that a new Pentecost is occurring in our time. But, if it is true, we continue to have no way of understanding it. No longer do we know what religious or spiritual experience might mean, at least for us. For a new eclecticism has shattered our established religious and theological categories. We have little if any sense of what either the subject or the object of such experiences might be, so much so that it would appear that the categories of subject and object are no longer relevant to our spiritual experience. If this is so, then this is a way of confessing that we simply do not understand that Spirit that may or may not be breaking into our midst.

In this situation, easy answers and affirmations are our greatest peril. It is noteworthy that the last religious author of unquestioned power and authority was Kierkegaard. For twentieth-century theology created a "nonreligious" mode of theological understanding, and that may well be its greatest achievement. No real theologian of the twentieth century employs either a religious or a personal language, and this is not accidental. The same can be said of both our artists and

THOMAS J. J. ALTIZER is Chairman of the Program in Religious Studies and Professor of English, State University of New York at Stony Brook. He was educated at the University of Chicago receiving his A.M. in Theology and Ph.D. in History of Religions from the Divinity School. His publications include *The Descent into Hell*, *The New Apocalypse*, and *The Gospel of Christian Atheism*.

our thinkers. Or, at least, they do not employ a language which is recognizably personal or religious. This should lead us to be profoundly suspicious of all contemporary religious and personal language, and most so when if appears in a "spiritual" guise. Who can the speaker now be who speaks of Spirit? How can anyone in our world have a sure sense of the nature and identity of Spirit? Is it any longer possible actually to speak of Spirit? If Spirit is now speaking, it is surely speaking in a strange and unrecognizable tongue. Perhaps, then, we are living in a "new" Pentecost.

Therefore a case method of theological exploration is fraught with dangers, particularly insofar as it relies upon case or personal histories. The fact that person and character as individual and unique centers of consciousness have virtually disappeared from our most serious literature should lead us to see the difficulty of now writing a case history. Can a person still be present in a case history, one whom we can name? Perhaps so, but it is my persuasion that to the extent that this is so we will be led to a false or illusory theological meaning. Let us see if this might be so in the case of "Anna Holmes." What most strikes the reader about this case history is that it is so easily resolved. Can this be possible? What is the resolution of "Anna's" problem? The discovery of the Trinity! And this on the part of one who believes that she has made an exodus from the Christian tradition. Can one take this seriously? I believe that we must, for it is just this kind of confusion which plagues us today.

We are informed that what was happening to "Anna" was an enormous and extraordinary conversion: "My coming into consciousness as a feminist corresponded directly with my coming into a new deep connectedness with God." But Anna discovers that she can't "exactly" pray to the Goddess of all wonder and life. Anna finds herself praying to the "Creator God," in other words, to the traditional Christian God. Thereby the Holy Spirit is "charging around" in Anna Holmes. Then Anna realizes that she has not really made an exodus, but is in exile; and this because she began to find that trinitarian language rang true to much of her experience. Can "exodus" and "exile" retain any meaning in this formulation? Anna is now a confessed and excited trinitarian, and she works with the doctrine of the Trinity in unusual ways. If so, we are not informed of these ways. We do learn a new identity of Mary Daly: "What Mary Daly did for me, really, was enable me to reappropriate my tradition at a deeper, richer, and more critical level." When the Roman Catholic hierarchy reads this, they may well hasten the ordination of women! Is the reappropriation of tradition what women's liberation is really about? What kind of feminist exile is this? None at all, of course, and this leads us to wonder if it is insignificant that a male is the author of this case history.

Yet this case history is almost a paradigm of those who can continue to speak an inherited religious language. For the cost of such speech is the loss of all genuine meaning, and this in the name of the Holy Spirit. Silence is one thing, meaningless speech is another, and if we can't distinguish them we are in a simply hopeless situation. Unlike silence, meaningless speech is not simply meaningless, it is inhuman. All too naturally, one questions whether "Anna Holmes" is a person named Anna Holmes. I do not believe so, for if I did, I would simply have to renounce the quest for theological meaning. Perhaps what is most significant here is that this case history purports to embody a meaning of God for us. Apparently God now means what He always did, at least to the conventional Christian. But now, at least, we can realize that this means nothing at all. Is this the way out of our theological quagmire? Or the way that the churches must choose today? Here, we truly are confronted with an Either-Or. Either meaning or meaninglessness, either human language or the language of the "Spirit." When God is identified with such a "Spirit," then not only an actual God, but also the human person disappears. And while a "spiritual" resurrection may well follow such a disappearance, there can here be no hope in a resurrection of the Body.

Selected Bibliography

Thomas J. J. Altizer, *The Gospel of Christian Atheism* (Philadelphia: The Westminster Press, 1966). My most forthright statement of the meaning of a Christianity embodying the self-negation of God.

John B. Cobb, Jr., *The Structure of Christian Existence* (Philadelphia: The Westminster Press, 1961). The best recent Protestant statement of the meaning of God within a global context.

Eric Gutkind, *The Body of God* (New York: Horizon Press, 1969). The most revolutionary Jewish understanding of the identity of God.

Paul Tillich, *The Courage To Be* (New Haven: Yale University Press, 1952). The classical Protestant statement of the God beyond God.
A New Catechism (New York: Seabury Press, 1969). The most radical contemporary Catholic teaching of the human meaning of God.

John B. Cobb, Jr.

Between Mary Daly's intention and her effect on Anna Holmes lies a distinction that goes to the heart of the Christian belief in God. They agree that the Christian God is Father of Jesus Christ. Daly calls feminists in the name of the true God to leave worship of this male, patriarchal deity. Anna Holmes finds that "Mary Daly has taught her to use Christian symbols and concepts to criticize and recreate" her own Christian tradition. The question is whether the new understanding of God to which Daly's incisive critique of Christian tradition leads Anna Holmes is a Christian understanding.

More generally, how much and in what ways can "God," that is, what we actually mean by the word God, change without divorcing us from our tradition and community? In the case before us, the issue is the maleness of the Christian "God." Can the Christian "God" become "Goddess," or neuter, or androgynous, or *gynandrous** and still be the Christian deity? Or is the Christian "God" bound up with maleness and the sanctioning of patriarchy? In other cases the issue can be about the absoluteness, immutability, and eternity of "God." Can one worship a relative, mutable, and temporal "God" or a "God" who is both absolute and relative, both immutable and mutable, and both eternal and temporal, and still be worshiping the Christian "God"?

John B. Cobb, Jr., is Ingraham Professor of Theology, School of Theology at Claremont. He was educated at Emory University and the University of Michigan and received his Ph.D. from the University of Chicago. He is the author of *A Christian Natural Theology*, *God and the World*, *Christ in a Pluralistic Age*. He is an ordained Methodist minister.

* *Gynandrous* is not a dictionary word. It is a way of suggesting that in the combination of the traits of the two sexes it is as appropriate to think of the feminine as primary as to place the masculine first.

If, as I do, one says yes to these questions, and even insists that the Christian is called to give up the one-sidedness of the tradition in favor of a dipolar concept of God, one is confronted with other concepts. What about the tribal deity of white Anglo-Saxon male American Protestants? Is that, too, the Christian "God"? Or do we want to reserve the right to reject some concepts and images of God, to say that some are Christian and others not? Surely we do, but does that require that the dominant concepts and images of the Christian heritage be accepted as defining the Christian "God" for all time, regardless of difficulties and limitations that appear? If so, then Christian belief in "God" is impossible for those who share in any modern view of the world; for concepts and images of God are bound up with world views and cultures, and these have altered greatly over the centuries.

We theologians are lucky that neither a simple yes nor a simple no to changing "God" suffices. If there were a once-for-all clearly established Christian meaning of "God," we would have little to do; but our role would be trivial if all concepts of God were equally acceptable. Since neither a blanket yes nor a blanket no suffices, we have the endless task of discriminating among changing concepts of God those which should be supported and encouraged and those which should be opposed. There are two main bases on which we can pursue this always risky and unfinished business.

One basis is "truth" in a sense that leads many theologians to philosophy. Philosophy does not get beyond concepts to the reality that is conceptualized; for the reality itself is never captured in our language. But philosophy does test concepts for their appropriateness to what the most critical inquiry points toward as reality itself. It can take account of the changing views of the world that scientific progress requires of thoughtful people. In this process, inherited ideas of God are repeatedly revised and even rejected. Since in worshiping God Christians mean to be addressing what truly is even apart from our own thought and worship, "God" must be repeatedly reconceived in the light of the best understanding of reality that is available. On this basis some emerging "Gods" can be encouraged and others opposed.

But this criterion is not sufficient for the theologian. This insufficiency is evident in the issue now posed by the feminists. Few ever suppose that God is literally a male. Yet the maleness of all the images of God has played a profound role in shaping Christian sensibility and attitudes and has even influenced philosophical reflection. Our response to God is shaped as much by our imagination as by our critical reflection, and our images must be evaluated, not so much as true or false, but as to how they shape our attitudes and emotions and the behavior that follows from these.

This evaluation cannot be once-for-all. In one culture or period the image of God as the Father of all may tend chiefly to free from fear, to break the power of hierarchy, and to overcome the boundaries that divide human beings. In other periods and cultures it may work chiefly to suppress women and to encourage patriarchalism. The theological task is to criticize images of God insofar as they work against human freedom and Christian maturity and to encourage new ones that carry forward the strengths of the old while avoiding their worst features.

Images cannot be forced. Anna Holmes found she could not pray to "the Goddess of all wonder and life." This is not because Christians have reason to believe that deity is more truly "God" than "Goddess." It is because the introduction of the image of Goddess would be disruptive at least in the context in question. Anna wants to reassure and comfort and to direct people to the power of healing and life, whereas an abrupt change of images would startle and create anxiety and distrust. But in other times and places women have found assurance and strength in addressing deity as "Goddess"; and the power of the cult of Mary shows that men, too, have needed female images for approaching God. In time female imagery about deity may be equally acceptable with masculine imagery. Theologians, both men and women, can work toward that end.

Philosophical concepts and religious imagery are different but related. Exclusively masculine religious imagery has supported and been supported by a philosophical concept of God as wholly active (the technical term is *actus purus* or pure act) and as unaffected by the sufferings of the world (the technical term is *impassible*). Female religious imagery can now take its place alongside the masculine more easily because there has already been a philosophical critique of the traditional concepts of God. Charles Hartshorne, among others, has shown that this impassible pure act can be only an abstraction incapable of love. The actual God must be the One who is supremely receptive as well as active, relative as well as absolute, mutable as well as immutable.

If we have overcome the supposed philosophical reasons for denying that God is affected by the world, rejoicing in our joy and suffering in our suffering, then we can recover and confidently employ a wider range of biblical images of God. We can also with disciplined imagination introduce new language. The masculine images that have dominated our tradition can be complemented by feminine images until a balance is achieved. We will advance, not by denying that God is like a father, but by affirming that God is also like a mother. The philosophical polarities of receptive and active, relative and absolute, mutable and immutable, can help open the way for the polar images of female and male. In the development of these new images leadership is primarily in the hands of women. This is a proper work of Christian theology in which Anna Holmes has a role to play.

Selected Bibliography

John B. Cobb, Jr., *Christ in a Pluralistic Age* (Philadelphia: The Westminster Press, 1975). Includes suggestions as to how theology is involved in continual transformation of images.

Charles Hartshorne, *The Divine Relativity* (New Haven: Yale University Press, 1964). A classic statement of the dipolar nature of God which allows for inclusion of both traditionally feminine and traditionally masculine aspects.

Schubert Ogden, *The Reality of God* (New York: Harper & Row, 1966). Shows how dipolar theism grounds the meaning of life and rightly expresses Christian faith.

Daniel Day Williams, *The Spirit and the Forms of Love* (New York: Harper & Row, 1968). Best comprehensive theological statement informed by dipolar theism.

PEGGY ANN WAY

Anna's pilgrimage speaks to us of possibility—not only for herself and other sisters, but for theology itself. Let us reflect on four of these possibilities.

First, it is important to note Anna's use of theology as *resource* to better understand her own experiences. Read carefully; you will also hear Anna validating theological understandings out of their congruence with her own experiencings. Notice what she said about trinitarian language: "It rang true to much of my experience." It is important to begin here, for it may not be apparent just how radical this is. Anna may or may not claim to have a formal theological method—but the method she tells us about is one where human, i.e. her own, experiences, are a part of the primary data for theology to consider and that they may even, indeed, validate the truths of theological concepts. You might note that this process usually occurs the other way around!

So Anna places a high valuation upon her own experiences—cares about them, risks acting out of them (i.e. she makes two "exoduses" as her experiencings guide her), seeks to find their congruence with conceptualizations others have offered out of their experiencings which are, believe it or not, the roots of most theologies. And let us not miss what happens: out of her critical and existential experiences of feminine consciousness she finds herself a "confessed, and excited, trinitarian"!

And I share with Anna the excitement of risking letting in the data—trusting the experiencings—for they might just serve to validate the essential truths which are so often masked in theological language and conceptualizations that have lost touch with their original fervor.

I find this happening among laywomen and women seminarians all

---

PEGGY ANN WAY was a member of the faculty of the Jesuit School of Theology in Chicago and has just accepted an appointment at Vanderbilt University. She has studied at the University of Michigan, Wayne State University, Chicago Theological Seminary, University of Chicago Divinity School, and Princeton Theological Seminary. She is the author of several articles and is a contributor to *Women's Liberation and the Church*. She is an ordained minister of the United Church of Christ.

across the country, and the possibilities are not only in their own lives, but for the very discipline of theology. For, however formulated, the method the Annas are lifting up is strongly experiential, risks root critique, insists on congruence between feeling and intellect, and conveys a joy not frequently present in theology as most of us have known it.

The *second* possibility arises out of taking seriously the fascinating continuum of growth with which Anna presents us. Let's trace its process: (1) an experience of discontinuity between home church and her own emerging values; (2) a period of seeking and finding space, while placing herself in situations where her "original religiousness" found less companionship; (3) a catalytic series of organizational and political events which gave a sense of corporateness—sisterhood, if you will, although Anna does not use that term—and gave permission and focus to her critical spirit; (4) a felt conversion process which found her feminine consciousness to be congruent with her God-connectedness!, and trusting its flow in working with real people (work that I, by the way, would call "ministry"); and (5) a repossession and rearticulation of her heritage, this time in congruence with her own values and experiencings.

Anna reminds us that we (and those who see us) don't have to be afraid of discontinuities, and that even the Church might be able to put in perspective and understand the meaning of combined personal/political statements such as those made by the women who participated in the exodus from Harvard Memorial Church. A sense of continuum amongst those participating in growth and change can both help to remove the threat and, perhaps because of this, make more lucid the message. In fact, those of you reading this might take more time to listen to the next personal statement that you hear or see that, at first feeling, offends you. Theology, you see, is also about personal statement and the ways in which personal histories touch into corporate meanings. And while I wasn't there, I'm sure that the conversations following the service, among men and women alike, would be deeply revelatory of a variety of theological understandings both of the nature of the Church and of the event that had just occurred. And just perhaps, those conversations are a part of theological dialogue! I only wish they could be named as such, with persons present to help clarify that the issues quite transcend personal feelings.

Of course it isn't all that simple, and that is the *third* possibility. Theology (that is, the discipline of) has a proud history as a critical resource. We need help in assessing personal feelings, in giving names to personal experiences, in sorting through different orders and depths of meaning. Anna found in Mary a person who could help her name and focus her critical responses—who offered her "the conceptual tools" to look at her own sense of discontinuity. But did you notice that the critical tools to assess the tradition were offered up by the tradition itself? That's what Anna tells us. And that's what Paul Tillich used to call the "Protestant principle." (The Catholics have it, too, by the way, and the evidence is that they have survived even longer!)

Now it must be said that I, too, have a critical sense and that, as theologian, I have a responsibility not to let it go even in relation to those persons and places where my valuings are most congruent. (You might have picked up by now that they are quite congruent with Anna!) But I need to know how important those first sixteen years of religious formation were for Anna. What if those experiences had not been there for her to repossess and rearticulate? Whose job is it to do that formation? A familiarity of language is somehow essential to fill it with new meaning.

Across the country I meet the Annas, seeking to move from discontinuity to congruence. And generally those whose pilgrimage moves with some joy have some history with which to become newly congruent. I am sure that it does not just begin with discontinuity, my friends.

I am intrigued also with theology's possible creative role in helping us sort through and mutually respect different personal statements. My own orientation and complexity of personality/values does not allow me to use worship as a political statement even as I recognize that, in its structure and languagings, it can be so viewed. Indeed, when I preached at Harvard four years later, I chose *not* to be political even when my requests for certain language and music had been ignored. For just as Mary wanted to symbolize our "Exodus from the patriarchal and sexist church," so did I want to symbolize our choice to stand there in the midst of it, telling of our own experiential truths even when the men say "idle tales!"

Now there are different theologies going there, and they can help us sort through the meaning of different personal statements. We need, I think, to know that which we choose—and when, and why. I myself want to hold onto my right to smile at Anna's wording: "About fifty of us walked together out of the sanctuary. The new media were there, and it was an exciting moment." Of course. But it was also an exciting moment when I first served communion with a Roman Catholic priest and there were no news media present—by choice.

I share this because I want so for us to be respectful of our many differences, so that the function of theology as critical resource is not only a tool against, but also a tool for.

I'm not sure what I think about Anna's self-understanding of living in feminist exile. For—and this is the *fourth* possibility—theology is also an historical discipline which helps us place events and meanings in perspective. I hear Anna claiming the congruence between her experiencings and the potential richness of theological language. She is free to speak of God the Father as one among many possible images, neither limited *to* or *from* it, and intentional in using alternative congruent images. But I do not hear her claiming congruence between her pilgrimage as woman—and the possible future impediments to it—and the pilgrimage of *any* Christian throughout the historical process who has claimed seeking over comfort, a desire for congruence-hard-won, or a critical and experiential stance in relation to that which has become so self-evident that it appears unchallengeable.

The issue is whether Anna's experiences of discontinuity and doubt, of concern for acceptance and the chance to be creative with people in a church or other institutional structure, are not normative for the growing Christian and only felt by Blacks or Latins or gays or women with more intensity and clarity and passion and commitment. I believe—theologically and historically and through the depths of my own experiences—that feelings like "exile" are the *normative* state for those who are called to keep the truth of the tradition alive. Pain and exclusion, despair and uncertainty are intrinsic for us—and not accidental. Thus I do not understand myself as living in, yes, a Jewish state of exile, but rather as living in the midst of the truth of the human situation, embodying the pain and possibilities of that gospel statement about the nature of human existence that quite transcends sexism or racism.

It isn't just being a woman, Anna—although it's certainly all of that. It's being the kind of person your pilgrimage states you are that sets you apart. And that is your pain and the glory. God be with us!

P.S. And so, Anna, you want more specific advice on what you should do? I cannot offer you that, nor, I think, can theology. Here theology comes closest to the offerings of Jesus: the offering is made, but it is yours to respond.

Through my own ministries I have learned the hardest lesson of all: I can only be responsible for the integrity of the offering, but not for the response. The dimensionality of your own life and faith experiences, with respectful consideration of a variety of theological and cultural analytics, must guide you in your own directions. Theology, at its best, can alert you to possibilities and pitfalls; the latter's "alerts" have perhaps rung the clearest notes for recent generations. I am myself beginning to believe that the pitfalls have been overdrawn and that the most truly transcendent call to ministry is somehow *through* the conceptual categories, theological and cultural, that appear to make "ministry in our time" an impossibility.

I find that not only utter nonsense but also historically naive. It is so tempting to make "particular difficulties," i.e. being a woman, having an imperfectly structured Church or society, lacking conceptual credibility, etc., the occasions to make ministry itself untenable. I would be less than honest not to confess that such "particular difficulties" have taken a tremendous personal toll—but they have also called forth from me at least a beginning wisdom, courage, and dignity that keep me seeking after—and finding—meaning in my own ordination.

No, ordination is not necessary to be about ministry. Surely it is the Roman Catholic sisters who do the vast bulk of ministering in that tradition. And now they, along with you, struggle with those hard issues: is the present Church structure one that you want to join? What will keep you from becoming "like them?" Has not a "cultic 'priesthood' " seen its last days?

These are vital—but, I think, "accidental" rather than "intrinsic" questions. Is God calling you, Anna, through and in spite of the analytics? Does ordination mean more to you than power and privilege? Can you "sit with" the integrity of others who make different decisions than your own—whichever way you go—and offer up to them as well as others that which is right for you? Because, through some mystery, your decision is *your* call?

Beware of all who offer limited options: you *must* be ordained; you must *not*. Follow your own heart and soul; your experiences to date indicate that you are as trustworthy as any of us who would offer you guidance.

Selected Bibliography

Robert J. Heyer, ed., *Women and Orders* (New York: Paulist Press 1974). A "neat" collection of essays relating an assortment of "ordination issues" to the Catholic Church, including Rosemary Radford Ruether, Ruth Tiffany Barnhouse, Emily Hewitt, Gregory Baum, etc. Clear, concise, simply written.

Letty Russell, *Human Liberation in a Feminist Perspective: A Theology*, (Philadelphia: The Westminster Press, 1974). Its very utilization of nonsexist language is a modeling of possibilities, and views consciousness raising as conversion opportunity.

David Tracy, *Blessed Rage for Order* (New York: Seabury Press, 1975). A methodological and substantive contribution that takes liberation thought seriously and just might help move some of us through some present theological confusions.

Peggy Ann Way, "An Authority of Possibility for Women in the Church," *Women's Liberation and the Church*, edited by Sarah Bentley Doely (New York: Association Press, 1970), pp. 77–94. An attempt to take "possibility" seriously without totally separating it from traditional sources and structures.

3

"Maker of Heaven and Earth"

Theological Introduction

THOMAS D. PARKER

The first article concludes with a confession of faith in the one God, who is the creator of "all things, visible and invisible," which is also a confession of our creatureliness. The Christian confession of faith presumes that the relation between God and the world is asymetrical: God is the origin and basis of all things and does not depend on creatures as they do on God. God exists *a se esse* (by his own being), as the medieval scholastics declared, while creatures exist *ab alio* (from another). Many theological statements express this thought:

> God hath all life, glory, goodness, blessedness, in and of himself; and is alone in and unto himself all-sufficient, not standing in need of any creatures. . . . he is the alone foundation of all being, of whom, through whom, and to whom are all things (Westminster Confession, 1646).

The idea of creation is located in two central texts of Scripture, although expressed in countless others as well: the first chapters of Genesis and the Gospel of John. The priestly writer in Genesis 1 states unambiguously that God created heaven and earth "in the beginning," and, by ordering the chaos ("dividing"), made the world we find around us. The living God is distinguished from the idols of the nations by the fact that God is Creator and works "mighty acts" of justice and righteousness in the world.

This basic article of faith is assumed by the New Testament writers.

It proved a staunch bulwark against denials of God as Creator of a good creation during the early years of the Church's life. The prologue to the Fourth Gospel speaks of all things being made "by the Word" which is the "true light" enlightening all persons, the "Word" which is God. In the Christian Scriptures, however, the accent falls strongly on the future dominion of the one God, who rules over creatures and draws them to their destiny in the "new age." God is the end as well as the origin of creatures. In this the Christian writers agree with strains of thought in the Hebrew prophets, and confess God the Creator as Governor, intimate with the creatures as well as distant from them as Creator and Lord. For St. Paul, the Word by which all things exist is the "Son" who shall "deliver the Kingdom to God the Father" so that God may be "all in all" (1 Cor. 15).

As a result of this twofold witness, theological expansion of the first article has generally added a doctrine of creation and of providence. According to the first, 'when God willed, in his goodness he created everything, creatures both spiritual and bodily'. Such creatures were good, because they were created by the Supreme Good, but they were changeable, and so subject to destruction and decay, because they were created out of nothing and endowed with freedom. According to this classic teaching, there is no such thing as a "nature of evil" because every "nature" is good insofar as it is a creature of God. But everything created is subject to corruption and can fall away from the good end for which it was made. The creation is the scene of a cosmic drama, played out in the lives of human beings, a drama of good and evil.

The second doctrine, providence, concerns the government of God over 'his' good but corruptible creation. Theological statements generally have insisted that God is not the author of evil but foreknows and allows evil in order to overcome evil with good. All things, indeed, are subject to the divine will, but some things, in their rebellion and corruption, are permitted to exist while others, turning from rebellion and corruption, are directed toward their proper end. The divine government establishes freedom among creatures and upholds human personal, historical responsibility. Further, it provides the background against which the "mighty acts of God" and especially the incarnation can be understood. Terms like deism and pantheism are used to characterize views which the classic theological tradition was forced to reject because of its notion of divine providence.

There are many disputed questions about almost every sentence in the above characterizations. Many theological traditions have extensive doctrines of predestination in addition to those on general providence while others accent the notion of free will. In some the extent of the corruption of creatures is strongly accented while in others their capacity to receive the grace of God is stressed. All traditions wrestle with these issues with seriousness, however, because at stake is the question of the righteousness of God, the reality of the redemption, and the relation between divine and human action.

The doctrine of God as Creator and Governor of all things has served to express several important elements of Christian belief. First, there is a limit set to all things. Creatures are finite, mutually condition each other, and have their principle of existence by divine gift. Second, within that limit, creatures are good, can increase and augment their life and come to their true destiny. Third, all things enjoy a continuing relation to God and therefore exist in a dependable order which is the basis of their freedom. Fourth, and perhaps most important, sin and evil are perversions or lacks (privations) of good rather than being principles in themselves. Thus the redemption of creatures is the fulfillment of their most proper destiny, whereas their final and total destruction is not. The work of salvation and of creation are in harmony with one another in God.

George and Marion

Marion Hathaway's eyes filled with tears as she turned away from the vacant stare of her husband of fifty-one years. Two weeks before George Hathaway had suffered the third stroke in as many days; he was completely paralyzed and could no longer speak. Marion turned again and quietly whispered, "George, you've left me alone to make the most terrifying decision in our lives. It's so hard to see you through all those tubes and machines. Why doesn't God let us die quietly and with dignity?"

Thorough testing by the hospital staff had given convincing evidence that the damage to George's nervous system was so extensive that there was no possibility for recovery of normal functions. George's heart was also seriously damaged by an attack which had preceded the strokes by four days. However, the heart condition had stabilized and the medical specialists now indicated that with intravenous feeding, oxygen, and later with constant medical care in a nursing home, George could live for weeks, even months, or years.

"Live," Marion mused. Her mind went over for the one hundredth time the brief but intense conversation she and George had shared just six months ago about what "living" meant for them. This exchange had been prompted by news of the suicide pact of two friends of many years, Elizabeth and Pitney Van Dusen. Marion recalled that Pitney, a theologian and past president of Union Theological Seminary in New York, had been handicapped by a stroke five years before; Betty was seriously afflicted by arthritis. Though "Pit" had lived two weeks longer than Betty, they had both intentionally taken an overdose of sleeping pills in the conviction that at ages seventy-

---

This case was prepared as a basis for class discussion rather than to illustrate either effective or ineffective handling of the situation.

seven and eighty they had lived "full and satisfying lives" in God's service; their written statements had said that the time had come to end those lives.

Marion remembered her reaction as one of both revulsion and deep admiration. She had tried to understand her friends' actions with awareness of their clear Christian commitment, but she also expressed to George her own faith in God's goodness. Life was his special gift. If we dare throw back that gift, aren't we expressing a lack of faith in his providence? God has purposes we don't understand; how do we dare decide when a certain life is over? Only God can make that decision.

"But Marion," George had intervened, "you and I have both lived in the assurance of God's gift of wisdom to make decisions, and his promise of forgiveness if we are wrong. We live daily in his promise of resurrection. If the extension of a helpless life were a terrible burden on someone I deeply loved, I don't see choosing to die as a denial of life. I am convinced that if I were in Pit's place I would do exactly the same thing."

At the time of this conversation George and Marion's lives were full and active. They did not linger on the topic of euthanasia nor did they come to any formal conclusions. The past week was the first time in many months that Marion had struggled with the question of whether one dares make a decision to end human life.

Marion Hathaway had always seen her role in life as a "helpmate" for her husband. In the past she had unabashedly told friends that it was hard for her to understand the independent "women libbers"; she "didn't know what she'd do without George."

For a number of years Marion was a talented teacher of both piano and violin and had been actively involved in local politics and community organizations, yet she had always given priority to George's work. In turn George had frequently been quite clear in expressing his dependence on Marion's companionship, her cheerful spirit, and her wise counsel. Though George had been very successfully involved in the business world, he was also deeply committed to his family. He and Marion had equally shared the responsibilities of raising their son and daughter, now both married with young families of their own. Even at eighty, George Hathaway was an extraordinarily energetic man. Though he was officially retired from the vice-presidency of a large electronics firm, he and Marion continued to travel extensively for business consultations. They had plans to move the coming October from their Long Island home into a cottage in Florida they had bought and were enthusiastically redecorating.

As had been true for the past fifty years, Marion and George were quite involved in the work of their local church. They both served repeated terms as ruling elders and considered the church an integral part of their lives. Since the severity of George's illness had become known, Marion had spoken at length with Rev. Jim Jewis, a respected pastor and devoted friend. Jim tried to help Marion sort out some of the issues with which she was struggling, stressing that the added years we receive by God—or that are provided by modern technology—were indeed an ambiguous blessing. Jim responded to Marion's questions about euthanasia by saying that he honestly felt that trust in God's faithfulness could lead a Christian responsibility to take either option. Consequently, as Marion's pastor, Jim confessed that he could offer his love and support, but it would be inappropriate for him to make the decision for her.

It was now six o'clock in the morning. Marion felt frightened and alone as she stood beside George's bed. She took his limp hand and closed her eyes. "Do I tell the doctors to let you go? We could face weeks or months of keeping the shell of your body breathing. But this would be an existence without your mind in dialogue, with no laughter, with no celebrating the joyous gift of life itself. I'm so afraid I can't care for you; we would both become painful burdens on our children.

"George, in my heart I know what you want me to do. So is my agony a lack of conviction that this could be God's will or my own terrifying fear that I simply cannot survive without you by my side? I have hoped and prayed that you'd be whole again. But in my heart of hearts all that I can see ahead is months of uselessness and pain. George, how can I decide what to do?"

Theological Briefs

GREGORY BAUM

After some reflection I am unable to let the story of Mr. and Mrs. Hathaway be the point of entry for a theology of God as Maker of heaven and earth. I am, of course, moved by Mr. Hathaway's broken body and by the anguished choice his poor wife is compelled to make. It is hard enough to make a sound decision when you are well and strong; how much more difficult it is when you are shattered, as Mrs. Hathaway, by grief, loneliness, and the darkness of tomorrow. Whatever her decision, I am certain, she will not offend the Creator of the universe. I refuse to regard the choice with which she is confronted as a moment of disclosure, bringing out the hidden significance of the Christian doctrine of creation.

In traditional Catholic moral theology, superannuated from many points of view, we had a sound principle of great help in this situation. We used to say—and I still subscribe to it—that people are bound to prolong the life of a patient by "ordinary," not by "extraordinary" means. Since Mr. Hathaway's complete recovery has become impossible, since even his regaining of consciousness is unlikely, since, moreover, the medical technology to make him breathe and feed him intravenously is complex and costly, the means used to keep him alive are, in my judgment, extraordinary. The story of Mr. and Mrs. Hathaway does not raise the difficult moral issue of euthanasia. The decision Mrs. Hathaway must make does not demand that she

GREGORY G. BAUM is Professor of Theology and Religious Studies, St. Michael's College, University of Toronto and Editor of *The Ecumenist*. He was educated at McMaster University and Ohio State University, receiving his Doctorate in Theology from the University of Fribourg, Switzerland. His publications include *Man Becoming*, *New Horizon*, and *Religion and Alienation*. He is an ordained Roman Catholic Priest and a member of the Augustinian Order.

wield power over life and death. Her moral reflection deals more directly with the extent to which she must go, under the circumstances, to prevent a dying person from dying. In my view, the dilemma of the poor lady does not bring out the hidden power of the Church's teaching on God as Creator.

In all honesty, I am a little annoyed that the story of George and Marion has been chosen as the starting point for a theological discussion on the divine authorship of life. I am a little annoyed because it seems to me that this story disguises the true reality of inflicted death in today's world and thus makes us insensitive to God's summons implicit in the doctrine of creation.

An unfortunate tendency in Christian theology makes us think that death takes place, normally and in most instances, in bed. Our theology creates the impression that after a long life mortality eventually catches up with us and we die. What such a theology disguises is the brutal fact that vast numbers of people, endless millions of them, do not die in bed but are killed by us in wars, genocides, starvations, and other institutionalized crimes. Theologians usually do not study human death in the light of Abel's death inflicted on him by a competitive brother, and of Jesus' death inflicted on him as troublemaker in the empire and as critic of his own tradition. We tend to create a theology of death and dying that persuades us that we are basically a society where people die in bed. Thus we leave no room in our theology for reflecting on the cruel reality of death in our age. While we must have compassion for the suffering of Mr. and Mrs. Hathaway, we should still affirm that to die in bed, at the end of a long life, surrounded by friends, is a great grace. Millions of people are killed, or die of starvation and exhaustion, while surrounded by faces that hate them. Since the Bible focuses on violent death, and since the prophets speak of the destruction of the powerless as crimes that cry to heaven, it is hard to understand why the Christian teaching on death has become so onesided.

God is the Creator of the world, the maker of heaven and earth—this is the teaching of the churches. And since Christian doctrine is not conceptual information about a distant divinity but the revelation of God's power and presence in human history, we must ask what is the redemptive meaning of this teaching. What is being said to us in this doctrine? How are we being addressed? What radical choices do we have to make involving faith in God as Creator of the earth? Again, I do not think that the story of Mr. and Mrs. Hathaway brings this out. I could end my commentary at this point. What I prefer to do, however, is to mention aspects of the world drama today that reveal to us the force and the meaning of the Christian doctrine of creation.

The teaching that God is Creator of the world sheds light on the burning question of world hunger. For according to the Church's teaching the earth and the fruits of the earth belong to God who made them and made them for his children. The food that is grown on the earth is meant to feed the people. Yet we have organized society in such a way that the earth feeds only those people who have money to pay for food. Private ownership of land and food seems to introduce a distortion in the order of God. Where does this private ownership come from? The Fathers of the Church thought that private property was connected with the world's fall into sin. We, as a society, no longer acknowledge that God is Creator of the earth: the fruits of the earth are no longer available to God's people but only to those who have money. In the Middle Ages, theologians took a more positive view of private property. They also acknowledged that God is the Creator of the earth, but they held that land and its ownership were committed to private persons so that these could take care of the land, take charge of its cultivation, and assume responsibility for distributing the food to the people who live on the land. Property was private, but its use was common.

In modern society, our self-organization has changed. We no longer believe that God is the Creator of the earth and therefore owns it; we have come to look at private property not as the duty to care for and distribute God's creation, but as the right to use and destroy it. People can do with their property as they please. The land and the fruits of the land are no longer for common use. Food has become merchandise. The producers and/or distributors have full control over food, they can do with it as they please, even, if it increases their profit, destroy it. The minerals and the oil hidden in the ground are the property of the company or the government that owns the piece of land. Contemporary society no longer believes that God is the creator of the earth and that all things are God's.

What does it mean to believe in the Church's teaching that God is the Maker of heaven and earth? Do we believe this by assimilating a particular concept in our intellectual life and by adding another predicate to our idea of the divinity? Or do we believe this when we are willing to perceive the world in the light of this teaching and recognize the land and its fruits as created by God as matrix of life for his people? Can Christians believe in God as Creator of the world when they actually hold in their hearts that people should have access to food only if they have money to pay for it? What is faith in God?

Land has become merchandise. It is treated like the goods we have produced, like tables and chairs. Commodities belong to those who make them, and hence we take for granted that they can be sold. But who has made the land? Land was created by God and belongs to those for whom he created it, his people. Land is the responsibility of the community. To buy and sell land like merchandise is to remove it from common use. Land speculation is a symbol rejecting the biblical God.

The teaching that God is creator of life also contains a message regarding peace on earth. Killing is against God's will. While this has implications for human decisions regarding the beginning of human life in the womb and the end of human life in old age (for abortion and euthanasia), the message of life speaks more directly to wider political issues that are not usually related to divine revelation. To believe in God as creator of life means to favor peace: it means to be committed to peace as the way of life in keeping with God's self-revelation. And since peace is not defined passively as the absence of armed hostilities but actively as concerted political action to overcome the conflicts that lead to war, the doctrine of creation has political implications. We do not love peace unless we are willing to examine the injustices in the social order, study the distribution of wealth and resources in the world, and favor political changes that permit all people to share in the goods of this earth. This does not mean, it seems to me, that Christians must reject war under any conditions. It is conceivable that evil people inspire a government to aggressive action in a manner that can only be stopped by war. But implied in the message that God is the Creator of life is the demand for social policies that seek to remove great social inequalities, overcome the domination of the many by the few, and reach for a worldwide social order that protects justice.

The final guarantee of peace and the resolution of conflicts is the conversation between equals. Nothing short of dialogue can firmly ground a peaceful community. But such a conversation is possible only among equals. Since dialogue across the difference in power is not a genuine conversation, dialogue becomes an instrument of peace–making only if it is accompanied by social policies that aim at the removal of inequality in power. Since the so-called Christian world embraces the more successful nations and controls the greater part of the world's resources, it is costly for Christians to accept the teaching that God is the Creator of life and that he demands the removal of inequalities and injustices from the global society.

As a society, in our actual self-organization as peoples, we reject the article of the Creed that God is the Creator of heaven and earth. Christians want to believe God's self-revelation in their hearts, even if this means that they must swim against the cultural stream and disagree in a thousand ways with the day-to-day, taken-for-granted self-understanding of contemporary society.

Since we are powerless to change society, since we cannot effectively oppose the free market in food, land, and minerals, since we cannot redistribute the world's riches in a more just manner, we easily feel that the social consequences of the Christian creed are not practical. They only make us feel guilty, they do not issue forth in realistic action. For this reason we are tempted to turn to the more personal consequences of the Christian creed and in this way "privatize" the biblical message. My reply to this is that even though we are powerless to change society at this time, we still want to perceive reality in terms different from the dominant culture and dream of an alternative society in keeping with God's will; the new consciousness may generate a social movement and as it is shared by more and more people, it may eventually initiate significant political change. In fact the only hope for the remaking of society is people's fidelity to their vision—in our case to the vision of society implicit in the Creed.

Selected Bibliography

The attempt to overcome the highly privatized understanding of the Gospel and recover its social power and meaning is the programme of several contemporary theologians.

Gregory Baum, *Religion and Alienation* (New York: Paulist Press, 1975), pp. 192–226, 266–294.
Johannes B. Metz, ed., *Faith and the World of Politics*, Concilium Series, (New York: Paulist Press, 1968), vol. 36, pp. 2–82.
Jürgen Moltmann, *Hope and Planning* (London: S.C.M. Press, 1968).

RICHARD A. McCORMICK

The case of George and Marion forces critical attention on the meaning of God's providence in our lives. This providence is itself an implication of the doctrine of creation, for in creating God orders His creatures to their proper ends or goals. For many centuries this ordering has been called in the Christian tradition the eternal law—the plan of divine wisdom insofar as it directs all activity and all change toward a final end. This eternal law is God's providence.

It is precisely the manner of our share in this providence that is at stake in Marion's decision. All creatures, precisely as creatures, are directed by the purposes of the Creator (the eternal law). But not all are directed in the same way. It is possible to be directed in a passive or active way by a plan or ordering. It is both the privilege and the responsibility of humanity, as created in the divine image, that one shares actively and in a higher way in God's providence. As St. Thomas noted, "he participates in providence by providing for himself and others" (*"Fit providentiae particeps, sibi ipsi et aliis providens" Summa Theologica*, I–II, q. 91, a. 2). The claims of this provision in concrete conduct are determined by human reason—illumined by but not replaced by faith—as it goes about establishing the proper relationship of persons to the basic values that define personal growth

---

RICHARD A. McCORMICK is the Rose F. Kennedy Professor of Christian Ethics, Kennedy Institute, Georgetown University and Senior Research Associate, Woodstock Theological Center, Washington, D.C. He was educated at Loyola University (Chicago) and received the Th.D. from the Gregorian University. He is a regular contributor to theological journals, has contributed chapters to numerous books, and is the author of *Ambiguity in Moral Choice*. He is an ordained Roman Catholic priest, S.J.

and flourishing. Simply worded, the instrument of God's providence over humankind is a person's rational nature—one's reason. That is why a person's participation in the eternal law or providence—a participation often misleadingly called the natural moral law—is above all the law of reason.

But what does faith-informed reason tell us where life decisions, such as that in the George and Marion case, are involved? A misreading here could lead to abandonment of responsibility on the one hand or on the other to an interventionism that is no less an assault on the human. In dealing with the basic value of human life, and in this sense in assuming its proper responsibility within the notion of providence, the Christian tradition has attempted to walk a middle path between the extremes of medico-moral optimism (that preserves life at all costs with all means) and medico-moral pessimism (that destroys life when it becomes burdensome or dysfunctional).

This middle path roots in a value judgment on the meaning of life and death. That value judgment could be put as follows: life is a basic good (as the condition for all other values and goods); but it is not the ultimate or absolute good. Similarly death is an evil, but it is not an ultimate or absolute evil. For this reason there is a limit on the means that must be used to preserve life. If there were no such limit, and we were obliged to use all means to sustain life, the meaning of life would be distorted and the achievement of higher values rendered more difficult.

What is the limit on the means that we must use to preserve our lives? It has been traditionally stated in terms of "ordinary" and "extraordinary" measures. There are two elements that functioned in the past in the determination of means as ordinary or extraordinary: hardship and hope of benefit. Thus if certain medical interventions or life-supports do not represent an excessive hardship to the patient and if they offer her-him reasonable hope of benefit, these are said to be ordinary—and obligatory. Contrarily, if they are excessively inconvenient or, even if they are not, they offer no reasonable hope of benefit (e.g., they would only prolong the dying process), they are said to be extraordinary—and as a general rule, not obligatory.

Two things should be noted about this vocabulary. First, the terms are extremely relative. They refer to *excessive* inconvenience, to *reasonable* hope of benefit. Obviously, their application can only be made by reference to an individual patient and his or her circumstance. Thus the terms do not answer all concrete problems; rather they provide a perspective or mental preparation to be brought to the decision-making process.

Secondly, the standard hardships envisaged by Christian thinkers are gradually disappearing. For instance, one such hardship was expense. If the expense of medical treatment would plunge a family into destitution, it was regarded as too great a price to pay. The patient would not have to use such means, though he or she was free to do so. In contemporary times, various agencies (government, insurance companies, etc.) are absorbing much of the burden of medical care. Something similar can be said of pain and most of the other factors that rendered means extraordinary. This means that increasingly judgments are made with an eye to a single factor: benefit to the patient. Will the means used simply prolong the dying process? Will it leave the person alive but with profound physical or mental disturbances? These and similar questions function in most decisions about artificial life-supports and medical interventions.

If that is the case, it is clear that the judgment about whether a particular means or life-support system ought to be used is increasingly made in terms of "quality of life" considerations. The term "quality of life" is regrettable because it is associated with a destructive history and some rather destructive possibilities. But the idea has always functioned in traditional attitudes and policies.

In summary, then, Christian reasoning has seen human responsibility toward life as *care for* the dying and desperately ill, not as *killing*. Its overarching concern is the form treatment should take, not whether treatment should be abandoned by killing interventions. Since the form of treatment has been determined by the overall good of the patient and the values that define that good, this approach—broadly shared across ecumenical lines—represents the best understanding of "death with dignity." In a technologically sophisticated age, there is always the danger that *techne* will replace the human experience rather than serve and support it. Concretely, there is the danger that "death with dignity" will be reduced to merely technological qualities (efficiency, cleanliness, painlessness, swiftness). When that happens, certain instrumental aspects of human experience are absolutized, and something of the human is distorted. It is in such an atmosphere that one begins to think of killing as a form of treatment indistinguishable from withdrawal of artificial life-supports.

For this reason, it is important to keep in mind two attitudes that function as controls and guides in the implementation of the basic value judgment on the meaning of life and death. One touches pain and suffering, the other interdependence. They have been stated excellently by an Anglican study group in their report entitled *On Dying Well*.

> 1. "The value of human life does not consist simply of a scale of pleasure and pain. Such may be the value of an animal's life. A dog's life, for example, may be valuable insofar as it is filled with doggy pleasure and devoid of doggy pains. But the value of human life consists in a variety of virtues and graces as well as in pleasure. These together constitute man's full humanity. They grow in soil in which action and passion, doing and suffering, pleasure and pain are intermixed. What a man is consists not only of what he does, but also of how he endures. A fully human life is inescapably vulnerable, as every lover knows, and even suffering may by grace be woven into the texture of a larger humanity. It is not that Christians believe that suffering is in itself a good, or that it necessarily ennobles. It may indeed destroy, and the alleviation of pain is a Christian as well as a human duty. But suffering as exposure to what is beyond one's voluntary control, suffering as undergoing, even as diminishment, is part of the pattern of becoming human. Even dying need not be simply the ebbing away of life; it may be integrated into life and so made instrumental to a fuller life in God" (p. 21).
>
> 2. "There is a movement of giving and receiving. At the beginning and at the end of life receiving predominates over and even excludes giving. But the value of human life does not depend only on its capacity to give. Love, *agape*, is the equal and unalterable regard for the value of other human beings independent of their particular characteristics. It extends especially to the helpless and hopeless, to those who have no value in their own eyes and seemingly none for society. Such neighbor-love is costly and sacrificial. It is easily destroyed. In the giver it demands unlimited caring, in the recipient absolute trust. The question must be asked whether the practice of voluntary euthanasia is consistent with the fostering of such care and trust" (p. 22).

Christian reasoning has answered that question with a negative and I believe the answer is correct.

It is within such general perspectives that the case of George and Marion ought to be approached. These perspectives will then be individualized to fit the facts of the case. Yet some of these facts are terribly unclear and make discussion of the case risky and hypothetical.

First, it is not clear what Marion sees as her alternatives or options. On the one hand there is mention of "euthanasia," of making "a decision to end human life," of "throwing back that gift (of life)." Furthermore, there is the recollection of George's statement that "if I were in Pit's place, I would do exactly the same thing." On the other hand, Marion asks: "Do I tell the doctors to let you go?" Therefore, is Marion debating (1) *"letting him go"* vs. continued use of artificial life-supports (oxygen, intravenous feeding); or (2) *killing* George vs. continued use of artificial life-supports? Indeed, does she see any difference? I do. We have responsibility for either decision, but because we must assume responsibility for both decisions does not mean that they are identical morally.

There may be any number of ways of explaining the difference between killing and allowing to die—some more problematic than others—but regardless of how the difference is explained, if it is concluded that we may not kill a dying patient (though we are not always bound to keep the patient alive), this can only mean that it is not for the patient's and our true good to do so. That means that, all things considered, killing is unreasonable. And if it is unreasonable, it would be at odds with our convictions about divine providence. For we share that providence in our rational natures.

Second, there is George's condition. He is described as "completely paralyzed," with "vacant stare," "could no longer speak," "an existence without your mind in dialogue." Is George *consciously experiencing* Marion's care and love, or is he beyond such experience? Is he capable of any communication so that he could be part of Marion's decision? Furthermore, is George in pain or not? Complete paralysis would lead one to believe he is not. Yet all that Marion can see ahead is "months of uselessness and pain."

These two points are not clear and they are vital to deciding what form of treatment is most appropriate. Why are they vital to Marion's decision? First, if George is in any way capable of making the decision to cease artificial life-supports, it is his prerogative and responsibility to do so. Secondly, the factors in light of which he (or Marion, if George is incapable of decision) would make his decision to continue life-supports or withdraw them are freedom, lack of pain, life expectancy. Because a person is the soul of his body and the body of his soul, no one of these factors can be absolutized in decisions about care for the dying. Thus it is not *human* care for the dying to maximize liberty at the cost of great and intractable pain. Nor is it *human* care for the dying to prolong life inconsiderately (i.e., with no consideration of increased suffering and diminished liberty). All of these values must be mixed and balanced. For it is not biological life for its own sake that is to be preserved, but biological life insofar as it is the basis for human existence. If such existence is no longer possible, it would hardly be reasonable and the implementation of God's providence to preserve such life.

The case of George and Marion raises many hard questions. Behind them all is the single crucial question: What is the Christianly reasonable thing to do and what are the criteria for discerning this? For what is Christianly reasonable is the execution of the providence of the Creator.

Selected Bibliography

Arthur Dyck, "The Good Samaritan Ideal and Beneficient Euthanasia: Conflicting Views of Mercy," *Linacre Quarterly* 42 (1975), pp. 176–188. This article examines the assumptions about mercy in the euthanasiast ethic.

Richard A. McCormick, S.J., "The New Medicine and Morality," *Theology Digest* 21 (1973), pp. 308–321. This examines recent literature on the distinction between killing and allowing to die.

On Dying Well (Church Information Office, Church House, Dean's Yard, SWIP 3NZ, 1975), pp. 1–27. An Anglican study group examines the ethics of care for the dying.

James Rachels, "Active and Passive Euthanasia," *New England Journal of Medicine* 292 (1975), pp. 78–80. Rachels argues that there is no difference between omission and commission in care for the dying.

John Macquarrie

The doctrines of creation and providence are among the most fundamental in the Christian faith. They are no mere speculative beliefs about the universe. Rather, they deeply affect our practical attitudes and decisions, as is brought out in the case of George and Marion. Clearly, it makes a great difference to one's feel for life, and one's attitude to the surrounding world accordingly, if one believes that the world has come into being through the power of a personal and loving Creator who still directs its history toward the fulfillment of His good purposes, or that chance and necessity are the ultimate forces to be reckoned with and that we ourselves are here because, as a French biologist recently expressed it, "our numbers came up in the Monte Carlo game."

It is wrong to think that the doctrines of creation and providence somehow make life easier, or that they reflect what is called "wishful thinking." They do indeed make possible an ultimate trust, but this is only at the cost of imposing a quite unique responsibility. The ambiguity is already plainly expressed in the Genesis stories of the creation. The individual is part of the creation, of the earth earthy, subject to natural laws; yet humankind is also the bearer of the image of God, and accorded dominion over the creation. Persons are in fact co-creators with God, for they have a share in shaping an as yet fluid and plastic world—a world in which the most fluid entity is human nature itself.

Abraham Heschel once declared that our attitude to the world must combine elements both of manipulation and of appreciation. It is the combination of these two opposing attitudes that is so difficult. Yet this is only one of many tensions in which we human beings find ourselves, when we consider that we are both part of the creation and yet its stewards, charged with an awesome responsibility. To be human, one cannot be just part of Nature, adapting oneself to its

---

John Macquarrie is Lady Margaret Professor of Divinity and Canon of Christ Church, Oxford University. He holds two earned doctorates from the University of Glasgow. His writings include *Principles of Christian Theology, Existentialism*, and *Thinking About God*. He is an ordained priest in the Church of England.

demands like a plant or an animal; but one cannot set oneself up as the absolute exploiter and manipulator of Nature, as if man himself were the ultimate and the measure of all things. The human condition is more complex, and it is this complex relation of persons to the world that comes to expression in the biblical doctrines of creation and providence more truly than in any other theory or ideology about humanity.

Let us keep in mind then this paradoxical demand of manipulation on the one hand, appreciation or acceptance on the other. It comes out very poignantly in the dilemma of Marion. There is certainly *appreciation* here—appreciation for the gift of life. With all our technology, we cannot bring life into being, and certainly not the life of persons on the human level. Marion has known that life in a wonderfully fulfilling way. She has known love and warmth, the joy of music and the arts, the satisfaction of being useful and wanted. She has shared this life with George. It has been a gift, and certainly not something that they have created for themselves. But here again is a paradox in human existence: we can terminate life, but we cannot create it or recreate it.

The reverence for life runs very deep in all religions—not only in Christianity but, notably, in Buddhism. This reverence is something to be maintained. Life is a mystery passing human understanding. Even if we discovered the physico-chemical properties of the living, and even if we were able to synthesize living organisms (and both of these possibilities may not be so far off), this would be only the tiniest step toward life in the full sense in which we know it as human beings. We rightly revere life, and, indeed, Albert Schweitzer built a whole philosophy on that fundamental appreciation for the mystery of life. In Schweitzer's philosophy, of course, *life* meant far more than simply the biological phenomenon, wonderful though that is. *Life* meant a universal will toward fuller being. And this is where Marion's dilemma is sharpened. Is George really living? Is this appendix in small print, so to speak, worthy to follow on the glorious chapters that constituted their real life together?

We note that she has been assured by the hospital staff that her husband has suffered irreversible damage. He can never fully *live.* Not only at the theological level, but also at the medical level there are nowadays new questions about death and life, and there is a strong tendency to understand death as occurring not when the heart ceases to beat or the lungs to breathe, but when the brain has perished. Incidentally, I do not think that at this point we are obtruding nontheological considerations into the commentary. It is true that the factual information about the state of George's nervous system, heart and so on is obtained by nontheological investigations, but the fact that the human being can acquire such knowledge or even has a duty to acquire it is part of the meaning of creation. It is part of this paradox that man is on the one hand a creature who ought to appreciate the creation and especially to revere life, and that he is on the other hand given dominion so that he ought to mold the creation and even in some cases manipulate life. The whole of medical science is a manipulation of life, and insofar as it has made life richer and happier, it has surely been good and in accord with the mind of the Creator.

But suppose that life in the full sense has come to an end, and it is certain that it can never be restored. Does reverence for life demand that George, who was once a real person, truly alive, should continue to "live" as a vegetable? Or is there not perhaps an irreverence for life here? Would this not be a denial of the dignity of life, almost a kind of obscenity, in keeping alive in a reduced biological sense one who was once alive in the full human sense? Would the manipulation lie in letting the person die, or is it not rather a manipulation and an irreverence to keep him alive in some reduced way although Nature is now ready to bring him to a quiet end? My own view is this: Where the personality (and/or brain) have been irreversibly damaged, there is no obligation to strive officiously to keep the biological processes of the body going—indeed, it might even be an affront to human dignity to do this. Hence my use of the word *obscene.*

It is a different matter, however, to take positive steps to end a life, e.g., by drugs, poisons, etc. Here the most dignified course may be just for the person to submit to the course of nature. Let us agree, however, that there may be borderline cases where the distinction cannot easily or certainly be made. In these matters, every case is unique, and needs to be studied carefully in the light of its particular character. At this point again factual information has to be related to the theological perspective, and one has to ask whether letting George die would be a positive act of terminating life, or whether keeping him "alive" is an officious and unwise interference with Nature. This is indeed a crucial point in Christian decision making, where reverence for life and the duty to be a good steward of God's gifts have to be weighed against each other and where the balance may be very fine. I should think myself that taking positive steps to terminate a life in which there is still some glow of personal being might well be an offense against that very deep and very sacred principle that we call reverence for life—reverence, that is to say, for the irreplaceable and unrepeatable; but it is quite a different matter to withdraw artificial life-supports from one whose personal being has already died. Even here, however, some searching of motives is required.

It is clear from what has been said that a doctrine of creation does not automatically solve any problems. It neither bids us preserve life or the merest spark of life in all and every circumstance, nor does it give *carte blanche* in disposing of matters according to our own convenience. It sets us in the tension of appreciation and manipulation, of knowing ourselves as creatures and yet also co–creators and coworkers with God.

What has been said about the doctrine of creation applies with equal force to the doctrine of divine providence. To believe in providence is not to believe that God has already determined everything for the best—that would be a kind of fatalism. But it is to believe that in the evolution of the universe and in the course of human history there is at work what Matthew Arnold called "a Power not ourselves, making for righteousness," and to accept our own responsibility of learning where righteousness lies and then working wholeheartedly with this Power not ourselves. There will be occasions where our attitude must be one of acceptance, where we must bow our heads in patient submission. There is a dignity about those old people, for instance, who accept that their lives must contract and who know when to withdraw from activities which they may once have held very dear. But there will be other occasions when we try to change to the very utmost of our power the circumstances which have overtaken us.

It cannot be stressed too much that belief in a creating and ordering God is no easy way out. It is neither a license for manipulation and exploitation nor an excuse for sitting back and letting things take their course. It keeps driving us to strain to the uttermost the powers of reason and conscience that are part of the gift of creation. We have to try to change the things that can be changed and ought to be changed, we have to accept with patience the things that cannot be changed, and ought not to be changed, and we have to learn to distinguish between them.

Selected Bibliography

John Macquarrie, *Principles of Christian Theology* (New York: Charles Scribner's Sons, 1966), especially Chapters 10 and 11. Sets forth the theological doctrines of providence and creation.

Hugh Montefiore, (ed.), *Man And Nature* (London: Jas. Collins, 1975). A report on the environmental question by a commission set up by the Archbishops of Canterbury and York.

Daniel O'Connor and Francis Oakley, eds., *Creation—The Impact of an Idea* (New York: Charles Scribner's Sons, 1969). A collection of essays dealing with the concepts of nature and society in the light of modern knowledge.

Thomas C. Oden

It is not surprising that Marion is troubled in conscience, for in addition to her dilemma, she is apparently getting encouragement from her pastor to think in permissive, "cheap grace" terms. Even if she and her pastor agreed, however, that euthanasia or treatment refusal were the best alternative, they would have difficulty convincing their physician that treatment should be terminated for a patient with cognitive function, spontaneous respiration, and all vital life signs. Standard medical practice says that treatment is terminated only when there is an irreversible cessation of vital brain and other

---

Thomas C. Oden is Professor of Theology, Drew University. He studied at the University of Oklahoma, Southern Methodist University, and received his Ph.D. from Yale University. His publications include *The Intensive Group Experience: the New Pietism*, *The Structure of Awareness*, and *The Promise of Karl Barth: the Ethics of Freedom*. He is an ordained Methodist minister.

functions. Even the broadest interpretations of "judicious neglect" of dying patients function with criteria not present in George's case. "Judicious neglect" is usually reserved only for those irreversible cases where there is terrible pain, and/or loss of all cognitive or sapient function, and/or imminent death, and/or grave burdens of care. George exhibits none of these conditions. We are speaking here not of a comatose or incompetent patient, but one who is able to understand, capable of responsiveness, not in terrible pain, and likely to live for some time. The physician cannot act to take life, even with merciful intent, and cannot legally omit an action which knowingly would sustain life. Furthermore, once a life-sustaining treatment is initiated, the moral predisposition is on the side of its continuation. However, in cases where the above conditions of "judicious neglect" are present, it is possible for the physician licitly to elect not to vigorously pursue treatment of certain new infections or emergencies in the best interest of the patient. But George's condition does not justify that. Marion risks a future of burdensome, incipient guilt if she colludes knowingly in an action causing death, however compassionate her motivation. For merciful intent, under present law, medical practice, and moral tradition, does not justify the taking of human life.

The task of the theological brief is to relate the situation to the norm. The situation is one of conflict between the value of relieving suffering and the value of life itself. The norm is the confession that God is the "Maker of heaven and earth," with the implication that God is giver of all things, including life under circumstances of stress and suffering.

The voluntary and direct taking of life, either one's own life or another's, is an irremediable injustice to oneself, to God, and to one's family and society. To take life is to dispose of it irretrievably, as if one were the legitimate authority over it. No person possesses legal and moral right to dispose of human life, either his own or another's, according to the Jewish and Christian traditions, however sympathetic one's motive. For if life is an inalienable gift of God, it cannot lawfully be renounced, even by the individual with his or her consent. For according to Jewish and Christian Scriptures, the individual does not have absolute right to self-determination over even his or her own bodily life, much less the life of another. "The innocent and just person you shall not put to death" (Exod. 23:7). Pope Pius XII has written that "a doctor worthy of his profession . . . will scorn any suggestions made to destroy life, however frail or humanly useless it may appear, knowing that unless a man is guilty of some crime deserving the death penalty, God alone, no power on earth, may dispose of his life." Following the commandment "You shall not kill," Jewish, Catholic, and Protestant teaching has condemned euthanasia and suicide as contrary to God's will.

Thomas Aquinas offers six arguments against suicide: (1) The taking of one's own life is contrary to the inclination implanted in every creature by the Creator which inclines one to care for oneself and to resist risks of death insofar as one can; (2) It is contrary to the call to be charitable, since charity also includes loving oneself; (3) You are a part of a family and a community which has no way of benefiting from your resources and possibilities if you are dead; so by destroying yourself you irremediably take away all potential values for all the communities to which you belong; (4) Anyone who takes his or her own life or another's, takes away something that God gives. Since life is sheer gift to humankind, it belongs to God alone to receive it back again in death, according to Deuteronomy 32:39; (5) "To bring death upon oneself in order to escape the other afflictions of this life, is to adopt a greater evil in order to avoid a lesser"; (6) Suicide is a particularly grave sin because "no time is left . . . to expiate it by repentance" (*Summa Theologica*, 2a, 2ae, 64.5). All of these arguments apply by analogy to premature treatment termination and the withholding of life support.

Although looking for suffering is a morbid act, the faithful Christian will accept life even under conditions of suffering as God's gift. Suffering may become an occasion for making reparations for one's own sins and for others. God Himself chose to take responsibility for sin even when it required suffering. The Apostles declared that they rejoiced "even in our present sufferings, because we know that suffering trains us to endure, and endurance brings proof that we have stood the test, and this proof is the ground of hope" (Rom. 5:5).

Life does not cease being an inestimable gift just at the moment when things become difficult or burdensome. Covenant commitment, according to Scripture, is tested through suffering both in the God-Israel relationship and in the man-wife relationship. Husband and wife have something special to learn about God's grace precisely amid their limitation and dependence which would not be learned if one or both were dead at their own initiative.

The value of life does not depend upon our pleasure-pain assessment of it, but upon God's granting of it, and valuing it Himself. For God chose to take upon Himself the specific burdens and conditions of human existence, even unto the cross and death. The hedonism which is engulfing our sensate society says simply: When life is not happy, give it up. When it involves more pain than pleasure, dispose of it. For Jewish and Christian consciousness, however, life is not understood as given merely for pleasure to be discarded when pain comes, but rather for the sanctification of personhood and for growth in responsiveness to God's grace even and precisely amid suffering when regrettably it comes. Human freedom has much to learn about its own source and ground precisely by means of struggling through its own specific limitations, not the least of which are suffering and death (cf. Søren Kierkegaard, *The Sickness Unto Death*, and Luther's "The Fourteen of Consolation").

None of us lives, and no one of us dies "for himself [or herself] alone. If we live, we live for the Lord; and if we die, we die for the Lord. Whether therefore we live or die, we belong to the Lord. This is why Christ died and came to life again, to establish his lordship over dead and living. You, sir, why do you pass judgment on your brother?" (Rom. 14:7–10). "You do not belong to yourselves," Paul declares further. "Do you not know that your body is a shrine of the indwelling Holy Spirit . . .?" (1 Cor. 6:19–20). On one occasion Paul himself prevented an impending suicide (Acts 16:27).

However public opinion may wax or wane on euthanasia, the Jewish and Christian tradition speaks clearly: Life is God's gift, not to be disposed of by human hands. Euthanasia has been viewed as a sin for the same reasons that suicide and homicide are sins: they arrogate to human self-determination that which belongs only to God.

Fantasize Marion Hathaway meditating on her dilemma directly out of the Confession of Dositheus (1672): "Yes, I believe that everything that exists is governed by your providence, God. You permit evil to exist, yet you are not the author of evil. You intend good to come out of evil. When we must face suffering, we pray that it may be overruled by some greater, even if hidden, good. It is as if you graft on to our struggles and alienations something better which we could not have foreseen or devised without them. It is your mysterious and ineffable will, only partly known by us. Yet the part that is known gives us confidence in that which is unknown."

How might good pastoral care advise Marion? It will listen empathetically to her struggle, and witness, from within her language frame, to the providence of God. It will help her to grasp that life is not only meaningful at those times we pronounce it to be meaningful to us. For the biblical understanding of God's providence views life as meaningful within God's frame of reference every moment, regardless of whether we perceive its meaning, and even when we are completely convinced that it is meaningless. This is exactly what faith in providence asserts: that the unfolding of time and history is meaningful precisely in those moments that seem totally meaningless. Pastoral care will help Marion and George enter into the potential learnings that are offered in the situation of facing death that are not available in ordinary human experiencing.

The question was put to Jesus regarding the man born blind: Who sinned—this man or his parents? Jesus' answer is still pertinent to circumstances such as George and Marion's: Neither the person's nor his parents' sins are the cause or meaning of this difficulty. This sickness has come on this person, said Jesus, in order that the work of God can be made apparent. Through our contingencies and illnesses, God shows us how He brings good out of evil, strength out of weakness, faithful celebration out of human limitations. The thorn was not removed from Paul's flesh, but precisely through it he learned that God's grace is "sufficient for every need." Suffering need not defeat us. Christian faith has no thought of making the value of life as God's gift dependent upon the amount of suffering we experience. It is through Jesus' death and resurrection that we learn that God's grace is present amid suffering to call us into radical trust.

Selected Bibliography

Gordon Kaufmann, *Systematic Theology: An Historicist Perspective* (New York: Charles Scribner's Sons, 1968). Note the excellent chapter on "The Providential Ordering of the World."

Søren Kierkegaard, *Fear and Trembling and the Sickness Unto Death* (Princeton: Princeton University Press, 1954). Stages of despair in relation to faith.

Martin Luther, "The Fourteen of Consolation," *Works of Martin Luther*, vol. 3 (Philadelphia: Muhlenberg Press, 1930). A timeless masterpiece of pastoral care.

Thomas C. Oden, *The Structure of Awareness* (Nashville: Abingdon Press, 1969), especially part one on guilt.

Wolfhart Pannenberg, *Basic Questions in Theology*, vols. 1 and 2 (Philadelphia: Fortress Press, 1970). A major contribution to understanding the resurrection.

4

"Jesus Christ, His Only Son, Our Lord"

Theological Introduction

THOMAS D. PARKER

The second article of the Creed is the central, and by far longest, article. Although succeeding theological discussion expanded the first and third articles considerably, the statement of belief in the second article remains fairly fixed among the Eastern Orthodox and the entire Western church, especially as fixed in the Nicene Creed and its interpretation in the Definition of Chalcedon (451).

There are two major reasons why the second article is the most amply developed in the Creed. First, the entire Christian faith hinges on the figure of Jesus Christ. The first article is prelude and the third article postlude to this center, apart from which there would be no Christianity. Some of the earliest creedal sources are little more than a confession of Jesus as Lord, together with the story of the passion and resurrection. The liturgical confession included in St. Paul's letter to the Philippians is an excellent example of this early stress (Phil. 2:6–11; versus 1 Cor. 8:6, 12:3, and 15:3–7). The Creed preserves this emphasis.

Second, the contents of the article are more like a divine drama than a list of beliefs. It is a "story" of the divine "second person of the blessed Trinity" who "assumed" human being to himself, was born of the Virgin, lived among us doing the works of the Kingdom and telling good news, suffered and died for us and for our salvation, was buried in the earth, was raised on the third day and ascended to the right hand of power, and rules until all things are transformed into the Kingdom of God. The Creed tells this story.

In the period of the early Church Fathers two great theological debates set the terms in which later generations would begin their own reflection. The first of them resulted in the statement that Jesus Christ, the only begotten Son of God, was truly "of the same essence as the Father." "Light from Light," he "came down from heaven, and was incarnated by the Holy Spirit and the Virgin Mary" and became human. This is the famous doctrine of the *homoousion* (of the same essence), that Jesus Christ is not merely like God, but himself fully God, although not all there is of God. This is what classical theology has meant by such phrases as *the deity of Christ* and terms such as *incarnation*, or, more recently, *eternal God-manhood.*

The second defined some of the limits within which the *homoousion* could legitimately function in theological discourse. It concluded by stating the full humanity and deity of Jesus Christ, and the uniqueness of the one in whom these two natures were joined "without confusion, without change, without division, without separation," who himself is not two but one "person" or *hypostasis.* The resulting idea of the Person of Christ was an attempt to do justice to the full humanity and deity of Christ and to protect the unity of his person. These concerns animated different sections of the ancient Church in their struggle against what many perceived to be false teaching or heresy.

Christology is concerned with the person of Jesus the Christ, his relation to God on the one hand and to humankind on the other. The Church Fathers reiterated again and again their belief that, whatever the work of Christ might be, he could only complete it if in his person he incorporated the reality and being of God *and* of humanity. As they would put it, only he who shares in both can overcome the alienation which is related to human sin and corruption. This is the ontological presupposition of the gospel.

In this developed form Christology insists on the uniqueness and universality of Jesus Christ: he is the only one in whom God is incarnate, and he is related to all persons, irrespective of race, sex, creed, culture or point in time, as their God and their fellow human being. However, this form raises tremendous problems for theological reflection: how can the infinite and unconditioned become finite conditioned without short-circuiting the meaning of these terms, and how can one person incorporate in his own history two complete and diverse "natures." Many critics, early and later, have puzzled over what they find to be an anomaly if not a freak rather than a statement of the profoundest mystery.

The consensus of official medieval Church theology is given succinctly in the theological statement of the Fourth Lateran Council (1215):

> And finally, the only-begotten Son of God, Jesus Christ, made incarnate by a common action of the Holy Trinity, and conceived by Mary ever virgin with the cooperation of the Holy Spirit, became a true man composed of a rational soul and human flesh, one person in two natures; and he pointed out the way of life more clearly. According to his divinity, he is immortal and impassible, yet according to his humanity he became passible and mortal.

This consensus is expressed with varying accents in the confessions of Western Christendom, while the Eastern churches keep it primarily in the words of the ancient creeds. Recent theological reflection among Protestant and Roman Catholics alike has sought new models for interpreting the Person of Christ, such as a "spirit Christology," a Christology of process, and various revisions of adoptionist Christologies.

Peace Child

Don Richardson sat cross-legged facing the elders of a Sawi (Sä′wē) village deep in the interior of West Irian in early 1963. These long-isolated people were headhunters and cannibals. Don lived among them for seven months, learning their language and customs. Much time had been spent pressing them to make peace despite their training for violence, and urging them to accept Jesus Christ as their Lord and peacemaker. He had come close to despair of never reaching his goals, so pervasive was the hostility. Now he had another chance.

The Sawi

In June 1962 Don Richardson established a camp in Sawi territory. He built a house and moved into it with his wife and young son. The next few months were spent learning the Sawi language and customs, using advanced methods of linguistics. During this period the people of two Sawi villages relocated nearby. He believed that the

---

This case study was adapted from Don Richardson's *Peace Child* (A Regal Press Book), by Prof. Jack Rogers of Fuller Theological Seminary as a basis for class discussion rather than to illustrate either effective or ineffective handling of the situation.

Jack Bartlett Rogers is Associate Professor of Theology and Philosophy of Religion, Fuller Theological Seminary and a Fellow of CSI. He was educated at the University of Nebraska and Pittsburgh Theologican Seminary, receiving his Th.D. from the Free University of Amsterdam. He has published *Scripture in the Westminster Confession: A Problem of Historical Interpretation for American Presbyterians, Confessions of a Conservative Evangelical*, and is an editor and contributor to *Case Studies in Christ and Salvation*. He is an ordained Presbyterian minister.

novelty of the new family and the practicality of things like nylon fishline, machetes, mirrors, etc. had drawn them and overcome the normally warlike ways in which the villages were accustomed to relate. That belief was unfounded; fourteen fierce, intervillage battles were fought within sight of his house during the first two months he lived among them. After that he lost count of the hostilities.

A Sawi child is trained to get his way by sheer force of violence and temper. He is goaded constantly to take revenge for every hurt or insult. Parents give examples as they carry out violent retaliation for anything that offends them. The Sawi hear a constant recitation of stories and legends exalting violence and treachery as traditional obligations. Those devising new forms of treachery become legend-makers, and insure their names being passed down in honor in the main body of Sawi legends.

In the peaceful times between fighting, Don Richardson tried to teach Sawi men stories from the Bible. They were generally not interested. Only once did his presentation get a ringing response from the Sawi. He reported afterward: "I was describing Judas' betrayal of Jesus. About halfway through the dsecription I noticed they were all listening intently. They heard how Judas had kept close company with Jesus for three years, sharing the same food, traveling the same road. That any associate of Jesus would conceive the idea of betraying such an impressive figure was highly unlikely.

"At the climax of the story, Maum (Moum) whistled a birdcall of admiration. Kani (Kä·nē′) and several others touched their fingertips to their chest in awe. Others chuckled.

"At first I sat there confused. Then the realization broke through: they were acclaiming Judas as the hero of the story. Kani leaned forward and exclaimed, 'That was a real *tuwi asonai man*' (Tōō·′wē ä·sō·nī′män)."

It took Richardson some time to understand the phrase. He later understood it to mean "to fatten him with friendship for an unsuspected slaughter." He realized that the Sawi idealized treachery as a virtue, a goal in life. Judas, to them, was a super-Sawi!

Don and his wife, Carol, discussed the problem over lunch as they always did. They had hoped together to bring the gospel to the Sawi while respecting Sawi culture. Now it seemed almost hopeless.

"God always has a way," Carol said. "There must be a way." They agreed to hope and pray for a key to the situation. Then the next day really serious fighting broke out again between Haenam (Hī·näm′) and Kamur (Kä·mûr′).

Reluctantly the Richardsons concluded that their coming and drawing two villages together had deprived these violent people of the mutual isolation needed to survive in relative peace. They determined that for the good of the people they would leave. Don told his decision to the chief men of each village. "Since you cannot make peace with each other, it is clear to us we ought to leave. If we stay here, it is only a matter of time until more are killed, and then you will be locked in a blood-feud which may take still more lives."

That evening a delegation of leading men from each of the villages came to the Richardson's home. "Don't leave us," one of them pleaded solemnly. "But I don't want you to kill each other," he replied. "We are not going to kill each other." The speaker steeled himself as he said, "Tomorrow we are going to make peace."

The Peace Child

On the following day the Richardsons watched as all the people of the two villages gathered. Emotions were at a high pitch and women were crying as two men from different villages approached each other, each with a tiny baby in his arms. Kaiyo (Kī·yō′) and Mahor (Mä·chôr′) stood face to face. "Mahor," Kaiyo challenged, "will you plead the words of the village of Kamur among your people?"

"Yes," Mahor responded, "I will plead the words of Kamur among my people." Kaiyo held forth his little son: "Then, I give you my son and with him my name." Mahor received him gently into his arms: "Eehaa! It is enough! I will surely plead for peace between us."

People of both villages thundered forth with shouts of triumph. People now began calling Mahor by Kaiyo's name. A man named Mahaen (Mä·hīn′), from Mahor's village, appeared at the front of the crowd. He presented his baby son to Kaiyo. Again the exchange of a child and names took place. The shouts of triumph from the two villages were mixed with anguished cries from the mothers and close relatives of the children exchanged.

The ceremony continued. Mahor shouted an invitation to people of both villages: "Those who accept this child as a basis for peace, come and lay hands on him." Men and women, young and old, filed past the two newly exchanged babies and laid their hands on them.

The children were next carried to the manhouses of their respective villages and adorned for a peace celebration. A leading woman of each village then held each child, while rows of former enemies passed by the children to confront each other. They moved to the throb of drums, meeting each other and exchanging names and gifts. After the trade, a wild dance ensued, symbolizing that the people of the two villages had now embraced each other. As long as the peace children lived, no one who had laid his hand on one could work violence against those of the village who gave him.

Richardson was moved and puzzled at first by this sudden reversal of warlike patterns. All his efforts to urge peace in the name of his God had failed. Yet this tribal ceremony had apparently succeeded, and held great power. Should he now go or stay? Was there a way of sharing the gospel he believed with people whose traditions were so alien to his own, without comprising what he believed or destroying them and their culture?

The Christian Message in West Irian

After two months of reflection and questioning to learn more of the peace-child custom, Richardson returned to talk with the elders of the Sawi villages. "When I saw you exchanging children, at first I was horrified," he began. "I kept saying to myself, 'Couldn't they make peace without this painful giving of a son?' But you kept telling me, 'There is no other way.' " He leaned forward and, in accordance with Sawi custom, placed his right hand palm down on the floor. "You were right," he said.

Every eye in the manhouse was fixed on him as he continued. "When I stopped to think about it, I realized you and your ancestors are not the only ones who found that peace required a peace child. *Myao Kodon* (Mē·ou′ Kō·dōn′), the Spirit whose message I bear, has declared the same thing—true peace can never come without a peace child." There was silence. "Because *Myao Kodon* wants men to find peace with him and each other, he decided to choose a once-for-all peace child to establish peace forever."

"Whom did he choose?" asked Mahaen. Richardson answered with another question, "Did Kaiyo give another man's son or his own?" "His own," they replied. "And, Mahaen, did you give another man's son or your own?" "I gave my own," he replied, remembering the pain.

"So did God," Richardson replied, looking sideways at the wall with a Sawi gesture meaning 'think about that.' He opened an English Bible and read a part of Isaiah's prophecy in Sawi: "Unto us a child is born, unto us a son is given; and the government shall be upon his shoulder, and his name shall be called Wonderful, Counsellor, the Mighty God, the Everlasting Father, the Prince of peace. Of the increase of his government and peace there shall be no end."

Mahaen looked at Richardson. "Is He the one you've been telling us about?" "He is," Richardson replied softly. "But you said a friend betrayed Him. If Jesus was a peace child, it was the worst thing anyone could do to betray Him," Mahaen continued. The room was quiet.

As he walked away, Richardson wondered about the future. He wanted to believe the Sawi could incorporate his message about Jesus Christ into their own traditions. Would the message of a once-for-all peace child be effective in changing the Sawi bent toward violence? And if it was, would the message be distorted beyond recognition?

Theological Briefs

Kenneth S. Kantzer

The ritual of the peace child is a beautiful and instructive drama by which the estrangement between two villages is dissolved and alien persons accept each other as brothers of one family. The tribal child thereby provides a remarkable illustration of the wondrous work of Jesus Christ, the God-given peace child for every village. In Christ, too, the estrangement between men is broken down. Through his work of atonement (at-one-ment) the Christ Child unites alienated men with God as their heavenly Father and with each other as children of one family.

Missionary Richardson's practical use of the drama of the peace child raises most of the fundamental questions related to Christian faith and the meaning of the Gospel. The first issue is that of the universality and uniqueness of the Gospel. Should not Richardson have quietly withdrawn from the scene since man's healing from alienation would already have been satisfactorily achieved within the framework of his own religious culture? Should he not, at most, have supplemented the role of the peace child by encouraging the villagers to extend its benefits to other villages and ultimately to the total global village? Or, perhaps, it would have been appropriate to exhort the tribesmen to faithful and vigorous application of the peaceful relationship and, even beyond a negative absence of hostility, to draw upon the peace child sacrament as a basis for positive good to those of alien tribes. "Love your [former] enemies!"

Kenneth S. Kantzer is Dean and Professor of Bible and Systematic Theology at Trinity Evangelical Divinity School. He was educated at Ashland College, Ohio State University, Faith Theological Seminary, and received his Ph.D. from Harvard University. He is the author of *The Evangelical Christian and Modern Views of the Bible* and *The Theology of Karl Barth*. He is an ordained Evangelical Free Church minister.

Richardson chose instead to avail himself of the tribal custom as a means to convert these villages to a wholly new and utterly alien religion—namely Christianity. For him the rite of the peace child is only illustrative of "the real thing." By thus insisting upon the Christ myth (Bultmann's definition) or "true" peace child, did not he become liable to the objections: (1) that the Christian missionary with his Christian absolutism is universalizing a contingent and particular fact of history (Lessing)? and (2) is he not demonstrating religious imperialism, a manifestation of contemporary Western imperialism (which has not proved notably successful in eliminating alienations within its own cultural rootage of the West)? At the very least, missionary Richardson could be charged with exhibiting a typical ecclesiastical narrow-mindedness.

To such charges Christians have insisted on the universal necessity of the specifically Christian message in the following sense: (1) The Christ revelation is for all—red, yellow, black, white, male, female, Chinese Maoist, American blue-collar hard hat, drunken bum lying in the gutter, and the president of the American Association of Manufacturers; (2) The Christ revelation bears what is crucially important to the life and experience of all. Without it there would be no true human fulfillment; (3) The Christ revelation bears all that is essential; and, in fact, the Christian revelation stands in judgment over all religions.

The Christian witness, of course, does not confront men in a vacuum; therefore, the Christian cannot afford to ignore the religious convictions and practices of others. Nonetheless, the Christian cannot present the Christ revelation as an amalgamation in which Christian faith joins hands in a syncretistic joint effort with other equally valid religions in which each contributes its insights. If one is true to his or her own traditions, moreover, one cannot even set forth Christianity as the consummation of the "natural religion" based on a valid but inadequate or at least incomplete revelation derived from the "starry heavens above and the moral law within."

The Christian witness, of course, must recognize ungrudgingly and in all honesty (and humility), the goodness and truth in other religions wherever one finds them. There *is* a valid revelation of the common (general) grace of God (Ps. 19). This explains humanity's well-nigh universal religious bent (Rom. 1:18–20) and also constitutes humanity's truly responsible existence before God (Rom. 2; Rom. 10:18; Acts 10:34–35). Great truths abound in other religions (the ethics of Confucius); and noble lives of civic righteousness, as well as religious zeal, are apparent (my Mormon neighbor). The Christian Scripture also provides solid support for Richardson's seizing upon the tribal peace child as a point of contact in preaching the Gospel (Paul in Acts 14 and 17).

On the most superficial level, of course, Christ is "better" than Buddha. He can "do more" for one than the tribal peace child. He is, for example, a model without sin; and his teaching is more noble—the Sermon on the Mount, love your enemies. No New Testament warrant, however, can be adduced for building Christ on the foundation of other religions reckoned as good but incomplete. Harsh and even bigoted as it may appear, other religions are reckoned as false (even demonic). It is far more true to the New Testament and to the Christian tradition generally to conceive of Christianity as conquering and displacing (most imperialistic of analogies!) than of building up or building alongside of or even building on top of other religions.

The reason for this has nothing at all to do with the idea that Christianity is a "better" religion than Hinduism (in spite of certain popular apologetics). The reason, rather, is to be found in the imperative of the reality of divine revelation. Not even the *idea* of the gracious God who loves persons and accepts them freely on the basis of faith alone represents the universal imperative of the Christian witness (note the various forms of redemptive Buddhism in India and Japan). The Christian imperative stems from the living reality of the gracious God who meets us and redeems us in Jesus Christ. In the Christ Child the sovereign Lord reaches out in love to humanity as the gracious Savior. By God's own initiative God conveys acceptance of the sinner, and through faith the believer accepts his or her acceptance. From this divine act of love there flows over the redeemed person a divine compulsion which issues in the great commission recorded in the Gospels and Acts to share with all people everywhere the story of the Christ who brings true human life and ultimate meaning to each person who finds God in Christ.

Not at all does this imply, as might be inferred, the triumph of the Christian religion. It is rather uniquely the triumph of God's revelation—his work and his word. Christ judges all religions. In one sense all religions, including Christianity, stand on the same level as human thoughts and words and deeds. The Christian religion is the true religion only to the degree in which it is a right response to the genuine revelation of God.

The story of the peace child, therefore, presents an inherent danger for all overeager witnesses to the truth—namely, to build upon the humanistic elements of life, to draw from common religious experiences and thus in effect to create, just in that measure, a "do-it-yourself" religion. This is the basic biblical thrust against the idolatry of false religions. It is not a rebuke because the representations of God do less than justice to the picture of the infinite God. Their inherent wrongness lies at the very start, for they are humanity's creation; and thus they represent a man-made religion ("the work of men's hands," Ps. 115:4).

With adequate warnings appropriately displayed, it is still possible and even desirable to use the peace child as an instrument of communication. It lends itself well as a point of contact to introduce the universal (and particular!) Christ Child. God himself wished to effect a reconciliation with man. But no man could or would make the sacrifice of the offering of his own child to become the peace child for such a reconciliation. Out of a heart overflowing with divine love, therefore, God provided himself as peace child. In the second person of the triune God (so we say), the eternal God chose to come down into the world to be conceived by the Holy Spirit in the womb of the Virgin Mary, to be born as a human baby, to live out his human life, and finally, to die. For treacherous men in their perfidy refused to honor the ultimate sacrifice and gift of God. They crucified the Lord of glory—the divine, once-for-all, peace child.

The Christian's conviction that God brings reconciliation to persons uniquely in Christ raises immediately further basic issues. On what grounds does the believer come to see that it is really God who has met him or her in Christ? How does a sinful person, alienated from God, from one's neighbor, and from oneself appropriate the divine gift of reconciliation? Is the good news of the reconciling Christ, crystalized in the preaching of the contemporary Christ, patterned after the kerygma of the New Testament? Or is it in the historically verified Christ—the "real" Jesus lying hidden under layers of New Testament tradition?

The answer must not be either/or but rather both/and. The Christ of the Church is the Christ of the New Testament and apostolic preaching. The Christ of apostolic preaching is the real Christ. The reconciling God who, here and now, meets us in the pages of Holy Scripture is not just the spirit of the Christlike God. Nor is the Christian story, as told by the Richardsons, simply the "universal" truth that human reconciliation is achieved through sacrificial self-giving—perfectly illustrated in the life and death of Christ, reduplicated (less perfectly, of course) in the Sawi peace child. The Christian Gospel is the good news of what God, in Christ, has done and will do for all persons everywhere who repent of their sin and commit themselves in faith to him and to his love and grace. Through personal faith in the Christ of the New Testament, who is the only real Christ, humanity encounters the contemporary Christ, who is also the living God bringing reconciliation to humankind.

So the story of the West Irian tribal peace child may not serve as the basis on which to construct our own humanly mediated and man-made (or partly man-made and partly revealed) religion; but it can serve as an illustration and as a point of contact which in turn becomes a point of departure for announcing the good news of the revealed God, who took the initiative once and for all to become for all men in their sin the true peace child, the God-man, through whom God has manifested his infinite forgiving love and worked his own work of reconciliation (on his side) and through whom humanity may become (on humanity's side) reconciled to God and to all his fellowmen and to the universal creation of God.

Selected Bibliography

Hendrik Kraemer, *The Christian Message in a Non-Christian World* (Grand Rapids: Kregel Press, 1956). In the light of Christian revelation all apparent similarities are dissimilarities. Points of contact are only to be found by antithesis.

Don Richardson, *Peace Child* (Glendale, California: Regel Press, 1974). A sovereign God prepares the way for the understanding and reception of the Christian message by creating natural and cultural analogies.

GORDON D. KAUFMAN

This case brings out in an interesting way some of the most difficult and profound problems with which contemporary reflection on the meaning of Christ must deal. The issue I want to focus on particularly emerges in the story as a development in the thinking of Don Richardson and his wife, a development the full significance of which they probably did not themselves realize.

Christian Faith and Christian Ideas

At the outset of the account the Richardsons are presented as persons holding what I would call a fundamentally ideational conception of Christian faith. They understood their task as Christian missionaries to be, in the first place, "to teach Sawi men stories from the Bible," that is, to teach the Sawi the basic Christian ideas. It was their understanding of Christian faith and salvation that led them to approach their task in this way.

From the earliest period Christians have found it useful and important to reflect on their faith in order to define and interpret it more accurately. Precise concepts and verbal formulas were invented and refined to insure that misunderstandings of faith, which would lead ultimately to its corruption or dissolution, could readily be detected and excluded. Thus, creedal formulas and definitions were worked out with great care and were officially adopted by the Church, or official bodies acting in behalf of the Church, as binding on all Christians. It was especially important to understand and accept the centrality of Jesus of Nazareth for faith; and the various stories of the Bible, as well as the later creedal formulations, were used to spell this out with the help of a variety of metaphors ("only begotten Son of God," "Light from Light," "of the same essence as the Father," etc.). This ideational development of Christianity, however necessary

---

GORDON D. KAUFMAN is Professor of Divinity, Harvard Divinity School, and an Advisor to the CSI. He was educated at Bethel College, Northwestern University, Yale Divinity School and received his Ph.D. from Yale University. His publications include *Systematic Theology: A Historicist Perspective*, *God the Problem*, and *An Essay on Theological Method*. He is an ordained minister in the Mennonite Church.

if Christian faith were to survive and grow, brought with it certain problems and distortions. Most notable was the tendency to regard the approved ideas and formulas as definitive and unchangeable dogmas. Faith became understood as a matter of assenting to or "believing" certain verbal formulations or ideas about God and Christ, sin and redemption.

Much of Christian missionary activity has been premised on these assumptions, and it was apparently with such an understanding that Don and Carol Richardson went to West Irian to minister to the Sawi. But to their consternation they discovered they could scarcely make themselves and their purposes intelligible to the people. The problem proved more serious than mere failure to communicate effectively. The arrival of the Richardsons in West Irian apparently was the occasion for two tribal villages to move nearby and thus into fairly close proximity with each other; this led to bloody conflicts in which villagers got killed. Far from improving the lot of the Sawi, the Richardsons had brought about a situation in which they were beginning to destroy themselves. So finally they concluded that "for the good of the people" they would have to leave.

The Meaning of Christ

This is an understandable decision, humanly speaking, but its theological significance should not be overlooked. It meant that the Richardsons had come to see that their basic Christian concern for the Sawi involved something deeper and more important than simply communicating the Christian stories and ideas to them: it had to do, really, with the quality and character of the lives and suffering of the people. More important than whether they learned Christian beliefs was that their mutual self-destruction cease, that they be able to live in peace even though without benefit of the Christian message. Hearing the Christian message, learning the Christian ideas, believing the Christian beliefs, was not, after all, the indispensable thing the Richardsons had earlier supposed. They were beginning to see that the meaning of Christ has to do more with the *quality of human life he made (or makes) possible* than it has to do with believing certain ideas or stories about him or subscribing to certain (creedal) formulas.

The conclusion of the story underlines this shift in understanding and at the same time begins to show the proper function of stories and ideas—and thus also of theology. When the Richardsons decided to leave, the Sawi villages agreed to make peace with each other, and their way of doing this required a dramatic sacrifice by each village: a ritual exchange of children was now to bind the villages to each other in a new way so that they could no longer be enemies. Thus, the reconciliation between them, for which the Richardsons had striven in vain with their evangelical approach, was accomplished by a ceremonial event rooted in Sawi traditional practices. Strikingly enough, this ritual involved a kind of giving and vicarious sacrifice—as genuine reconciliation of deep human estrangements almost always does—not unlike that spoken of in the Christian story. The Richardsons were able to recognize these analogies and see that precisely this sort of actual reconciliation and peacemaking, with resultant human fulfillment, was what Christianity really was all about. Their Christian stories, thus, could now become vehicles of a further and fuller illumination of the actual communal life and problems of the Sawi; these were no longer largely abstract "truths" which they were asking the Sawi to "believe."

We are not told whether Richardson and his wife realized that this recognition implied a considerably different understanding of the meaning of Christian faith, and the significance of Christian ideas and language, than that with which they began their work. But it obviously does. Is the meaning of Christ to be understood as primarily (though of course not exclusively) a matter of subscribing to certain ideas (about God, Christ, humanity, etc.)? Or is the primary significance of Christ fundamentally nonideational, having to do with the basic quality, style, and character of human life? If the latter, it will, of course, not be possible to dispense with the use of verbal and conceptual formulations, but they will have a secondary and instrumental role: their function will be to help facilitate the life of reconciliation and love rather than simply be bearers of "truths" which must be "believed." Ideas, concepts, verbal formulations—especially those about "God" and "Christ"—will be used by thoughtful Christians only insofar as they help to promote the upbuilding of human community and the realization of free personhood, for these are the actual incarnation of Christ in contemporary life.

Traditional Christological Language and Contemporary Faith

Once this proper subordination of the ideational to the existential in Christian faith is recognized, much of the theological difficulty for moderns with traditional christological talk can fall away. That talk was attempting to express and interpret the mystery and wonder felt by ancient Christians that somehow because of their relationship with Jesus of Nazareth, they were no longer living at odds with the fundamental Source and Creator of all life and being, nor at odds with each other, but were finding reconciliation, peace, and fulfillment. They expressed this in terms of the myths and metaphors through which they understood the Source and Foundation of human life as well as their relationship to this ultimate reality—now re-created in and through Jesus.

Understanding, and even approving, all this, there is no need whatsoever for us to feel bound by those ancient formulations. We must begin rather (as did they) with the actual and existential concerns at the heart of Christian faith—the realities of reconciliation and love, of freedom and trust and loyalty—and see what Jesus Christ has to do with these matters; then we will be able to work out for ourselves (with the help of 2000 years of Christian reflection) christological formulas and ideas appropriate for our own situation and faith.

We will begin to see, perhaps, that the kind of absolute self-giving exemplified by the cross (and by the "peace child" of the Sawi) is often the price that must be paid by the innocent in order to bring some sort of peace to humankind. And we will begin to understand that it is precisely to such lives of self-sacrifice that Christians are called. So far as we recognize that genuine human fulfillment comes only in this way through self-giving ("whoever loses his life for my sake and the gospel's will save it," Mark 8:35), we will see a kind of universal significance or meaning in Christ and his cross, and we will grasp this person and this event as revelatory of the ultimate realities of human life. And from that stance and in that respect we will be able to understand again what was affirmed of old, that what we encounter in Christ is "of the same essence as the Father, . . . true God from true God." The old creedal formulas may come to have new life and meaning for us, though we will probably more naturally and normally express ourselves in somewhat different metaphors.

Of course, if we do not discover the story of Jesus to be in this way genuinely illuminative of what is really significant in human life and of how human life is to be lived, and thus actually empowering an existence of love and reconciliation, we will not be inclined to develop a christocentric—that is a Christian—theology at all, and our allegiances will fall elsewhere.

Christology is at the heart of Christian faith, not because it is somehow true that Jesus is (was) God's literal "son," and Christians are obliged to "believe" this, but because Christians in fact find the meaning and problems of their existence illuminated decisively by the man on the cross: because of him, and in relation to him, they come to grasp and better understand both who and what they are (what is "truly human") and what is the ultimate reality with which we humans have to do (what is truly "divine"). Christians have attempted to express these matters in many and variant myths and metaphors, ideas and formulas, over the centuries. This same centrality and significance of Jesus is the principle issue for contemporary Christian faith and theology.

If Christian faith is in fact about the realities of actual estrangement and reconciliation in human life, the Richardsons' decision to stay with the Sawi was probably the right one. But this was at least as much because of what the Sawi had to teach the Richardsons as because of what the Richardsons could offer the Sawi. The Sawi sacrifice of a "peace child" had enabled the Richardsons to see that genuine reconciliation is brought about through actual human giving and sacrifice, not primarily through "believing" (Western) Christian ideas or formulas. This more profound understanding made it possible for them to enter into community with the Sawi as partners and equals; the stance of superiority, with which they as "teachers of the truth" coming to "ignorant heathen" had begun their work, was broken. And thus the Richardsons could offer their lives—and their story of Jesus—to the Sawi in a way that could become truly significant, and possibly normative, for Sawi life and culture. More important than that: the Richardsons could now become missionaries of a more profound Christian reconciliation back to the Americans who originally sent them.

SELECTED BIBLIOGRAPHY

Gordon D. Kaufman, *Systematic Theology: A Historicist Perspective* (New York: Charles Scribner's Sons, 1968), especially chapters 3–4, 11–14, 27–29. Giving a much fuller elaboration of the christological position taken in this brief, this work attempts to show, through systematic interpretations of the major Christian doctrines, that Christian faith is essentially concerned with human history and historicity.

John Knox, *Jesus: Lord and Christ* (New York: Harper & Row, 1958). An influential and significant interpretation of biblical materials on Christology by a noted New Testament scholar, providing helpful background for the position taken in the brief.

H. Richard Niebuhr, *Meaning of Revelation* (New York: The Macmillan Company, 1941), especially chapters 2 and 3. A seminal interpretation of theology as dealing with the revelatory events and images carried in a historical tradition, rather than focusing primarily on doctrines and creeds.

DOROTHEE SOELLE

The case study "Peace Child" moves on two clearly distinguishable levels, which one could call, in a literary sense, setting and content. The activities and interpretations of the missionary belong to the setting, while the content is the tribal ceremony in which peace is inaugurated. In sociological terms, these levels can be described as Western industrial culture and primitive fishing and hunting society. Politically the two are ordered to the First and Third Worlds, respectively. Theologically they represent the opposition between Christianity and paganism.

It is important to be clear about the fact that not only the mission-

---

DOROTHEE SOELLE is a member of the faculty of the University of Cologne and Visiting Professor of Theology at Union Theological Seminary (New York). She studied at the Universities of Cologne and Freiburg, receiving the Ph.D. from the University of Gottingen. Her publications in English translation include *Christ the Representative*, *Political Theology*, and *Suffering*. She is a member of the Evangelical Church of Germany.

ary but also the narrator of this story belong to the white Christian, industrial world and adopt its valuations. The Sawi are introduced as headhunters. It does not occur to anyone that the culture represented by the missionary has produced far more effective forms of headhunting, for instance the body count. In the narrator's view, hostility and violence are characteristic of the Sawi; the question *why* their legends "exalt violence and treachery as traditional obligations" is not raised. Their violent proclivities are presupposed as something natural. It is not asked whether they might have historical causes which might even be traceable to experience with colonial powers. The superiority of the First World, which has nylon fishline and the Bible, and in which children are not reared "to get their way by sheer force of violence and temper," appears in every sentence of this case study. We can read it as a document of an unbrokenly naive cultural imperialism, an imperialism in which we are all caught up.

Theological questions about the content and significance of this story make sense only against this background, and they can become productive only when we reach a clear awareness of where we as inquirers live (in the First, i.e. the rich and satisfied World), when we live (after Auschwitz and Vietnam), and under what social conditions we live. This awareness must accompany our thinking, our praying, and our doing of theology.

A simple question, but perhaps the most important one, which we can put to this text, is this: where is Christ in this story? Has the missionary brought him along, as it were, in his pocket? Does he belong to the First or to the Third World? The case suggests an answer when it connects the Christian message to the ritual of infant exchange the Richardsons have experienced. The ritual—the cultural and religious means of expression in the Third World—is used to illustrate and enrich that which is already present in the First World. The missionary "has" the truth in the biblical stories which he can tell, but he can communicate it only after he has found a point of contact. Truth is understood here as essentially verbal. Peace is proclaimed and told about: this alone is the task of the missionary.

The entire theology of the First World is verbalistic in the extreme; i.e., it is full of words, it is kind to words, and it overestimates words. At the same time it is poor in gestures; it employs only one form of human expression and subordinates all others to it. Above all, however, it is irrelevant to action. We have plenty of talk about peace, but we live in a state of organized belligerence. Our peace child does not function to build the peace and mediate our tribal feuds. The case study lays great stress on the figure of Judas, but we must read at this point against the grain, if we wish to become aware of our traditional verbal bias. The Sawi identify verbally with Judas, but they go about constructing peace. They become an "instrument of his peace," to put it in the words of St. Francis. We in the First World identify with Christ, but we betray his peace. Peace is established rather by the allegedly primitive and violent Sawi. So it is that if I am actually looking for Christ, I seem to find him in the ritual of the heathen and not in our own corrupted tradition.

What consequences are we to draw for Christology from this supposition? What does the story of the peace child of the Sawi teach us about Jesus Christ? I return to the ritualized drama of the tribal culture. What kind of a God must this people have who bring about a secure peace by exchanging their own children? He is in any case not the God of Abraham. None of these fathers is summoned by a remote invisible being to slaughter his son. The laws of blood do play an elemental role, but in the exchange of the children the old natural ties are historicized and humanized. It is a question of interpersonal exchange overcoming hate, not of obedience to an incomprehensible God. At this point, then, the question becomes whether the Sawi, who obviously can cope with their murderous wishes better than we, need Christ at all. At least one must ask if they need the Christ of the missionary, the Christ of the First World. Is it not rather the case that Christ, the bringer of peace, is already among them? And won't the missionary do well to pack his bags and come right home, in order to evangelize us by telling how this wild and violent tribe makes peace? What is the actual distribution of peace and violence? Who should be converting whom in this situation?

What we need is a Christology *from below*. To articulate such a Christology is difficult, because the tradition affords little help. The tradition has privatized our relationship to peace, just as it has individualized and privatized our relationship to the peace child. We consider it to be progress that we do not physically threaten and kill one another, but instead shut up a growing percentage of the population in mental institutions, ghettos, or large-scale concentration camps (as in South Africa). The Christian tradition has not helped us to analyze the structural violence under which we live and with the help of which we have become rich and powerful.

Our Christology is thus as well-meaning and as helpless as the attempts of the missionary with nylon fishline and Bible. It is a Christology which operates from above: sociologically, politically, and theologically. It is not able to give articulation to the lives of the people around us. It does not give meaningful expression to the theologians who write Christology nor to the lay people who hear and read it.

Some of the painters and woodcarvers of the waning Middle Ages portrayed Christ in the clothing and shoes of a peasant. They used him, in other words, to clarify the situation of the afflicted and exploited peasants. It is important to use Christ and to let oneself be helped by Christ through this use. To need someone is a deeper relationship to him than to revere him. Our Christology will succeed in articulating us as the brothers and sisters of Jesus Christ on the way to the cross when it seeks to place itself in the lowest possible position, and to see the history of Jesus Christ not through the eyes of God, but through the eyes of those most wronged and humiliated by the world. Today that means through the eyes of the planetary proletariat which we call the Third World.

I can do no more here than name a few of the necessary conditions of any such Christology from below:

1. It will contain an abandonment of cultural imperialism and its theological exclusiveness. This Christology will not bring the Christ to the Sawi but will discover that he is already there: that God is at work in the exchange of children. It will not destroy but strengthen the Sawi tradition and help the people to understand it better. But theological exclusiveness and cultural imperialism are also important features of theology as it is done in the First World. Middle-class people as theologians and ministers are bringing the Christ to the poor instead of seeing him already there. The most Christlike forms of peace-making in modern times are to be found in the struggles of the working classes, which have developed nonviolent ways of fighting for justice such as the strike and boycott. A contemporary example is the United Farm Workers movement in California. A Christology from below will discover Christ sooner in the labor movement

than in the churches, understanding that Christ is greater than whatever we label Christian.

2. A Christology from below will contain an understanding of the cross of Christ which is not authoritarianly oriented to his unique suffering, but rather fraternally comprehends the cross of all the world's humiliated. Christ came to the cross because he went too far in loving people, not because a heavenly father elected him as the special victim to be punished. To stand under the cross, then, does not mean to adore him as a totally other being and in so doing to alienate oneself even in a purely religious sense. It means to go as far as he went, he who is our elder brother. The consequence of going a little bit further than we usually do is that we are fired, discriminated against, finally eliminated. The cross is the expression of love destroyed by society as it now is.

3. A Christology from below will contain an understanding of the resurrection from the dead as the currently occurring and still to occur liberation of all peoples. Resurrection was and is an object of faith, not of observation. Those who have eyes to see can see it happening among our young people, who are beginning to abandon their inherited way of life, which consists of production and consumption, and to make the cause of universal human liberation their own.

This Christology will be inclusive, fraternal, historical, and social. The century in which Jesus Christ was crucified knew more crosses than his. The highways of the Empire at the time of Spartacus' revolt were laden with the crosses of slaves. We do not understand Golgotha as long as we do not recognize Christ in the crosses of these slaves and as long as we do not see the peace child at work in the bombed out hospital of Bach Mai in Hanoi.

Selected Bibliography

Jose Miqucz-Bonino, *Doing Theology in a Revolutionary Situation* (Philadelphia: Fortress Press, 1975). The best introduction to Liberation Theology.

Frantz Fanon, *The Wretched of the Earth* (New York: Grove Press, 1968). Introduced by Sartre, a classic (and a must) for all understanding of the Third World.

Dorothee Soelle, *Political Theology* (Philadelphia: Fortress Press, 1974). Coming out of a more academic discussion with Rudolf Bultmann, but leading to the same consequences as Miquez-Bonino.

Dorothee Soelle, *Suffering* (Philadelphia: Fortress Press, 1975). Personal and collective forms of suffering reflected under the questions of how to abolish and what to learn from them.

David W. Tracy

The question of the "peace-child" Christology articulated in this case raises in a new form but not in an entirely new manner the classical questions of Christology. Since the New Testament itself includes a pluralism of Christologies—a pluralism continued and even enriched by the history of creedal statements and individual theologies in Christian life and reflection throughout the centuries, there would seem no initial general reason to distrust the attempt of a peace-child Christology formulated within and for yet another cultural context.

To recognize, indeed to affirm, the fact of pluralism in Christologies is not synonymous with suggesting that there remain no criteria by means of which we may challenge any particular Christology's appropriateness for Christian self-understanding. Indeed, one may affirm the relative adequacy of a particular Christology not only for a particular cultural setting but also for its more universal or at least its universalizing possibilities.

The fact that the Richardsons have already decided to articulate a peace-child Christology, at least for the purposes of establishing some peace between the warring peoples, is indicative of their tentative commitent to a pluralism of Christologies. It also seems to be the case, however, that the troubled conscience of the Richardsons has

---

David W. Tracy is Associate Professor of Philosophical Theology at the Divinity School, University of Chicago. He was educated at St. Joseph's Seminary, Cathedral College and the Pontifical Gregorian University from which he received his S.T.D. He is the author of *The Achievement of Bernard Lonergan* and *Blessed Rage for Order: The New Pluralism in Theology*. He is a Roman Catholic priest.

two principal foci: first, their very presence as Christian missionaries has occasioned, however unintentionally, the desperate situation described. In this particular situation, the troubled conscience of the Christian cannot but ask: is our peace-child Christology simply a desperate attempt to alleviate, perhaps even transform, a situation which our own actions have occasioned? Is this peace-child Christology, therefore, simply a human, a moral, and also an *ad-hoc* and not necessarily Christian theological response to the desperate character of this concrete situation? This last question serves to clarify the central theological dilemma with which the Richardsons are faced: are there any explicitly Christian warrants or backings which would allow one to call the "peace-child Christology" an authentically Christian Christology? To seek for such Christian warrants and backings is, in fact, to search for theological criteria relevant to judging the Christian status of this or any particular Christology.

Among such criteria, the following seem relevant not only to the question of the peace child but also to the wider question of the relative adequacy of any particular Christology. The first criterion is the need to affirm the radically christocentric character of Christian self-understanding. Included in any understanding of Christocentrism, moreover, are the focal questions of uniqueness and universality involved in the Christian affirmation of Jesus Christ. Although these two questions serve as constants in christological understandings, the answers they have received are various.

In one sense, the problem is not peculiarly Christian. For one may presuppose as fact what history and commonsense alike testify: that any specific religious tradition starts with some moment or occasion of special religious insight. If the language and the experience appropriate to that occasion bear universal implications; if they are not at the mercy of psychological or sociological forces which adequately explain their meaning without remainder, then we may describe this religious tradition as a universal, a major religion. Universality, then, implies two characteristics: the religion arises from a special historical occasion of religious insight, and the special religious experience and language are sufficiently evocative of our common experience to bear the claim of universal existential meaningfulness. As this latter claim is clarified—for example, through the *logos* tradition of Christianity—the full import of the special occasion is felt with more and more existential force. The special occasion of the preaching and person of Jesus of Nazareth clearly meets these criteria. For as the Christian religion develops in and beyond the New Testament period, one finds that this process of universalization is radicalized to the point where he who preached the Kingdom becomes himself the focus of the preaching.

This strange history—an intensification process which includes at one and the same time a universalization of religious meaning and a radicalization of the special occasion—allows one to see the peculiar complexity of christological interpretation. As that complexity has been clarified in the mainline Christian tradition, one finds the insistence that all Christian self-understanding of God, humankind, and cosmos is irretrievably christocentric. As that complexity has been developed in the history of christological reflection, one finds the concept *Christocentrism* accepted as constitutive of the Christian religion. Still, Christocentrism has been understood in two radically different ways in Christian theology. In a first and still widely influential form, *Christocentrism* means that only and solely God's "special revelation" in Jesus Christ is meaningful for authentic human self-understanding. This form of Christocentrism (more accurately labeled "exclusivist Christology") may be found in most forms of Christian fundamentalism, as well as in such sophisticated and non-fundamentalist theological forms as the Christology of Karl Barth and various evangelical Christologies.

In this case, not only the troubled conscience of the Richardsons, but also the lack of any exclusivist language in the peace-child Christology itself frees this Christology from the familiar dilemmas of all exclusivist Christologies. The question recurs, however, whether any real alternative to exclusivity can still merit a Christian label. At precisely this point the Richardsons could, and, in my judgment, should appeal to the second major kind of Christology in the Christian tradition, viz. an "inclusivist" Christology.

For this second major alternative, one finds a claim for Jesus Christ that does place an understanding of his role and person at the center of Christian self-understanding; that does believe that this understanding of Jesus Christ is universal in its applicability to the human situation. Yet this alternative does not believe it either necessary or Christianly appropriate to employ exclusivist language. For this second inclusivist christocentric position, the disclosure manifested by the Christian proclamation of Jesus Christ *is* disclosive of all reality; is meaningful for the fundamental existential questions of our existence; is central for an understanding of the transformative limit-possibilities for human existence present in the affirmation of Jesus Christ as Lord. What that special occasion ("special" or "categorical" revelation) manifests is the disclosure that the only God present to all humanity at every time and place ("original" or "transcendental" revelation) is present explicitly, actually, decisively as *my* God in *my* present response to *this* Jesus as the Christ.

This tradition of an "inclusivist Christology," moreover, is present implicitly in historical Catholic Christianity's appeals to the theological motif of the "universal salvific will of God" and in liberal Protestant Christianity's reformulations of "Christocentrism." In fact, for this latter inclusivist understanding of Christocentrism, the question of a theocentric anthropology is the constant amidst the pluralism of New Testament, creedal, and later theological Christologies. For the crucial meaning of any Christology is in its definitive response to the fundamental existential questions of our lives as human beings. This response demands that our fundamental faith, hope, and love in the faithful, trustworthy, and loving God manifested in Jesus the Christ be affirmed over and over again in however many culturally diverse forms.

In that case the following questions move to the forefront of any discussion of an analysis of the peace-child Christology: Is the image of God re-presented here the image of a loving source, sustainer, and end of all reality? The description of *Myao Kodon*, the Spirit whose message the Reverend Richardson proclaims, seems clearly none other than the God who is love. Is the image of human possibility re-presented in a particular Christology, one whose symbolic force genuinely transforms what must be called the evil even sinful inclinations of the human spirit? In this case one must affirm that, by any transcultural ethical standards, treachery and violence must perforce be listed among those evil inclinations. The creative manner by means of which the violence and treachery of the local mores is broken and transformed by the powerful and, for that culture, properly re-presentative story of the peace child seems a sure indication that the peace-child Christology, like the great line of particular Christologies before it, performs the unique and universal role of any good Christology. For here the rearticulation of the decisive event of Jesus Christ as the peace child is proclaimed in such manner that the gracious, eventful, giftlike character of God's transforming power and love breaks into this particular human situation. It might also be noted that West Irian violence and treachery are at least openly proclaimed as virtues rather than disguised in their more muted, but no less lethal, modern forms—for example, in the "discreet charm of the bourgeoisie."

Yet this last observation may lead to a final if still tentative conclusion: by the criteria of the inclusivist Christology outlined above, one may welcome the peace-child Christology of West Irian. By those same criteria, one may also hope that the Richardsons and other Christian missionaries would also develop Christologies representing the need of and possibility for a transformation of our own Western, personal, societal, and cultural violence and treachery. Do only the peoples of West Irian need that personal and societal transformation provided by any authentic Christology?

SELECTED BIBLIOGRAPHY

Van A. Harvey, "Faith, Images and the Christian Perspective," in *The Historian and the Believer* (New York: The Macmillan Co., 1966), pp. 246–93.

Schubert M. Ogden, "What Does It Mean To Affirm 'Jesus Christ Is Lord'?" in *The Reality of God* (New York: Harper & Row, 1963), pp. 188–206.

Karl Rahner, "Atheism and Implicit Christianity," and "I Believe in Jesus Christ: Interpreting an Article of Faith" in *Theological Investigations* vol. 9 (New York: Herder & Herder, 1972), pp. 145–69.

David W. Tracy, "The Re-presentative Language of Christology," in *Blessed Rage for Order: The New Pluralism in Theology* (New York: Seabury Press, 1975), pp. 204–40.

5

"Suffered Under Pontius Pilate"

Theological Introduction

THOMAS D. PARKER

The basic pattern of suffering and death, resurrection and ascension, and return in glory is common to all Christian theology, and is contained in all the major creeds and confessions. It is the dramatic story of the dying and rising Christ that is the heart of Christian faith, as it is the focus of major sections of the New Testament, especially the Pauline and Johannine strands (see especially Rom. 3, 5–6; Eph. 4, John 3 and 1 John 4).

The Apostles' Creed and the Creed of 381 are unique in the mention of Pilate, and only the Apostles' Creed mentions the descent to Hades. These short statements summarize the entire life of Christ, the content of the four Gospels, in one word, *suffered,* and concluded with the one word, *descent*. The Christian story is the story of the humiliation of God in our midst, the conflict between creatures caught in the net of corruption and the one who has come to set them free. It is the story of the suffering of the Son of God for the salvation of humankind. The stress on the dramatic structure overshadows the content of any one scene and is the meaning of the divine play.

In contrast to the Apostles' Creed the Confession of Justin, given as a statement of Christian belief, stressed the life of Jesus Christ as teacher:

> And (we worship) the Lord Jesus Christ, the Servant of God, who had also been proclaimed beforehand by the prophets as about to be present

> with the race of man, the herald of salvation and teacher of good instructions.

This emphasis received little theological expansion until the developments in theology following the Enlightenment, when a consideration of the life of Jesus became centrally important. The early, but subordinate, tradition of Jesus as teacher understood the content of the divine drama of sending Jesus Christ into the world for sinners in terms of his words of good news and works of love. Jesus appeared as the teacher of righteousness and advocate of the weary and heavy-laden, whose mission was to lead us from untruth and bondage to sin to divine truth and freedom from sin.

The two forms of confession are, of course, united in that unique body of materials, the four Gospels. There we find both the drama of death and resurrection, with the hope of return in glory, and a divine work of ministry doing the works of the Kingdom and calling persons to faith. Except for scattered statements in some confessions that hint some importance for the life of Jesus, however, the entire confessional tradition, East as well as West, concentrates on the "passion story," with the Gospel materials considered as prologue, or, in some cases, the first events on the way to the great work of salvaion.

The "great work" itself was explained as a "sacrifice for our sins." The confession of the Council of Toledo (675) put it in ways that expressed a wide consensus:

> According to the truth contained in the Gospel, we believe that in the form of his assumed human nature he was conceived without sin, born without sin, and died without sin. He alone was made sin for us, that is, was made a sacrifice for our sins. Nevertheless, he endured the Passion itself for our offenses without any change in his divine nature; he was sentenced to the death of the cross, and suffered true bodily death.

In later reflection theories were developed to interpret this great work. The notions that Christ wrestled with the powers of evil and was victorious, or that he was the bait given Satan or the ransom paid to release sinners were supplemented by notions that the work of Christ demonstrated God's love to move us to repentance or that Christ's death was satisfaction for the justice of God, a treasury of merit sufficient for the salvation of all humankind. This latter view developed into an idea of death as punishment for sin and of a vicarious suffering of pain to appease the wrath of God against sin. In some of these the "objective" side was stressed, while others emphasized the "subjective" side.

In all these ways, and others developed in recent theological work, the passion story is seen to be more than a story of Jesus' life and fate; it is the story of all humankind lived out in his life. In Pauline terms, we are identified with Christ in his death and resurrection, sharing his sufferings and his glorious future. The passion story is the story of the life of faith: a constant dying to sin and arising to new life in the Spirit (cf. Rom. 6, Phil. 3). In this way Jesus' act is exemplary for Christians (Phil. 2) and a proclamation of God's love (Rom. 5). The theme of struggle and liberation is taken up in most strands of New Testament teaching, as in 1 Peter, and provides a contact point for contemporary theologies of liberation and of the future.

St. Paul's statement in Galatians 2 refers us to the deepest levels of identification:

> I have been crucified with Christ; it is no longer I who live, but Christ who lives in me; and the life I now live in the flesh, I live by faith in the Son of God,who loved me and gave himself for me.

This identification with Christ in suffering and in glory is applied to persons and communities, and finally to the entire race and to the cosmos which, transformed, will join in the celebration of the "liberty of the sons of God."

Ben Phillips Dies—Funeral Today

Had he known that they would call on him to "make some remarks," as was the custom in black services, Ned Turnbull might have found an excuse not to go to the funeral at all. Though not a close friend of Phillips, Turnbull respected him as a colleague in the movement and wanted quietly to pay "last respects." Ben's death was indeed a tragedy, particularly for the poor people of the city. So, hurriedly, Turnbull gathered his thoughts to say something or to refuse graciously. If he did preach, what could he say?

Ben had grown up in Midville and attended college and seminary right there. During the early sixties, as a young pastor of Midville's Fourth Baptist Church, Ben rallied sisters and brothers for the struggle. Soon the whole area began looking to Ben, among others, as a major civil rights advocate. When a campaign developed for Midville Black Voter Registration, Ben had helped lead it. His forceful speeches and his intense, personal care of poor black people (not characteristically members of "Fourth") stood out in the memories of many Midvillians. When Dr. King came to Midville in the course of the campaign, he noted publicly and complimented privately the

---

This case was prepared by Prof. Louis B. Weeks of Louisville Presbyterian Seminary as a basis for class discussion and does not represent either effective or ineffective handling of a situation.

LOUIS B. WEEKS is Associate Professor of Historical Theology, Louisville Presbyterian Theological Seminary. He is a Fellow and the Case-Writing Coordinator of the CSI. He studied at Princeton University, Union Theological Seminary (Virginia) and received his Ph.D. from Duke University. He is the author of *Religion in the New Nation*, editor and contributor to *Casebook on Church and Society*, and coauthor of *Case Studies in Christ and Salvation*. He is an ordained Presbyterian pastor.

abilities of Ben Phillips in organizing and leading the local people. Dr. King had subsequently invited Ben to assist him elsewhere, from time to time. Ben had been among the real leaders of many civil rights campaigns in various American localities.

Turnbull got to know Ben Phillips in the process of Midville's second civil rights movement—the attempt to have passed a city open housing law. Phillips led the marches; and on one occasion when a number of demonstrators were arrested for "disturbing the peace," they shared a cell in the city jail. Turnbull was released after six hours (Phillips held overnight as an instigator). However, during that time they had talked together about the movement and the city, and Turnbull from that day considered Ben Phillips one of God's really beautiful people. Ben had faith that people would actually change in the U.S. He even thought that Midville's new law, once passed, would make a difference, help open Midville's societal patterns to blacks "up and down the (economic) ladder."

After the marches and the meetings, an ordinance did pass in the city in 1968. Racial discrimination did not cease, however. Apartment leasing seemed to open up a little, but black homeowning was still contained in Midville. If anything, color housing patterns became more distinct after the code had been adopted. Ben Phillips' name dropped from the front page of the newspaper, but occasional features focused on his work at the metropolitan hospitals and jails. He was, according to a sympathetic reporter, "the unofficial chaplain of poor black people in Midville institutions." Turnbull remembered one quotation from Ben in particular: "For the middle class, there might be a dream. But for poor folk—nothing."

Phillips gradually stopped attending meetings of the Midville Ministerial Association, where Turnbull had seen him most consistently. Ned missed their occasional conversations there as well as the greetings they had frequently shared. Phillips called Turnbull in July, 1973, and made a request. Would he recommend Ben for the job as staff executive for the Mayor's Committee on Education? "Sure," said Ned, who wondered but did not ask if these new responsibilities would mean a change in Ben's pastoral relationship with Fourth Baptist. Turnbull wrote a glowing letter of recommendation and received two weeks later a postcard informing him that Ben had been hired for the job.

Right before Christmas, he chanced on Ben at a party. Even in the brief encounter, Ned felt Ben's strain and frustration in trying to achieve a foothold for the city's poverty-stricken blacks by working through the "establishment." Ben, already a little drunk, talked about painful memories: "It hadn't been worth all the trouble. . . . Dr. King was the lucky one, because he wouldn't have to see America as it degenerated. . . . Hey, remember the good times when we were marching. . . . Wonder what happened to ole' Charles Schaeffer? . . . Some days it would be nice to be back out on the streets, egg in our faces and fighting us head on. . . . Hang in there, Brother Turnbull."

There were rumors at the ministerial association that Ben drank too much. Perhaps as a consequence of the struggle for quality education with setback after setback in the Midville Board of Education—or perhaps because he was facing a possible divorce.

Then the automobile accident happened. As a friend shared with Ned, "that accident put an end to Ben's frustration and his quest for the oppressed and the poor—at least in this life."

As Ned sat in the pew, listening to the choir, he thought about Martin Luther King. Life snuffed out in a Memphis motel before his dream for America could be realized. Now Ben Phillips, cut off before the new educational proposals could be acted on, let alone implemented. Maybe Ben was right—"It wasn't worth all the trouble."

Turnbull looked out over the faces of those people quietly finding places in the sanctuary of the Fourth Baptist Church. There were not very many, in comparison to the hundreds Ben had known and worked with. The faces of the former leaders of the civil rights movement were absent. The congregation was filled with the weary but smiling people of this city's poor. So what was he to say?

Theological Briefs

DAVID B. BURRELL AND OLIVER F. WILLIAMS

How does one deal with principalities and powers? When the wave of initial enthusiasm which pulses through a movement has been spent, where does one go from there? What steps are available? Which one should I take? If understanding, as Wittgenstein observed, is knowing how to go on, who can help us to find a way, tossed up on a trackless beach? When the inertia of customary arrangements and accumulated compromise emerges to restore the maze of barriers and blinders, how can a person find a way, and where can that person find the heart to go on?

These are the questions which Ned Turnbull's plight raises for us, and raises acutely, for it appears that he has dealt with them little better than most of us. Turnbull had come to know Ben Phillips in one of those momentary troughs in the onward wave of the movement, and found him—in that luminous moment—a beautiful person. After the movement crested, they lost contact—Ben moving into city hospitals and jails, Ned busy with other things. Since Ben frequented

---

DAVID B. BURRELL is Chairman of the Theology Department and Associate Professor of Philosophy, Notre Dame University. He studied at the University of Notre Dame and the Gregorian University in Rome, receiving his Ph.D. from Yale University. His publications include *Analogy and Philosophical Language*, *Exercises in Religious Understanding*, and *Arguments of the Philosophers: Aquinas*. He is an ordained Roman Catholic priest, C.S.C.

OLIVER F. WILLIAMS is Assistant Professor in the Theology Department, University of Notre Dame and Director of the Professional Theology Program. He did both graduate and undergraduate work at the University of Notre Dame and received his Ph.D. from Vanderbilt University. He is a Fellow of the CSI and the author of several published cases. He is an ordained Roman Catholic priest, C.S.C.

the ministerial association meetings less and less, Ned had little occasion to see him. Nor did he seek Ben out; it was Ben, in fact, who asked him the favor of a recommendation—for the Mayor's Committee on Education, no less—and Ned was grateful for the opportunity to turn a key for him. Then there was the chance meeting at the party. . . .

The enthusiasm generated by a movement offers us a peculiarly aesthetic purchase on a human situation. Carried along by the sheer right of our convictions and impelled by the utter wrong of the *status quo,* we are thrown together and pitch in alongside one another, often to the point of exhaustion. But for all that we apparently share, the motion itself can insulate us from the very people whose plight moved us to action, as it can keep us from testing one another's mind and heart. Paradoxically, we seem to taste the suffering of the people we came to help, as well as the poverty of those who came along with us, only after the movement has subsided. When we cast about for what to do next, our own inability to come up with an answer dissolves the illusion of power and brings us up against our own personal poverty. Here is the precious moment—when we can feel the want of those we came to help, share the anxieties of those like us who wanted to help, and ask what it is we might do, together. Here is the turning point, where an aesthetic perspective dissolves, and a stark ethical alternative opens up to us. But there are many such alternatives; which one should I take?

There is no answer to that question, of course, for there is no step predetermined for us to take. But there are criteria, and they come in an order neatly inverse to the one we spontaneously adopted in the movement. From among the avenues open to us, we must first select those which lead us to share the plight of the persons whose situation first aroused us. Only then are we permitted to choose the path we might judge most effective, or the one most congenial to our talents.

How do we know to invert the order in this way? From what we learned of the instant successes in the initial wave of the movement. Seeking effectiveness first, we addressed the media directly in a language calculated to affect a liberal constituency of conscience. We hoped that way to influence those in a position to make decisions affecting the lot of many. So went the theory; an explicit statement of the unconscious priorities by which most of us operate. But the media as well as that very constituency—ourselves—found itself imbedded in institutional arrangements that rendered our early successes quite impotent. The old alliances reasserted themselves and inertia restored the *status quo*.

What about us? We tend to succumb to that same inertia and those same arrangements—albeit nagged by a conscience that will not allow us to take comfort in our otherwise comfortable circumstances. What to do? Place ourselves in a situation where we are forced to share the lot of those whose lot awakened our concern, where we must learn to listen. Submit ourselves to those principalities and powers, enough at least to feel their sting. Learning what it is not to control one's destiny, we will come to understand how suffering—undergoing rather than managing things—becomes a key to a new sort of life. That is, we will have learned how to go on. A number of avenues will open before us, each one offering a way of submitting to what we once set out to eliminate, of participating in what we had hoped to solve.

We are driven to this response out of desperation and out of hope. Desperation at the failure of a problem-centered approach to offer any inward grasp or alleviation of a human situation; hope born of the story of Jesus. The promise sown in Jesus' submission to the powers, and his death at their hands followed by his resurrection to and by the Father, is a promise of a way through. Participating in the powerlessness of so much of humankind, Jesus nonetheless forged a way through that submission to a new kind of life. This is not another lawlike prediction that suffering begets enlightenment, but something quite novel: that submitting to the point of extinction carries with it a pledge of new and eternal life.

We must turn to the Epistle to the Hebrews to renew our faith that in Christ we have the suffering love of God, the ultimate gift. The costly, total self-giving that ended with death on the cross manifests the radical quality of the Father's love and opens the way for us to follow in his path. Our belief that life comes through death is given expression in the great hymn of the Epistle to the Philippians (2:6 ff.), and we know that for us this means that by entering into our humanity, and making the cares of the poor our own, we too can share in his exaltation. Through him we have the power of becoming sons of God.

Ben Phillips and Ned Turnbull both acknowledged this story; each preached it, in fact, to different gatherings of believers. Each faltered some, as most of us do, when it came to believing that it actually pointed a way to follow. Yet one suspects that Ben may have enacted it better than he or we could say, as the plight of those he so wanted to help gradually overwhelmed him. Perhaps Ned will catch something of this. If he does, he will certainly speak it out. Will articulating it help him to adopt it as a rule of life? Will Ben Phillips' enactment of the passion narrative bring that way home to Turnbull better than the story of Jesus' death and resurrection has been able to do? What does it take for this story to take its measure of us?

As Ned reflects on Ben's life, he may come to see the world from Ben's point of view, he may pass over to Ben's standpoint and begin to have a feel for Ben's life story. It is helpful here to think of conversion to Christian faith in terms of a change in story. Just as Jesus trained his disciples by telling them stories and providing a new language for them to "live into," so too the process of total conversion to Christian faith involves a "living into" the Christian language with all the changes in habits and attitudes that such a move entails. By participating in Ben's story we can begin to shape our own story with fresh insight and perspective.

Rather than ask "Did Ben have faith?" Ned might better say "What story was Ben in?" and this of course quite naturally leads to "What story am I in?" From being involved with Ben's life story, we can glean some insight on just what story we are in, and what we might have to do to be in another story. Ben's life, as an attempt to appropriate the story of Jesus, enables the statements of theology to come to life. It may even offer a fresh perspective on the gospel.

Hearing Ben's story will help all of those in the congregation understand what it means to live the gospel. The narration of his life will set the context so that insight into the Christian gospel is actually available for all who will listen. And Ned's recounting of Ben's life should not gloss over all that points to the sin and tragedy, the principalities and powers involved in a human life. "It hadn't been worth all the trouble. . . . Dr. King was the lucky one because he wouldn't have to see America as it degenerated." For as we realize the failure in Ben's life, we might discover new challenges in our own. And as we experience the sin shot through our most noble endeavors, we come to see the scope of the Father's love and power. We too then have the courage to say with Ben, "Hang in there, brother."

Selected Bibliography

David B. Burrell, *Exercises in Religious Understanding* (Notre Dame: University of Notre Dame Press, 1975). Examines the thinking of Augustine, Anselm, Aquinas, Kierkegaard, and Jung and develops the theme that the most important things in life are not really understood unless we are prepared to incarnate them.

John S. Dunne, *A Search For God in Time and Memory* (New York: The Macmillan Co., 1967). Grapples with the problem of evil and suffering within the Christian tradition in a fresh and insightful way.

Oliver F. Williams, "Thought Vs. Action in Ministerial Programs: A Misplaced Debate," Washington, D.C.: Seminary Newsletter Supplement (Nov. 1976), NCEA Publications. Argues that reflection on the unity of the "being" and the "doing" of Jesus offers much promise for a contemporary understanding of ministry and for devising effective ministerial programs.

Eric G. Lemmon

At first blush one might be expected to moan, "Poor Ben Phillips." Here is a man whose life was spent chasing the impossible dream, in a quixotic assault on the windmills of poverty and injustice, in a halcyon delusion that he could bring in the Kingdom of God. And on the surface of the matter the appraisal is probably not too incorrect. After all, how much more can a man lose than his life, doing what he perceives to be right, and straining the fiber of his life to work out his faith practically? What has changed? Not much. What has been the reward? Little, if anything at all. Aren't these the criteria for adjudging a life wasted?

The Christian faith is not nor may it be blind to the realities which hold us by virtue of our existence. To look at a life like Ben Phillips', and to say something glib or to ignore the great grief of soul

---

Eric Gregory Lemmon is Assistant Professor of Theology at Gordon-Conwell Theological Seminary, South Hamilton, Massachusetts. He studied at the University of Arizona, U.C.L.A. and received his Th.D. from Fuller Theological Seminary. He is the author of several articles and is an ordained Baptist minister.

and anguish of spirit that this man and his friends must know, is to be blind to the real dilemma of life. Life is most often not just, and injustice hurts as few things can. Many a man who raises a voice or strikes a blow toward a cherished and good objective finds himself reeling from the experience, topsy-turvy and unable to touch base with the reality of his vision. Who hasn't said, "Is it worth it?"

This question is not new. Hardly. The question is at least as old as Job—"Curse God and die"—and as old as the writer to the Hebrews. The difference between Job's motley helper and the insight of the author of Hebrews is that the first had no Christian perspective, and the second did. And this perspective does not make *a* difference; it makes *the* difference! Very little of the human predicament goes unnoticed in the Bible, and the one posed in "Ben Phillips" is no exception. In Hebrews, the second chapter, the writer, from his perspective of Hebrew culture, poses the same question in cosmic dimensions. What's wrong?

From our twentieth-century perspective, in the light of DNA research, pacemakers, agroeconomics, orthomolecular psychiatry, etc., the question seems less ponderous, even less important. But from the perspective of the human spirit, the quest for justice, the bent for freedom, the search for the elusive good and ultimately the need for rest of mind and heart—is mankind really much better off than Job's comforters? Ben Phillips apparently didn't think so. Or at least his life and the turns that it took don't seem to indicate any great hope in the consummation of all things—not even a measure of simple personal fulfillment. What's wrong? In the light of the human predicament, the author of Hebrews says that whatever it is (Paul in Romans labels it "sin") we have Jesus—he's right! This orientation to life is what distinguishes Christianity from other well-meaning and well-doing approaches to life. Here, according to Christian faith, and here only, can Ben Phillips's life and frustrations find meaning. If Ned preaches Christ, not simply as exemplary, but as substitutionary, then he commends Ben Phillips's life and ministers healing to those who hear him.

This Jesus whom we have is not just any religious figure. He is not simply a strikingly important revelational event. If he were only this, he would be one among many and rather than easing the dilemma, he would complicate it. This falls short of the biblical teaching concerning

Jesus and falls short of the real need of man generically, and of individuals like Ben Phillips. The Bible does not teach Jesus is a Lord, but he is *the* Lord; not simply *my* Lord, though he is that, but *the* Lord of life and even of the material, universal, and cosmic order (Phil. 2:6–11; Col. 1:14–19; 2:2–3; Heb. 1:1–3; 2:10). Jesus is not simply the Christ of man's spiritual and internal existential needs, he is the God of life—material and spiritual. Jesus Christ is not only a man among men; he is God's man for men. And he is God's man because he is God. The intellect boggles at this affirmation, and well it should; but nevertheless, the biblical writers and the Church historically have set this affirmation as the *sine qua non* of faith—formal and personal.

Furthermore, this is not only a nice way of talking "God-talk." This is an ontological existence—a real being who coordinates in himself both man's need to have spiritual integration and his need to have sense made of the turmoil of everyday life and events. It was necessary, says Hebrews, that this man should be one with us (Heb. 2:9–15). This is not some philosophical conception to give us insight; this is a man who suffers the same pain and the same frustrations as you and I, yes, as Ben Phillips. He is zealous, selfless, concerned, self-giving, to the point of dying. Yet this life of a good man is spurned by his own generation. He is not simply frustrated, but ridiculed and rejected, betrayed by friends and sold by enemies. He falls victim before the impersonal forces of governmental bureaucracy and political expediency. And he dies. Albert Schweitzer says that he dies, crushed beneath the wheel of history (*The Quest for the Historical Jesus*). Poor deceived Jesus—no better off than Ben Phillips.

But the Christ and his message do not die in ignominy, awaiting to be resurrected only in the fond hopes of feebleminded albeit stouthearted disciples. This would not satisfy the mind and the heart. The basis of faith is ontological and the substance of faith is historical or it is nothing. It is like trying to feed a starving man by reading to him from a cookbook! Mere words—but no substance. What use is a Jesus who lives on only in the wishes and memories, worse yet, the delusions of his disciples? What comfort can Ben Phillips get from a myth—regardless of its philosophical message? Is he to deny the flesh and blood existence which is his every day? Is he to give himself unstintingly for a dream or many dreams which give some appearance of hope, but only die, perhaps felled by an assassin's bullet? Or is the Christ, Jesus the Christ, actually resurrected? Is he alive uniting man's concrete world with his spiritual world? Alive in his body, not simply in hope? Alive in his humanity, not simply in a religious proclamation? Alive—not simply in God's mind or our minds? But alive—body and spirit? Ben Phillips doesn't need to have died in vain. What is it but vanity if he dies for some impossible dream? Let him do what he understands—eat, drink, be merry. But if Christ is risen—body and spirit, there's hope, Ben Phillips.

This hope lies in who this man Jesus is, God-for-us. But it lies as well in what he has done. In the first place he has identified with us. Not simply in some sympathetic or even empathetic, way (many men do this) but in a factual, concrete existence, a human life bearing human responsibility, human passion, human distress, human agony, and human death. By virtue of his unique relationship to God (Col. 1:1, Heb. 1:13) what he endures as a man is (a) intensified by contrast with the beatitude and serenity of God; and (b) because of his being the God-man, given cosmic value. When he lives a human existence, God lives a human existence; when he suffers, God's nature is involved in the suffering, and when he dies, God, who by definition cannot himself die (death is reserved for the created order) is touched by death and knows it from within the experience itself. So miraculous and complete is this identification between Jesus Christ and God, that his life and death have infinite, cosmic value. He is not one among many; he is God-for-us. And as such when he suffers for "what is wrong," because of the distance others have put between themselves and God, he is able and fit, worthy, to represent humanity before God in the universal struggle which we face between the demand of God that we belong to him and our bent to belong only to ourselves.

This latter is the heart of what the Bible calls "sin." Humanity's independence and all that flows from it is the nub of the human predicament. But Jesus Christ unites man and God again. He unites them in life, in death, and in resurrection. He also unites them in a legal and real transaction which allows God to be united with individuals who have spurned him and his demands. God is, to put the matter biblically, just and the justifier. Justice and love and mercy are united in Christ personally and in his work forensically. This is why theologians have called this atonement, "at-one-ment."

There is, of course, no etymological connection between atonement and at-one-ment, but the idea is there. We have been brought back into phase with God, because God gave us someone equal to the task. As Karl Barth has suggested (*Church Dogmatics*, III-1), the image of God in man is at least that man is in a relationship of dependence with others even for life itself (Gen. 1:27). But we are also dependent on a relationship with God who is the source of life, but whom we willfully ignore. This attitude of heart and mind and the deeds which flow from it, separate persons from God, make them unnaturally independent. This estrangement is so deep that only radical means can rectify it. This is why the author of Hebrews says "Such a man was necessary." Once God decided to help us, then there was no other way than this. This is why Jesus is the Messiah (Promised One) of God. It is also why he is the Christ (Lord). All this is summed in the fact that this real man, who was also God, suffered with us and for us, represented us before God in all his infinite and cosmic dimensions, and then he was accepted by God on our behalf.

The resurrection is the token (sign) that the life of Jesus Christ the man was worthy of the life of Jesus Christ who is God. Being worthy, death has no hold on him; life conquers death. *Christus victor* is enthroned as representative of those who trust him. The resurrection is as well a token of life in Christ (as in Adam all die; so in Christ shall all be made alive. (1 Cor. 15:22). So that our lives which, left to themselves, ultimately end up in the dust of the ground whether we are nominally successful or whether we are not, are resurrected in Christ. If Ben Phillips knew this, he will not have lived in vain, for whosoever loses his life for my sake, the same shall find it (Matt. 10:39); even if in this life we experience failure, famine, peril, or sword as the Bible puts it—and even death itself—because he lives—we too shall live! "God was in Christ reconciling the world unto himself, not imputing their trespasses unto them; and has committed to us the word of reconciliation" (2 Cor. 5:19). If Ned reminds the poor collected to mourn Ben Phillips of this and reminds the members of Fourth Baptist Church, they can understand that life does not consist in what a man possesses but in how he possesses his life.

To live is Christ. To reconcile is Christ. To minister to the physical man and to the spiritual man is Christ. To break partitions and to set at liberty captives is Christ. And as he was in the world so are we. Faith doesn't rest on creeds, as if creeds were more than words. When this equation is made, it is a red herring. Faith rests in the realities which the creeds represent, but this reality includes true history or the whole Christian enterprise is nonsense. No dead, archaic words these, but the bread of life in the word of life. Because he lives, we too shall live, and not in vain, Ben Phillips.

SELECTED BIBLIOGRAPHY

Karl Barth, *Church Dogmatics* IV/1, IV/2 (Edinburgh: T. & T. Clark, 1956, 1958). Reflects on the transcendent and immanent nature of Christ's atonement, and on his person.

Emil Brunner, *The Christian Doctrine of Creation and Reconciliation* (Philadelphia: The Westminster Press, 1952). Discusses theologically the human predicament and God's provision in history in Christ.

Eric G. Lemmon, *The Nature of Biblical Faith* (Pasadena: Fuller Theological Seminary). Emphasizes the historical ontological object of faith and its experiential confirmation.

Leon Morris, *The Apostolic Preaching of the Cross* (Grand Rapids: Wm. B. Eerdmans Publishing Co., 1956). Sets out the biblical basis for a faith grounded in historical verities.

ARTHUR C. MCGILL

The case of Ben Phillips confronts us with the destruction of life—with death—in three different modalities. There is, first, the systematic, centuries-old oppression of black people, against which Ben Phillips directed his life. This is the living death of starvation, sick-

ARTHUR C. MCGILL is Professor of Theology, Harvard Divinity School. He was educated at Harvard University and Yale Divinity School, receiving his Ph.D. from Yale University. He is the author of *Suffering: A Test of Theological Method*, *The Celebration of Flesh*, and coauthor of *The Many-Faced Argument*. He is an ordained minister in the United Church of Christ.

ness, destitution, and degradation. Secondly, Ben's own vitality has withered away before the realization that all his efforts have failed, that the killing power of the white establishment remains undiminished. Ben knew that, when measured by its results, his life of dedicated service "wasn't worth the trouble." He sank into despairing alcoholism. Third and finally, the automobile accident ended Ben's life completely.

Ned Turnbull's task—and ours—is to bring Ben's life and death into the light of the existence of Jesus Christ.

As Ned discovers, this is not an easy task. For Jesus throws upon our existence a strange and difficult light and overturns our basic assumptions. Nowhere is this more striking than with regard to the significance which the New Testament and many of the Christian traditions attach to Jesus' death. The New Testament is quite emphatic that Jesus' death is not an accident, is not a disaster, and is not primarily the work of evil-doers. On the contrary Jesus' death is viewed as life-affirming, as the essential and indispensable event in the way in which God through Jesus brings renewed life to humanity. So crucial is it, in fact, that all those who would attain that life are called upon to "take up his cross," that is, to pass through the kind of dying which occurred in Jesus. That death is God's way of bringing us to life. Until we die that death we will not find the fullness of life.

How can Jesus' death—how can any death—be life-giving?

In his various letters Paul develops one view. Paul finds that Jesus lived his life constantly and comprehensively in the posture of *thanksgiving*. He did so, according to Paul, because in all ways and at all times he knew that he was receiving his reality from God. God was the on-going basis and origin of himself, of all humanity, and of the whole cosmos. In other words, in all his life-acts Jesus did not live on the basis of an identity which he possessed. His identity, his being, was constantly coming to him from God's loving activity. There was no moment and no regard when, to himself or to others, he was simply the reality which he possessed, simply his own self. Always and in all ways he was receiving himself from God. At his center was not his own act of having and holding onto his own reality. At his center was God's activity of giving him himself, God's parenting activity.

Jesus' center, then, was no longer in himself but in God. To know

Jesus properly is to know him as he knew himself, namely, as constantly constituted from beyond himself. According to Paul, through Jesus we are to understand ourselves and one another in exactly the same terms. "What have you that you did not receive?" Paul asks. Nothing, not even ourselves. "If, then, you really received it as a gift, why do you take the credit to yourself?" (1 Cor. 4:7).

From this vantage point Paul easily identifies that fundamental perversity which marks human life. This perversity is rooted in the tendency of people to live, not on the basis of the activity of God, but on the basis of their own capacity to have and to hold onto some bit of reality as their own. Whether or not they think that God once gave them their reality makes no difference. They now relate to themselves by the technique of having, and not by constantly receiving themselves, as a gift from God. They find their identities within the circle of their own beings, in terms of that reality which they imagine belongs to them. For Paul this being by virtue of possession is the essential form of human evil, and all the monstrosities of oppression and envy and anxiety in human life arise from this.

In terms of the new kind of identity which is actualized in and through Jesus, death loses its sting, its ultimate power. For death does indeed empty us of everything within the circle of our being. It kills our bodies and our souls. It ends our possessed being. However, if our reality is continually constituted, not by what we can hold onto as our own, but by something wholly outside of us, that is, by God's activity, then the death which dispossesses us of all the reality which we have does not reach to God and does not there destroy the root and basis of our being. As Paul writes, whether we live or whether we die, we belong to God through Jesus Christ (Rom. 14:8).

People have learned to live perversely, to live out of themselves, on the basis of their own reality. They do not take on this new christic kind of identity with magical suddenness. Their growth in this new identity is a slow and convulsive process. In this process death plays a crucial and climatic role. For as long as people do possess some bit of reality, it is never brought out how much they may be clinging to that bit for their being. Only in relation to their dying, only in relation to the end of all their possessed being are they liberated from every secret impulse to have and are perfected in their life of pervasive thanksgiving. The whole of the Christian life, so far as it seeks to uproot evil, is a willing movement toward death, a practice of dying —of dying with Jesus—a learning to live in thankful receptivity and not by the technique of having. Only at death are we purified of every strategy of being by possessiveness.

Jesus' resurrection represents the entrance of human existence into a domain liberated from all having, where therefore God's bestowing activity is manifest in all things and through all things. Resurrection does not mean that the dead get back what they lost through death; resurrection is not the reinstitution of having and the reappearance of perversity. Only the dead in their destitution, only the totally and thoroughly dead who have willed their dispossession and loss of all having—only they are in the condition to enjoy the fullness of the life of constant receiving. The resurrected are the dead as such, those who have nothing of their own possessing but who are alive wholly from God.

The life of Ben Phillips is marked by the oppression of many blacks—an on-going death—and by Ben's own despair and death. These take on an unexpected significance in the light of Jesus.

The oppression of black people by the establishment is not some momentary forgetfulness or some accidental failure of love. That oppression brings to light the essential character of the technique of having by which the middle class lives. Middle-class existence is now tyrannized by that technique. Because the people of the middle class live by holding onto themselves, holding onto their possessions, holding onto their achievements and holding onto their kind, they cannot be receptive at the center of their beings and therefore they are cut off from love. The energy of possessing carries inescapably within itself the anxieties of greed, envy, domination, and exploitation. The degradation and destitution imposed on the blacks is an outer expression of the savagery which middle-class people have executed upon themselves by their enslavement to possessiveness. Therefore, to resist middle-class oppression, as Ben Phillips has done, is to oppose, not just some bad people, but that style of life which carries all the energy of evil, and which Jesus, with his life of radical receiving and radical giving, sought to eradicate.

As we consider Ben's working life, we must remember that the horizons of Jesus are not the horizons of middle-class affluence. Because of its seeming power and arrogance and secure self-contentment, the establishment can hypnotize us. Entranced by its illusions, we come to believe that any blacks who are cut off from affluence are cut off from life. This is not so in the horizons of Jesus. For there the technique of having is itself exposed as the essential lie, the fundamental sickness, the nightmare of destructive conflict and isolation. In the struggle against oppression the aim is not to enable everyone to possess and to share in that sickness, but to enable human existence to receive more freely and to give more freely.

Even while the struggle against oppression goes on and at times seems hopeless and futile, those oppressed are not separated from the Lord of life. Though cut off from having, they are not cut off from God. And within the horizons of Jesus, their dispossession is not without its meaning, its capacity to humanize, its role in the reordering of human existence to the love of God. Precisely because, through the positive significance of death in the perspective of Jesus, a newness of life may grow in the most terrible darkness, because even there people learn to become more fully receptive and more freely self-expending, that growth gives them the power to continue the struggle against oppression.

Where were the voices reaffirming this vision to Ben Phillips in his despair? Where were the neighbors to sustain him in his process of undoing and dispossession, in the movement of his life into the shadow of the cross? Who reminded him that the Christian way is not simply a series of outer victories over the social environment but also an inner breaking and emptying where new dimensions of fellowship and humanity come into play? Who will tell us that his self-offering, his risking of himself against principalities and powers wholly beyond his power and his being broken on the rack of their crushing immovability—who will tell us that in all this Ben advanced along the way of Jesus that many of us never reach?

Obviously Ned Turnbull will not tell us these things. Ned apparently knows nothing of the positive meaning of death, has never realized that death belongs part and parcel to the overcoming of evil and the perfecting of love. Because the practice of dying has not been at the heart of his ministry, because for him death has never been an essential element in the transformation of human existence, when he comes to the funeral he obviously will have nothing to say. Ned is probably a middle-class minister, that is, a minister of the technique of having. In that perspective, Ben's death—like Jesus' death—can never be anything more than a senseless accident.

The approach of the Christian community of Christian individuals and of Christian ministers like Ned Turnbull to the positive meaning of death does not occur at funerals. It occurs in the midst of life. It grows out of the realization that what we cling to as "life" is itself the most subtle death, is itself that which separates us from God who is our authentic life. The realization that our enemy is not out there in the waiting cancer or the speeding automobile, but is the very life to which we cling with passionate intensity—this realization comes to us from the existence of Jesus. By our daily encounter with Jesus' kind of life, the secret possessiveness that lies at the heart of our will for life may become apparent to us. Only then may we also realize that the death which ends our possessive existence, the death which empties us of everything we possess as our own may itself be liberating and not simply destructive.

In all sermons and in all counseling, the Christian minister seeks to foster these realizations in the community to which he or she carries responsibility. It is a difficult calling in middle-class America, because there the belief in one's *own* being and one's *own* name and one's *own* possessed reality is so deeply entrenched. To discover the arrogance, the exploitive inhumanity and the godlessness of that possessiveness is what the Christian venture is all about.

Selected Bibliography

Phillipe Ariès, *Western Attitudes toward Death, from the Middle Ages to the Present* (Baltimore: John Hopkins University Press, 1974).

Oscar Cullman, "Immortality of the Soul or Resurrection of the Dead?" in Krister Stendahl, ed., *Immortality and Resurrection* (New York: Macmillan Co., 1965).

Arthur C. McGill, *Suffering: A Test of Theological Method* (Philadelphia: Geneva Press, a component of Westminister Press, 1968).

Preston N. Williams

"Suffered under Pontius Pilate" was a phrase probably added to the Creed in order to date Jesus' life and death. It is the first bit of solidly historical evidence in a Creed filled with supernatural or non-natural images. In between creation and divine birth, resurrection, and ascension is "suffered under Pontius Pilate." A faith which is distinguished for its stress on God's acts in history gives to its adherents in this Creed an encounter with suffering and death as their first fully historical event.

The event of Jesus' encounter with Pilate is both modern and perennial. Modern in that it poses once again the problem of capital punishment. A problem about which states and nation states are still disturbed. Perennial in that it points to the inescapable relation between religion and state. A person's religious belief, if held seriously, gives direction to one's life as a citizen of a state; on occasion severe conflict or tension results. Jesus' mission and message may have been purely religious, but it sought to give guidance and direction to masses of people, and many, including Pilate, came to see it as a threat to the absolute sovereignty of the state. Civic control and unity required capital punishment. Jesus was crucified. Jesus may not have been a religious or political revolutionary, but the people, religious authorities, and Pilate perceived him to be both. The State acting upon the ambiguity put him to death. Jesus and Ben Phillips thus come to have one thing in common. People saw in their religious activities political implications.

The explicit nature of Ben Phillips' political interpretation of his ministry and the implicit nature of Jesus' political message may cause some to wonder about the validity of this association. After all, Jesus was neither a Zealot nor a civil rights leader. Nonetheless Pilate's

---

Preston N. Williams is Houghton Professor of Theology and Contemporary Change, Harvard Divinity School. He was educated at Washington and Jefferson College, Johnson C. Smith University, Yale Divinity School and received his Ph.D. from Harvard University. He is the editor of *Ethical Issues in Biology and Medicine* and the author of numerous scholarly articles including "Black Religion and Black Experience" in *New Theology No. 8* and "The Ethical Aspects of the 'Black Church/Black Theology' " in *Quest for Black Theology*.

presence in the Creed, Jesus' death by state action, and the sign on the cross, "King of the Jews," underline the deep significance of even these implicit connections. There is less than a porous wall between religion and the state. Religion and the state are inevitably entangled because the religious person is also a citizen, and religious values have consequences for one's understanding of his or her duties as citizen. The first concern of one seeking to understand Ned Turnbull's dilemma is not to interpret Ben Phillip's death, or to eulogize him in a manner pleasing to the black congregation, or to speak to the guilt of some whites and the callous indifference of other whites. What Turnbull and we need is an insight into the political dimension present in many aspects of religious activity.

Ben Phillips' ministry was like Jesus', a religious ministry dedicated to enabling persons, especially the poor and the oppressed, to see themselves as children of God and persons of worth and dignity. It differed qualitatively from Jesus' ministry but built upon it because the Western Christian church and community, together with persons of good will, had over the centuries come to believe that the sacredness which the individual received from the hands of God could only be honored when persons received from the state and society certain basic rights. Thus Phillips added to his ministry a concern not present in the white secular and religious community which had already achieved the right to vote, to equal and fair treatment in public places, to equal access to the available housing in the community, and to equal educational opportunity. By seeking to universalize and make identifiable the political and social dimension of a religious value, the dignity and worth of persons, Phillips gave to his ministry a political coloring not present among white Christian ministries in Midville and exposed the political assumptions present in much of the community's religious life.

What appears to be a point of affinity with Jesus' ministry turns out to be a source of contradiction. Ned Turnbull and Midville's white Christians are not at-one with Jesus because they depart from Jesus' affirmation of human dignity and worth. The interrelatedness of human dignity and civil rights is made evident by the fact that failure in political or civic aspects of life lead to failure in religious and church life. The white and black societal patterns were separated in church life, clergy associations, Christian fellowship and personhood, hospitals and jails, neighborhoods and schools. Because white Christians failed to attend to the political or civic aspect of their faith, Midville became two communities, one black and one white.

Present in our case study also is the suggestion that the political community is the place where God's judgment is delivered. The high priest and countless religious leaders since Pilate's day have exhibited wisdom as well as shrewdness in carrying seemingly religious matters to civil authorities. They know that faith and morals when lived out can transform a society rather than simply make for cohesion and order. Thus God's judgment is carried out in the midst of society although God's ways are not man's, and God's rewards and burdens may not coincide with those distributed by the state. It was by his actions in the Roman state and before Pilate that Jesus fulfilled his fidelity to God. This included accepting crucifixion as well as rising from the dead and ascending to God's right hand.

While neither Ben Phillips nor Ned Turnbull died in order to affirm their loyalty to God, both had to carry out in the political area action witnessing to their commitment to God. Their records were spotty in regard to every form of piety. Unlike Jesus they were sinners. Yet Ben Phillips had come to realize something about God's dealings that Ned had not yet learned. Ben knew that religious judgment occurred in political encounter and decision. Religious faith was lived in the community as well as the home and church. Ben therefore saw in the degeneration of the American dream—the hope that the religious notion of equality and dignity would pervade all society—God's judgment upon the soul of America. Ned Turnbull, white Midville, and white America did not and do not perceive that judgment. They saw Ben Phillips and Martin Luther King, Jr., as regrettable failures and their cause as not worth the trouble. Their lack of interest in reconciling white and black Americans attested to their lack of concern with that for which Jesus died.

The Creed, by stating that Jesus descended into hell before he ascended, reminds us that his goodness resulted not from escape but from involvement. The Gospels tell us this in many ways. In the parable of the Good Samaritan and in the encounter with the Samaritan woman we receive cues about his racial attitudes and in the stories of the rich young ruler and the woman caught in adultery indications about his attitude toward class and petty moralisms.

Jesus' actions and teaching declare him to be at all times an affirmer of human worth and dignity regardless of the consequences that follow from rejecting societal patterns. Ned Turnbull and his white co-religionist were blind to that moral and religious vision. As Ned Turnbull preaches, one hopes he catches a glimpse of the political dimension of Jesus' gospel and the need to make human dignity substantive as well as formal.

Selected Bibliography

Cone, Cecil Wayne, *The Identity Crisis in Black Theology*, A.M.E.C., Nashville, Tennessee, 1975, Chapters I, II, and III. An allegation that most black theology is reductionist, an attempt to indicate what must be done to remove the reductionism.

Cone, James, *God of the Oppressed*, New York: Seabury Press, 1975 No. Nine, pp. 195–225. A criticism of Preston N. Williams' views concerning black ethics and a statement of Jim Cone's position.

Williams, Preston N., "Criteria for Decision-Making for Social Ethics in the Black Community", *The Journal of the Interdenominational Theological Center*, Vol. 1, No. 1, Fall 1973, pp. 65–79. An essay attempting to suggest criteria for determining black social ethics.

———, "James Cone and the Problem of a Black Ethic", *Harvard Theological Review*, Vol. 65, No. 4, October 1972. A critique of the exclusive nature of some black theology.

———, "Ethics and Ethos in the Black Community", *Christianity and Crisis*, Vol. XXI, No. 9, pp. 104–109, May 31, 1971. An attempt to illustrate some of the ways in which the black perspective on society differs from that of whites.

6

"In the Holy Spirit"

Theological Introduction

THOMAS D. PARKER

The third article of the Creed professes faith in God the Spirit, "equal in power and dignity" to God the Father and God the Son. It lists the works of the Spirit which have to do with the salvation of humankind, viz. the Church, the communion of saints, forgiveness, the resurrection of the body, and eternal life. Some of the earlier versions of the Creed had merely the statement about the Holy Spirit, without any expansion, while the Nicene adds:

> the Lord and Giver of life, Who proceeds from the Father, Who is worshiped and glorified together with the Father and Son, Who spoke through the prophets. . . .

In this form, the article represents the theological work of the Cappadocian Fathers, whose theological tracts on the Trinity gave attention to the third person as well as to the *homoousia* of Father and Son and their relations. For the Cappadocians, Father, Son, and Spirit were a threefold manifestation of the divine *ousia* (being, essence). Their full trinitarianism gave the person and work of the Spirit its first consistent expression. Until the debates between Nicea and Constantinople, the Holy Spirit had not been a center for theological thought. Indeed, the simple trinitarian statement of the baptismal formula and the reality of the life and gifts of the Spirit had been the carrier of this element of belief, without any felt need for an expanded theological statement.

The ambiguity of theological thinking about the Spirit is traceable to the New Testament itself. Along with the baptismal formulas there are confessional statements which are binitarian, such as 1 Corinthians 8:6. The Holy Spirit is related to the power of God which raised Jesus from the dead (Rom. 1:4), enables the faithful to say, "Jesus is Lord" (1 John 4:2) and is the source of the gifts received by the community (1 Cor. 12). For St. Luke, the Spirit is clearly God's gift to the young Church, a sign that the Kingdom of God is present in the world as well as to be consummated in the future. For the Johannine tradition, the Spirit is sometimes identified with the Living Christ, in a way of thinking that is chiefly concerned with the Father and the Son. One looks in vain for a theological statement on the Spirit comparable to those concerning the person and work of Jesus Christ.

In the development of theological statements, the article on the Spirit became a point of difference between the East and West. In 589 the Council of Toledo added the term *filioque* ("and the Son") to the Creed, making it read, "Who proceeds from the Father and the Son." This change, rooted in the trinitarian thought of St. Augustine, ties the person of the Spirit to that of the Son, and therefore to the visible structures of the Church and to its ministry of Word and Sacrament. In the Eastern churches Pentecost is typically seen as a new work of God, not a continuation of the incarnation so much as a new gift to a humanity prepared to receive it through the work of Christ. In turn, the incarnation itself is seen as a work of the Spirit who works for the perfection of the creature from all eternity.

As theological reflection developed the concerns of the third article, the stress was laid on other phrases, especially those concerning the Church, forgiveness, and revelation. They were more pertinent to the Church struggles emerging in various times. Many were content to agree with the statement "the Holy Spirit is the soul of the church" (*Mystici Corporis*, 1943) and go on to more urgent matters. Others, opposing such an identification of the Church with the Spirit, insisted that the Spirit works "when and where and how he pleases," echoing the idea of wind in the Gospel of John (chapter 3), seeing the work of the Spirit primarily in relation to individuals, their conversion and growth into the image of Christ.

If we consider the theological output of the Reformation and responses to it as commentary on the doctrine of the Spirit, then it must be said that concern for the Spirit occupies a central place in Christian reflection. Indeed, from the time of Schleiermacher, Christian existence as life in the Spirit has been the central focus of much theological reflection.

In the contemporary theological world, two elements in the classical discussions are being highlighted: the special gifts to the Christian community and the general presence of the Spirit in all human culture and history. First, a new discussion is taking place around the spread of "charismatic" experiences in many churches, such "charisms" as speaking in other tongues, the gift of healing in Jesus' name, prophetic discernment and the like. It is still an open question how the classic confession of faith will be influenced in the light of these new conversations. A part of this discussion is concerned with the formation of a "spiritual community," asking about the shape of life together in which the gifts are used for building up the common life of Christians working and, in some cases, living together.

Second, a new discussion is beginning with respect to theologies of liberation, of history, and of culture to inquire into the meaning of the more universal work of the Spirit which is the background for many of the biblical texts. To see the Spirit's presence in movements for justice and peace is not new, of course; theologians have long spoken of the "hidden Christ" who meets us in the figure of the oppressed, along the lines of the parable of the last judgment in the Gospel of Matthew (chapter 25). What appears to be new is seeing these historical movements rooted in the development of all creatures, of the whole cosmos as it is destined for the Kingdom of God, transformed, renewed, and perfected.

Jim Barton

"I first knew Jimmy when I was one of five women from the church who took turns driving him, daily, to the cerebral palsy clinic. At three Jimmy could stand if his braces were locked and someone held his hands. When I would walk him to the door of the clinic, I would lock his braces to a standing position and help him move his legs. All the time he would try to talk and not a word could be understood. I can still see that helmet on his head as he smiled good-bye, and I recall thinking that he would never make it in this world."

The friend of the family who spoke these words had known Jimmy since infancy. Karen and Roger, his parents, had found out about his cerebral palsy shortly before he was baptized at the age of three months. For the next ten years they lived under the burden of Jimmy's handicap that drained them and left the family in difficult financial straits.

During these years, Jimmy would panic when he first tried things, but tests showed that he had a keen mind. He was nearly helpless but he never gave up. His smile was beautiful and his teachers and therapists adored him. But his parents bore their burden heavily.

Karen would come to the church nearly every day, hoping to share her difficulties. A prayer group had started at the church primarily in the hopes that it would meet the needs of Karen and others like her.

This case was prepared by Prof. Thomas D. Parker of McCormick Theological Seminary and Ms. Katherine E. Irwin as a basis for class discussion rather than to illustrate either effective or ineffective handling of a situation.

KATHERINE E. IRWIN is Chaplain at Loyola University Medical Center, McGaw Hospital in Maywood, Ill. She studied at the University of Detroit, Marygrove College and McCormick Theological Seminary, where she received her M. Div. She is an ordained Presbyterian minister.

Some were making discoveries in their own faith, but Karen had only become more bitter and angry with God.

One day Karen came in waving a piece of paper. "This lady in Illinois has invited us to bring Jimmy to a healing service. They promise to lay hands on Jimmy for healing." One of the staff members of the church asked her if she were going. "Of course we're going. This lady said that all things are possible with God and she told us to just pray a prayer for more faith all the way over to Illinois." The minister called on her and they talked about the problems that might result in Jimmy's life if the healing was unsuccessful. They went off anyway, praying and making Jimmy pray the whole way.

The Bartons came home thrilled. The healing service had been beautiful. They had told the family to watch for signs of gradual healing since instant healing had not occurred. More faith was needed. A "joy-filled" Karen called a prayer meeting of all her friends and of some devout Christians she had heard about. Witnessing to all that had happened, she charged people to praise God for Jimmy's recovery. One of the friends who had driven Jimmy to the clinic was there. She relates, "I couldn't wait to leave. Now I had two images in my memory. Jimmy in a helmet going to the clinic and now ten-year-old Jimmy looking around for a place to run and not finding any."

Weeks went by and nothing happened. The doctor said that new medication would have to be started because the shoulder muscles were weakened. Karen went into a depression, and the family experienced severe strain. Only concern for Jimmy kept things together.

Jimmy began coming to the youth group at the church. Everyone agreed to form a car-pool and pick him up for every meeting and activity. At sixteen Jimmy was still badly handicapped, but he could walk without braces and he could type with two fingers. He attended the group faithfully, but he would never pray. When everyone bowed heads, he stared straight ahead, grimly.

Jimmy decided to go along with the group when they went to a youth rally at a charismatic fellowship in a town across the state. He couldn't resist the music, the warmth, the love in the group, and the complete lack of pressure. No one had a plan for him. There was faith but no one was setting boundaries. Hearing people sing and pray in tongues, as a normal part of the service, seemed strangely comfortable. When a branch fellowship was started in St. Louis, Jimmy was a founder, but he never discussed it with his family.

One night, in a small group, Jimmy spoke of his desire to be filled with the Spirit. The leader said, "What are you hoping for? Why are you asking for the gifts of the Spirit, Jimmy?" Jimmy stammered out that he wanted to be used by God to bring other people into the Kingdom. It was not healing he wanted so much as to be a person God and other people would really love without effort. Then he started to cry.

All ten of the young people, together with the adult leader, began to pray silently, laying hands on Jimmy. Then the leader prayed out loud, in the name of Jesus Christ, for the power and protection for Jimmy. The room was electric. Jimmy began to speak beautifully, in "tongues." His speech was clear. But the loveliest gift was the silence that followed. There was peace. Jimmy radiated. And those who were with him felt a love almost overwhelming.

Four years later, Jim Barton attends the state university. He lives in a men's household of a charismatic community. He is active in the Presbyterian Church his parents attend and teaches in the church school. Both parents have experienced the "filling of the Holy Spirit" as Jim had. They completed advanced degrees and teach in the public school system.

Jim drives his own car, plays tennis, rides a bicycle, and walks to every class carrying his own books. He can be understood when he speaks. The family friend says, "I notice the change because I have been away. His family never thinks to mention it. He still has cerebral palsy. Yet, when you are with him for a time, you hardly notice it. What I do see is that he commands attention. His friends love him without effort and he radiates. Jim has authority. He has come so far. I want to believe that this is a miracle."

Theological Briefs

J. Massyngberde Ford

Jimmy Barton's case is very typical of the many changes which the Pentecostal experience has achieved in numerous lives. Only the extreme skeptic could deny that some of these are almost miraculous happenings (see D. and K. Ranaghan, *Catholic Pentecostals* [New York: Paulist Press, 1969] and R. J. Voigt, *Go to the Mountain* [St. Meinrad: Abbey Press, 1975]). However, one must ask whether the case might lead one to attribute too much to faith healing and the prayer group experience and not enough to other sources of the grace of the Holy Spirit?

There are three premises with which one must begin this evaluation (1) the role of the Spirit in sacraments (not only baptism and confirmation but also the Eucharist); (2) the diversity of the gifts of the Spirit; and (3) the relationship of the Spirit to the theology of the cross.

One may proceed through the case and note the various activities of the Spirit. One observes that Paul in 1 Corinthians 12:4–6 has made a very important point when he says that there are different *gifts* (*charismata*), *ministries* (*diakoniai*) and *works* (*energēmata*). Respectively these may be equated with (1) a combination of supernatural grace and human talents; (2) social concern and work which involves a special love for the persons whom one is serving; and (3) a directly supernatural gift which is quite unobtainable by human

J. Massyngberde Ford is Associate Professor in Biblical Studies, Notre Dame University. She was educated at the University of Nottingham and the University of London, receiving her Ph.D. from Nottingham. She is the author of *The Spirit and the Human Person*, *The Anchor Biblical Commentary on Revelation*, and *The Spirit and the Human Person*. She is a member of the Roman Catholic Church.

endeavor. Paul states emphatically that all come from the one Spirit and he implies that all are equal in the sight of God. Paul sees the source of all the gifts in the sacrament of baptism (1 Cor. 12:13).

Throughout Jimmy's life all the manifestations of the Spirit have worked and, one hopes, continue to work. First, Jimmy had received the Spirit in baptism, as had his family and friends. Second, Jimmy witnessed both *diakoniai* and *charismata* from his family, from the car pool, and from the people working in the cerebral palsy clinic. It is significant to note that, when the people helped him, Jim responded with a smile, that is, a manifestation of the joy in the Spirit even in tribulation (cf. James 1:2–4 and Phil. 4:4–5). Third, in his early life Jimmy was gifted not only with this spiritual joy but also with endurance. Both he and his helpers were going through an experience which is aptly described in 2 Peter 1:3–8 as the progression from one virtue to another. Fourth, one notes, too, Jim's intellectual gifts which he received from the Creator Spirit (cf. James 1.5). Naturally these talents are bound to have had an important effect on his life as he grows older especially after adolescence.

In this case Karen does not appear to be a very heroic figure, but is this first impression an accurate one? She is faithful to prayer (cf. 1 Thess. 5:17) especially ecclesial prayer, where the action of the Spirit is especially powerful. She begins a prayer group whereby implicitly expressing her need of human companionship as well as divine aid; this is very wise. It is not necessarily wrong for her to express bitterness and anger towards God, for the prophets, the psalmists, and the saints of the Church have felt that they could lay bare their emotions before God (cf. the confessions of Jeremiah 11:18–12:6; 15:10–21; 17:12–18; 18:18–23; 20:7–18, the book of Job and many of the psalms). Further, could not one see in Karen a situation of which Paul speaks in Romans 8:26–28, the Spirit helping us in our weakness even with inarticulate groans? Although Karen's enthusiasm about the healing service and her "making Jimmy pray the whole way" seem to have elicited wise cautions, they indicate her faith that miraculous healing can occur and her return from the service with a healed soul. However, her anxieties are realistic. She does appreciate that God does not perform miraculous healing in all cases.

The case says that "nothing happened for weeks." In fact something did happen. The doctor provided Jimmy with new medication. This is also a ministry of the Spirit. We are told in Scripture to honor both the physician and the pharmacist (Sirach 38:1–8). Thus the answer to the healing service may have been new medication from the doctor to whom God had given the Spirit's gift of wisdom and insight.

The family suffered. There is nothing sinful about this. They were kept together by love for Jimmy (cf. Col. 3:12–14 which is one of the readings for the feast of the Holy Family). The fruits of the Spirit were manifest even if the miraculous gifts (the *energēmata*) were not. This is important because the fruits of the Spirit as listed in Galatians 5:22–23, Philippians 4:8–9 etc. are a manifestation of the Personhood of God, his attributes, and are always indispensable both for the individual and for the Christian community. However, the gifts are a manifestation of the activity of the Spirit and are dispensable. God uses them when occasion arises but they are not essential either for the life of the individual or for the Church. However, the religious intensity of the family took its toll on Jimmy. When he attended the youth group he never prayed. This is the natural result of too much religiosity in the home.

Jimmy was drawn to the charismatic fellowship through the youth group. It is significant that there was "complete lack of pressure." The effect of the music, the warmth, and love can be seen in a purely psychological light but it is also legitimate to view it as Spirit-graced. The lack of pressure is important because the Spirit always respects our personshood and our free will. Jimmy's motivation for wishing to receive the gifts of the Spirit (more precisely to receive more of the gifts of the Spirit) was a mixture of the wish to serve and a certain "selfishness" although it is not wrong to wish to be loved. Through the prayers of his friends Jimmy receives what is commonly known today as the "baptism" or "release of the Spirit." This is an experiential sense of the presence of God usually accompanied by sensible (felt) devotion. In Jimmy's case it was also accompanied by the gift of tongues, that is speaking a "language" not learnt in a human way. Although there is much discussion about the gift of tongues, even those who do not readily espouse it admit that it does bring about a certain elation which can be a genuine joy and peace in the Spirit or euphoria (see John P. Kildahl, *The Psychology of Speaking in Tongues*, [New York: Harper & Row, 1972], pp. 45–46 and 60).

From the time of the Pentecostal experience onwards the case study seems to suggest that all is well, the goal has been attained, both Jimmy and his parents have made distinct advances both spiritually and academically. This is good, indeed very good, and one is encouraged to find that Jimmy and his parents are active in their Presbyterian church as well as Jimmy's belonging to a Pentecostal men's household. However, the last paragraph of the case leaves the reader with some uneasiness. The statements "his friends love him without an effort" (did not Jimmy's former friends and therapists love him without an effort), "Jimmy commands attention," and "Jim has authority." We are not told any details concerning this, but one cannot help entertaining some misgivings when one realizes that tongue-speakers do see themselves as special people (Kildahl, p. 67).

Jimmy lives in a household. This may be good depending on whether the community is governed from an authoritarian or a democratic stance. Some communities foster much dependence both upon authority leaders and on the community, and they build up a certain barrier to keep away the pain of the world. The individual ego becomes merged into the community ego (see B. Zablocki, *The Joyful Community*, [Baltimore: Penguin Books, 1971]). One would have felt happier if Jimmy had tried to keep in touch with his friends who suffered from the same disease or if there were an indication that he showed vital social concern.

The sense of uneasiness generated by the final paragraph of the case leads to some general warnings about some aspects of the Pentecostal movement. Church history witnesses to the fact that most charismatic movements eventually succumb to biblical fundamentalism, elitism, authoritarianism, lack of social concern, and extreme legalism. Many become sects. Recent criticism of the Catholic Pentecostal movement (William G. Storey, *A. D. Correspondence*, May 1975 and six articles by Rick Casey in the *National Catholic Reporter* from August 15th to October 1975) has shown quite plainly that the present Charismatic movement has not avoided these pitfalls. Two of the most powerful centers of the phenomenon, South Bend, Indiana, and Ann Arbor, Michigan, have a complete paraecclesial structure with officers parallel to bishop, presbyter, and deacon; a teaching magisterium which is regarded as almost infallible; a formal catechumenate lasting six weeks; and post "baptism of the Spirit" courses to initiate people into covenant communities which include a severe disciplinary system. The leaders are often ahistorical in their outlook and seek to cast away nearly 2,000 years of history and culture and to establish communities modeled on New Testament patterns. Women are taught to be completely submissive and to accept Pentecostal male leaders, not Catholic priests, as their spiritual directors. Dissent from the tenets of the leaders is followed by exclusion, sometimes accompanied by shunning.

These aspects of the movement can be "redeemed" only by the leaders listening humbly, attentively, and fearlessly to criticism and by carefully altering their life-style to be more consonant with twentieth-century life. It is the fruits of the Spirit which will enable them to do this and to learn to live with ambiguity and creativity.

This is not a psychological brief, but perhaps we could chart Jimmy's psychological and spiritual maturity by a simplified form of the Maslow chart:

1. physiological needs, provided by his parents and friends through *diakonia* and *charismata*
2. safety (security, order, stability), given by his parents and therapists and later by the youth group and charismatic household; (*diakonia*, *charismata*, and *energēmata*)
3. love, belongingness (family affection), beginning to show in Jim's work for the church and school, will develop more when he relates to women and contemplates either marriage or consecrated celibacy
4. identity (self-respect, self-esteem, success) certainly helped by his charismatic experience, but it would have been helpful to have more information about the type of household in which Jim lives. Is Jim's identity one with the group or his own real personality?
5. commitment (focus, direction)
6. self-actualization

The development of the last two may be impeded if Jimmy is subject to authority figures, to public manifestation of conscience or, if he reaches a position of authority, this will develop when he learns and practices collaborative authority and/or democracy. At that point he would be less likely to desire to "command attention" and try to make his friends "love him without an effort." Indeed, somewhere in his life experience even Jimmy, who has always carried a cross, will have to meet creative conflict and "enemies," "opponents" or "dissenters." When he deals with these successfully with the aid of the fruits of the Spirit (cf. 2 Cor. 1–9), he will emerge as a more mature man and be able to direct his own life with less dependence or no essential dependence on the community, and he will reach self-actualization (cf. Eph. 4:11–16, esp. 4.).

It may be that the Pentecost experience was a grace-filled one through which it was very necessary for Jimmy to pass, but not one in which he should stay lest his psychological and spiritual development be impeded. Incidentally, nothing is said about Jimmy's relationship to women, and women often carry many fruits of the Spirit which must complement the male for his full maturity.

The writer wishes to make two additional points which go beyond the case. First, the work of the Spirit should be focused on an ecclesial plane rather than individual salvation and, second, the gift of the Spirit is very closely associated with the glory of the cross. Indeed, as Krister Stendahl observes "the Christian before the courts is the only one to whom the Scriptures promise the gift of the Spirit. No one individual is otherwise promised a special gift of the Spirit. . . . In the courts is the confrontation that has the promise of the Spirit" (Stendahl in Michael P. Hamilton, *The Charismatic Movement*, [Grand Rapids: Wm. B. Eerdmans Publishing Co., 1975]).

Thus Jimmy Barton's case has illustrated the workings of the Spirit through the Church (in this case Presbyterian), through the communion of saints (all those who were friends to Jimmy), and through the resurrection of the body a glimpse of which is caught in the healing of Jimmy's soul and mind and, to some extent, his body. He (or She) is seen to be the source of "every gift and created grace" for Jimmy.

SELECTED BIBLIOGRAPHY

J. Massyngberde Ford, *Ministries and Fruits of the Spirit* (Notre Dame: Catholic Action Press, 1973). This is a simple exposition of the gifts and fruits of the Spirit intended for the average lay reader.

J. Massyngberde Ford, *Which Way for Pentecostals?* (New York: Harper & Row, 1976). This describes two types of Pentecostalism which have emerged in the Catholic Church, one type is losing its Catholic tradition, the other is wholly integrated.

Donald L. Gelpi, S.J., *Charism and Sacrament, A Theology of Christian Conversion* (New York: Paulist Press, 1976).

"Pentecost Continues, Charismatic Renewal," *Origins* 48 (May 4, 1975) pp. 754–757. The Charismatic renewal in Canada; its strengths and weaknesses by the bishops of Canada. A document of great pastoral significance which can be a guide to laypersons and pastors alike.

Simon Tugwell, O.T., *Did You Receive the Spirit* (New York: Paulist Press, 1973). This is especially important because of the inclusion of Orthodox pneumatology.

KILIAN MCDONNELL

Experience as Possibility

Can a person experience God, be directly touched by his presence, have some immediate contact with his living reality? This question with which the case of Jim Barton confronts us has troubled contemporary theology. The answer which emerges from the biblical text is an unqualified yes. Jim sought God, stumbled toward him, experienced him and came to know him. There is an ancient pattern here. The Israelites, whom Yahweh had chosen, stumbled toward him and came to know him in the same way they knew everything else, by experience. "I will take you for my people and I will be your God; and you shall know that I am the Lord your God, who has brought you out from the burdens of the Egyptians" (Exod. 6:6, 7). They

---

KILIAN MCDONNELL is President of the Institute for Ecumenical and Cultural Research and Professor of Theology, St. John's University, Collegeville, Minnesota. He was educated at St. John's University, University of Ottawa, Catholic University of America, and has the Ph.D. in Protestant theology from the University of Trier. His publications include *John Calvin, the Church and the Eucharist, The Charismatic Renewal and the Churches,* and he is the editor of *Holy Spirit and Power: The Catholic Charismatic Renewal.* He is an ordained Roman Catholic priest, O.S.B.

knew by experience that Yahweh was their God because he freed them from Egypt.

In the New Testament it is the Holy Spirit who mediates the knowledge and experience of God. Specifically the Spirit leads one to proclaim "Jesus is Lord" (1 Cor. 12:13). A characteristic element in the Church's preaching has been the offer of the personal experience of the Spirit (Acts 2:38; Rom. 8:9; Gal. 3:2; John 14:26; 1 Pet. 4:14). To have experienced the Spirit does not make one a special kind of Christian. It is simply part of normal Christian expectation and awareness.

If Jim really experienced God, then he stands not only in the biblical tradition but in a long postbiblical history. The patristic-monastic theology of the Middle Ages had the experience of God as "both the principle and the aim of the quest" (Jean Leclercq). St. Bernard's (11th c.) motto might well have been "I believe in order to experience." He wrote: "Which among you has not at some time or other experienced in the depths of his conscience, the Spirit of the Son crying 'Abba, Father'?" William of Thierry (11th c.), a disciple of Bernard, said that a person lays hold of God "more by taste than by understanding." Here we must avoid turning experience into a kind of religious anti–intellectualism.

Experience as Power

Granted that such a thing as religious experience exists, how does one know that Jim had one? This points to the ambiguity of Jim's situation. Not everyone who claims a religious experience has had one. But the indications (not proof) that Jim had an authentic, if lower case, experience of God are there. He sought God, he did not isolate himself from other seekers, he grew in his relations with others, he loved to taste the Lord in silence, he underwent a personal as well as physical change.

Why should an experience of the Spirit change Jim? The Spirit is "the Finger of God" (Luke 11:20). In the biblical text finger of God is a sign of power and in the later tradition the finger of God came to be that by which God touches others. To be touched by the finger of God is to experience his power. Could one really experience the "Lord and Giver of Life," be touched by the power which raised

Jesus from the dead (Rom. 1:4) and remain unchanged? To have remained unchanged would have been a sign that Jim did not experience God. What would one say if in the light of this experience Jim began to conceive of the Christian life as a movement from peak experience to peak experience, from mountaintop to mountaintop? To think of the Christian life as wholly experience-oriented in this sense would be distortion of the gospel. The Christian walks in light, joy, and praise, but also in darkness, sorrow, and doubt. To be a Christian is to be baptized (dipped) into both the death and the resurrection of Christ.

Yahweh freed Israel from captivity in Egypt and by this act the Israelites experienced him there where they suffered the oppression of slavery, where their lives were "unbearable with hard labor" (Exod. 1:14). In the New Testament the healing miracles of Jesus were experienced as the presence of the Lord there where persons suffered from diseases and were in pain. For the moment let us suppose that in the wonder of a cure God presented himself to be experienced by Jim there where he was suffering. What is this experience of the miraculous? Does the miraculous presuppose that God lives beyond our ordinary experience, in some realm beyond time and history, in some way out there? Then when God wants to work a miracle he dashes into our time element, breaks into our history where he makes an exception to what some call the laws of nature (in this case the processes of a body ravaged by cerebral palsy), lets himself be experienced, effects a cure and then dashes back beyond time and history to the great timeless beyond which is his proper element. I pose some basic questions: Is a miracle an intervention in our lives and laws by God who lives beyond our lives and laws? Is a miracle a wondrous experience of God who is by definition beyond experience because he is above and beyond time? Is a miracle a radical disruption of the normal pattern of human existence? Or, to put it more crudely, does God break the laws of nature to work a miracle?

Experience as Presence

Is it not possible that God lives and is to be experienced there where Jim and Karen live and experience themselves, in that "room" where they are conscious of themselves, where they move and act, where Jim struggles with such basic activities as walking, talking, eating. Is it not possible that God lives in the same time and history where Jim lives, not in some great timeless beyond? Must a miracle be an intervention from beyond, a suspension of the "laws of nature" to prove that God is God, that he is real? Could it not be that the Lord of creation works a miracle by manifesting his presence (which is not the same thing as proving his presence) in "nature" and through "nature," heightening in a wondrous way those recreative powers that are there by virtue of his ultimate lordship? This may still be an intervention, but it is not from beyond but in history and time. Many persons in time and history intervened in Jim's life and are experienced by him. His mother and father, his friends. Why not the Holy Spirit? Why not the Lord and Giver of life?

There are some rather embarrassing details to Jim's story. One is his unsuccessful visit to a faith healer. This is embarrassing first because the healer did not heal. But what sort of judgment would we make if Jim had experienced God in a cure at this time? In philosophical terms I ask the question: Is a theory true because it works? Are there not other reasons why a thing works than because it is true (wish fulfillment, for instance)? In theological terms I ask the question: Is the working of a miracle proof that the Holy Spirit is acting? False christs and false prophets also work miracles (Matt. 24:24; Mark 13:22). This points to the ambiguity present when trying to decide whether God has been experienced in a healing (1 Cor. 12:9). One removes the ambiguity of whether a healing has religious meaning or not, whether it is a true experience and manifestation of the Spirit or not, by the process of discernment (1 Cor. 12:10; 14:2–4). The whole community, which is the local church, makes the judgment on religious experience.

Experience as Mutuality

The faith healer told Jim and Karen to pray for more faith. Isn't this a bit clumsy? Is the healer suggesting that if Jim does not experience God in a healing, the fault will be their lack of faith? On the other hand, didn't Jesus ask a similar question of the two blind men who came to be healed? "And Jesus said to them, 'Do you believe that I can do this to you?' They answered him, 'Yes, Lord.' Then he touched their eyes, saying, 'Let it be done to you according to your faith.' " Faith, like experience, is a dialogue of two liberties, Claude Tresmontant reminds us: the liberty of the Holy Spirit and the liberty of man. If faith is simply the liberty of man, clenching its fists and screwing up determination to do something or believe something, then what Jesus asks is monstrous. All the burden is on the blind men (or on Jim and Karen), and if they cannot muster the strength to make the leap of faith, they have no one to blame but themselves. Faith is that mutual exchange between the liberty of the Holy Spirit and the liberty of man. Experience is by definition a mutuality. And when the liberty of Jim experiences weakness and fear, it turns to the liberty of the Holy Spirit for strength and cries out "I believe Lord, help my unbelief" (Mark 9:24).

I think Jim experienced a healing. Is the meaning of that healing exhausted by the new physical abilities Jim has of walking, driving, bicycling, and by the new authority with which he speaks? First, healing is not intended to inaugurate in a dazzling way an era of happiness on earth without pain. It is rather a sign that Jesus is present in Jim's life, that the kingdom of God is in some initial way already here. Jim's healing is a sign that no restriction can be made upon the promises Jesus made. "Whatever you pray for in faith you will receive" (Matt. 21:22). Those promises bind God today as they did when Jesus lived. And the promises are available to Jim and to us.

Experience as Wholeness

Perhaps more importantly, the manifestation of the Holy Spirit in the gift of healing in Jim's life tells us something about salvation. Man is really not a rational animal. He is a seeing, loving, fearing, hoping, contemplating animal and it is that totality which is saved. The Spirit is manifested not just in Jim's soul but in that totality which is Jim Barton. Is Christianity just a philosophy of the soul, or just a metaphysics of the human spirit? God is not really interested in souls—his salvation has to do with persons and their total personal histories. Jim's healing is a sign of cosmic healing in that ultimate future when the lordship of Jesus will triumph (Eph. 1:9, 10; Gal. 4:4), and all creation is summed up and reconciled to the Father in Christ. In Christ "all things hold together" (Col. 1:17) including materiality and bodiliness. Ultimately God does not heal by halves.

Jim's healing is a sign of the cosmic nature of salvation: moon, stars, mountains, rivers, fish, and fowl, and also the total human person. The whole created universe is to be recapitulated in Christ, transformed, and handed over to the Father.

Another embarrassing detail in Jim's story is the crying episode. With justification that immediately puts us on our guard. Though the principle should not be pushed too far, one can say that the higher the emotional content the more suspect is the religious meaning of a person's experience. Having said that, I wonder if it is truly a sign of Jim's emotional unbalance if the experience of God is reflected in his whole self, including his emotions. Or are worship and praise only something we do conceptually? Why cannot a person respond to the experience of God by using all his or her faculties to worship, including a restrained use of the emotions? If one were to look in the whole mystical-ascetical tradition from the fourth to the seventeenth centuries, one would find that persons like John Cassian (4th c.), Peter Damian (11th c.) and Robert Bellarmine (17th c.) responded to God's immediacy by the gift of tears—tears of joy for God's love, tears of sorrow for their own and others' sins. In the Roman Catholic church there was a set of Mass prayers in the old missal (*Orationes Diversae* 21) in use until the 1960s, entitled "For Asking the Gift of Tears." Weeping is a very human act and can be an expression of the experience of God in prayer. Obviously not every shedding of tears has deep religious content, and sometimes it can be simply a sign that a person is upset.

Experience as Community

Jim's experience of God came through various communities of believers and it forged new personal bonds of some depth with their members. Both he and his parents found new meaning in their church. So the experience of the Spirit and the lordship of Jesus was not strictly a private affair. Yet it was also a profoundly individual experience. It affected Jim not only in his relation to others but touched him from within so that he prayed in a new way, he loved the silence which followed the invocation of the name of Jesus, he was at peace. There was a new fire and authority within. And it was deeper and more lasting than a warm feeling, a momentary glow.

This reflects the patterns of how the Spirit acts in lives. The Spirit blows where he wills and his activities are not coterminus with the life of the Church. But the Church is in large part a creation of the Spirit. The difference between the company who followed Jesus and the Church is the gift of the Spirit. Both Christ and the Spirit are constitutive of the Church—before Pentecost there was no Church. The Spirit was poured out on the Church precisely because she is to proclaim the good news by the power of the Spirit. We all know the dangers and pitfalls inherent in being a chosen instrument, but that does not change the fact of being chosen. So it is not with an infallible necessity but with a certain propriety that Jim's experience of the Spirit and that of his parents resulted in a new love for and commitment to the Church. For Jim's parents this life in the Spirit has led them to the service of others in teaching in the public schools.

In summary Jim's experience of the lordship of Jesus through the power of the Spirit led gradually and in a not unlikely manner to a measure of physical healing and to Jim's interior transformation. Jim's experience touched Karen and his father and resulted for all of them in a greater participation in the life of the Church and in service to the world.

Selected Bibliography

C. K. Barrett, *The Holy Spirit and the Gospel Tradition* (London: S.P.C.K., 1947). A scientific exegetical study of the Holy Spirit in the Gospels of Matthew, Mark, and Luke.

Hendrikus Berkhof, *The Doctrine of the Holy Spirit* (Richmond: John Knox Press, 1964). A great systematic theologian reflects on six doctrinal themes with historical insight and theological acumen.

George Hendry, *The Holy Spirit in Christian Theology* (Philadelphia, The Westminster Press, 1956). Not a systematic treatment but an attempt to relate the Spirit to certain doctrinal areas such as Christ, the Church, the Word, the human Spirit.

Kilian McDonnell, ed., *The Holy Spirit and Power: The Catholic Charismatic Renewal*, (Garden City: Doubleday, 1975). A symposium on central themes such as the person of the Spirit, Baptism in the Holy Spirit, Christian initiation, religious experience.

"Theological and Pastoral Orientations on the Catholic Charismatic Renewal," (Communication Center, P. O. Drawer A, Notre Dame, Ind., 1974). A document drawn up by an international team of theologians and pastoral leaders explaining the theological basis of the charismatic renewal.

THOMAS D. PARKER

Jimmy and his parents face the difficulty of dealing with cerebral palsy, a serious physical handicap. In addition, there are psychological, social, and financial burdens incident to the disease. They must discover what health means for them and what caring and love demand under circumstances more difficult than most of us face. It is hard to read this case and not be impressed by the extent of the parents' love and the strength of their hopes, the willingness of neighbors to do what they can, and Jimmy's own efforts to find a full life.

At the same time there is a group of persons called "handicapped," into which Jimmy and those like him are put by the rest of us, whether they want this or not. Handicapped people are those you take special pains for, make allowances for, and rescue whenever possible. The resentment against this literally explodes in Jimmy; he wants nothing more than to be loved "without effort" and to help others find their way "into the Kingdom," as he puts it in one dramatic moment. The distinct impression this leaves one with is that the "healing" so deeply desired is a healing of Jimmy's relationships and self-image as much as his bodily functioning. It involves his parents, his friends, and the Church quite as much as Jimmy; yet no one ever asked Jimmy what *he* wanted.

It is sad the family felt they had to go to another state to find spiritual help, even though the case tells us how much very real help had been given in their own community: the tutoring, the prayer group, the exercising and the rest. Healing is one of the major "works of the Kingdom" in Jesus' ministry and in the ministry of the young Church. Christians have always built hospitals to care for the sick and prayed for health. I ask myself whether there is too narrow a view of healing in many churches, separating healing of the mind and spirit from healing of the body. There is obviously much love and care, so much deep faith in God and trust in God's providence; why is a "healing ministry" so often relegated to small groups alongside the "mainline" churches?

At the same time I am glad that there was a charismatic fellowship in which Jimmy felt loved, and began to believe that he was not defined by his handicap, but by his potential for full life under God. The case shows both the institutional Church and the small fellowship as ways in which the ministry of Jesus takes place today. Surely faith in God in response to the gospel was nourished in the parish church. Health includes the forgiveness of sins and the fruits of the spirit Jimmy found there. But health also includes a depth of personal relationships and physical well-being, the release of a capacity to grow and flourish, which Jimmy found in the charismatic fellowship, and which his parents later found for themselves.

According to the New Testament, the outpouring of the Spirit upon the people of God, their bodily well-being, and the forgiveness of sins were bound up together with their expectations for the "Kingdom of God." Jesus announced that the Kingdom was "at hand," and his own ministry of forgiveness and healing gave reality to that announcement. What we know of the earliest communities of Christians indicates that forgiveness and healing were central to their common life. Moreover the "gifts" of the Spirit and the universal reign of Jesus as the Christ were the source and goal of the new life they shared together.

This case suggests to me answers to three important theological questions related to this New Testament witness. First is the question of the location of grace. There is no separation of the so-called natural and supernatural, or the ordinary and extraordinary works of God in Jimmy's life. Medical help, loving attention, prayer, and a service of healing are all a part of the outcome. Grace perfects the creature and leads it to what it may be under God. There is an immediate relation of every creature to God as well as many mediated ones. The grace of God is found in a personal relation to God (faith) *and* through the agency of other persons (love) and things. My own theological tradition (Reformed) teaches a doctrine of common grace echoed in the convictions of Christians of many persuasions that God is at work in "all things" and not just in a special sphere of life called religion or the inner (spiritual) life.

Second is the question of the meaning of health. Whenever creatures flourish as they may in a vital balance with other creatures and within their own life, we may speak of health. In the case, Jimmy's growth and development in all dimensions of his life is a movement toward full life, toward health. In this sense of the term, there may be sick and healthy handicapped as well as sick and well "normal" people. Health is a well-being, not an ideal body, a perfect situation, or excellent achievement. All of us exist in the struggle to maintain a vital balance in our own lives; are we unhealthy because we are not perfect? Jimmy's handicap was an obstacle to his flourishing until he gave it to God. It is so no longer; not only is the disease stemmed, it is being overcome. I believe that this overcoming may include organic change or may not; in either case this is a secondary question.

Third is the question of what is a miracle. Some will deny that what happened to Jimmy is a miracle, for it seemed to come about through ordinary processes and be well within the range of what is possible for human beings. Others will affirm that it was a miracle, for the prayer of faith was answered in a particularly beautiful way by the One who is the source of all life and health. The key to this seems to be what expectations we have when we use a term like *miracle*. It is clear that the faith of Jimmy and his parents grew into an expectation of fullest human life for them all, and that they were in a position of looking for God's grace. Some of us never see because we never look.

We usually mean by miracle something out of the ordinary, unexplained and mysterious. Many things once thought of as miraculous no longer strike us as such because conditions have changed. But if miracle means a direct, divine intervention into the course of events that works by cause and effect, then neither the unusual nor the usual is being interpreted with much theological acumen, I am afraid. Such a view would make ordinary providence mechanical and the extraordinary magical. How much more adequate to speak of the divine energy and order operating in a world that is open to that which is new and without precedent, in an on-going creation, than of a fully fixed and determined world violated from time to time by a willful intervention from outside. Process theologies represent one common way of reflecting on this.

Beyond these three questions lies the more general problem of how we understand the person and work of the Spirit of God. The term *spirit* is drawn from the basic life act of breathing. It is a term used for the liveliness of creatures as much as for the life of God. When the Creed of 381 declares the Spirit the "Lord and Giver of life," this basic idea is affirmed: the finite energies of creatures have their source in the uncreated energy of God, and reach their destiny by the same divine source. The human spirit is not so much a part added to us, say to our bodies and minds, but the liveliness of our person in all its dimensions. Likewise, the divine Spirit is not a part of God, but God as such, as the Living One who makes all things new. In the words of the ancient creeds, the Spirit is *homoousion* (of the same being) with the Father and the Word.

The Reformed doctrine of the Spirit places emphasis on the work attributed to the Spirit in the glorification and perfection of creatures. In relation to the Christian community this is a work of sanctification and in relation to the world as a whole it is a work of transfiguration in which all things come to their fullness in God. In relation to the case, there is a merging of these two foci of the divine energy. The Reformed expressed this view in their traditional phrase *Word and Spirit*, God's presence actively to reconcile and renew the creation. Irenaeus used the figure of the two hands of God to speak of Word and Spirit, the divine order and energy apart from which nothing exists or reaches fulfillment.

Seen from this vantage point whatever makes for a pattern of human existence in the world in which persons flourish on every level of their being is the work of the Spirit. Since human existence is inconceivable without its biological, psychological, social, and cultural dimensions, human flourishing cannot be limited to one or another of these aspects. A "spirited" life involves the whole person mentally, emotionally, physically, etc. It is understandable but unfortunate that the term spirit has often been limited to our higher capacities, our self-consciousness, for example. Intellect, artistic sensibility, creativity, religious feeling, and the like are genuine manifestations of the human made alive by the Spirit, but so are labor, sexuality, emotions, and sensuality, to name but a few "lower" capacities. If the inner and personal aspects of our lives live by the Divine Spirit so do the outer, communal, and typical aspects of our lives. All human capacities "come alive" when they are energized by the Spirit, including our capacities for faith, hope, and love as Christians.

The life in the Spirit witnessed in the New Testament reflects both our new being and new functioning as Christians. The "fruits" of the Spirit (Gal. 5) are the qualities of being: love, joy, peace, gentleness, and the like. The "gifts" of the Spirit (1 Cor. 12) are intensifications of our ability to function in certain helpful ways: speech, healing, administration, discernment, teaching, etc. In both instances what is named flows from the divine energy and makes us flourish.

It is sad that we so often settle for a diminished life. Our energy is sapped and our aliveness recedes when we are out of phase with what is going on around and inside us. Instead of being energized by our relations to other creatures and the divine ground of being, we are cut off and we set our own energies against their source and setting. Instead of being reinforced and carried along, we fight the flow of things and become worn out. "Be the flow of the universe," the sage from the East advises us, while Jesus promises those who believe in him "rivers of living water" flowing out of their center. The promise of the Christian faith is that we may be filled with the Spirit, fully alive, and so "healthy" in the most important sense of that word. No one has to live as though half dead.

The miracle in Jimmy's and his parents' lives is a work of the Spirit in our midst. It is fitting for Jimmy and those around him. His life has opened up. In fact the evidences of the disease are receding. Who would wish to refuse thanks to God for what has happened in his life, or to appreciate his witness to the power of the Spirit?

Selected Bibliography

Arnold B. Come, *Human Spirit and Holy Spirit* (Philadelphia: The Westminster Press, 1959). Drawing on classic and contemporary sources, this book offers an interpretation of the work of the Spirit and the human potential for personal growth.

Gregory of Nazianzus, "On the Holy Spirit," Fifth Theological Oration, in Edward R. Hardy and Cyril Richardson, eds., *The Christology of the Later Fathers, Library of Christian Classics*, vol. 3 (Philadelphia: The Westminster Press, 1954), pp. 194–214. A classic patristic treatment of the deity of the Spirit.

Morton Kelsey, *Encounter with God* (Minneapolis: Bethany Fellowship, Inc., 1975). A sketch of theological possibilities and problematics of the doctrine of the Spirit, written from the viewpoint of sympathetic interest in the charismatic movement.

Paul Tillich, *Systematic Theology*, vol. 3 (Chicago: University of Chicago Press, 1963), part 4, "Life and the Spirit." A systematic theological consideration of the doctrine of the Spirit and its ramifications for the Church as a "spiritual community."

J. RODMAN WILLIAMS

This story is a dramatic representation of the difference in human affairs between a situation in which the Holy Spirit is experienced as present and active and one in which there is minimal understanding and experience. The perspective is quite different after Jimmy's attendance at a youth rally and charismatic fellowship. What is depicted as effecting the critical change is the experience of being "filled with the Holy Spirit."

Prior to the youth rally and charismatic fellowship the narrative carries forward two strains. First, there is a kind of indomitable courage and determination on the part of Jimmy, his parents, and a number of friends. Despite all outward appearance that Jimmy could never make it in this world, he would not give up; in fact by age sixteen Jimmy, while handicapped, was able to walk without braces. One senses that the Holy Spirit as "Lord and Giver of life" (Constantinopolitan Creed) was present creatively enabling Jimmy's halting but steady progress. Also, whatever the failings of Karen and her husband, there was a marked persistence to find a way for Jimmy's healing, and a determined faith that God could and would bring it about. It is likewise impressive to observe the Christian friends who established a prayer group largely for Karen's sake; noteworthy also is the readiness of distant persons to lay hands on Jimmy for healing. Thus there were remarkable evidences of the Holy Spirit as Comforter. It is not too much to suggest that here was the Holy Spirit "proceeding from the Father and the Son" (Council of Toledo): the

J. RODMAN WILLIAMS is President of Melodyland School of Theology and was previously Professor of Systematic Theology at Austin Presbyterian Theological Seminary. He studied at Davidson College, Union Theological Seminary (Virginia), and received his Ph.D. from Union Theological Seminary (New York) and Columbia University. He is the author of *The Era of the Spirit, The Pentecostal Reality*, and *Ten Major Doctrines of Christian Faith*. He is an ordained Presbyterian minister.

Father who is "the Father of mercies and God of all comfort" (2 Cor. 1:3), and the Son who himself sends the Comforter (John 14:16). One might add that however inadequate were some of the consolations and actions of friends, they were more than human sympathies. For such expressions of intended helpfulness were those of people in the believing community, the Church, which is the fellowship of the Holy Spirit. If the Holy Spirit is "the soul" of the church (*Mystici Corporis*)—wherever the Church is found—then the Holy Spirit was active even in these faulty ministrations.

The second strain bears much less evidence of the Holy Spirit's activity. On the one hand, there is Karen's early bitterness and anger against God, and at a later date her deep depression when God seems to have failed her. There is little sense of the Spirit's joy and consolation wherein every situation can be met affirmatively and creatively. Further, Karen acts in coercive manner so that Jimmy is forced to pray all the way to the healing service, and despite Karen's laudable belief in God's healing power (an aspect of the Holy Spirit's work), she seems to demand immediate action rather than allowing God freely and sovereignly to move in his own time and manner. "Where the Spirit of the Lord is, there is freedom" (2 Cor. 3:17); but this is little demonstrated in Karen's relation to Jimmy or to the Lord. On the other hand, the minister who called on Karen showed even less spiritual sensitivity. He could have affirmed, along with Karen, the possibility of healing and its witness to the Spirit's power and grace, while encouraging her to leave the issue in God's sovereign hands so that she might be prepared if healing did not occur. Instead he focused totally, and negatively, on the resulting problems if Jimmy were not healed. The minister therefore was quite unable to meet Karen affirmatively, and thus pastorally and spiritually. The Holy Spirit as "soul" of the Church was less evident in this case than in that of Karen and her friends.

We may now reflect upon the radical difference in the tone of everything connected with the charismatic fellowship. There was no pressure exerted on Jimmy to conform to the style of the group, no calculated plans for his next steps, no boundaries set on what might occur. It was a Spirit-filled group in praise; singing and praying in tongues were a normal part of their fellowship; and love was abundantly present. All seemed to Jimmy "strangely comfortable" (recall the Holy Spirit as "Comforter"). The consequences were significant: Jimmy later, in a small charismatic group, rather than asking for healing, expresses his desire to be "filled with the Spirit" so as to be more fully used by God; hands are laid upon him; and then Jimmy speaks beautifully in "tongues"; his long stammering speech becomes momentarily clear; and praise, love, joy, radiate forth.

The continuing results are also significant. Jimmy becomes active in his church, his school, in athletics; and there is about him a striking combination of authority and love. Though the cerebral palsy is not fully gone, his parents, who have likewise come to experience the "filling of the Holy Spirit," hardly notice it, and no more is there mention of frustration, bitterness, and depression. They have also moved ahead to complete advanced degrees and teach in the public schools. One senses a fresh breath of life in both Jim Barton, who now attends the university, and in his parents. Whatever the difficulties that undoubtedly remain, the whole situation has been transformed by the reality of the Holy Spirit.

The story about Jim Barton can make for a fresh appreciation of what it means to say, "I believe in the Holy Spirit." This simple statement in the Apostles' Creed originally stemmed from the experience of "the reality of the life and gifts of the Spirit" (Historical Section, *supra*). If meaningful in our own day, this expression of belief in the Holy Spirit needs to be based on experience. The early historical development in the Constantinopolitan Creed wherein the Holy Spirit is recognized as "Lord and Giver of life," to be worshiped and glorified equally with Father and Son, and the later development in the West wherein, according to the Council of Toledo, the Holy Spirit is said to proceed from Father and Son (*filioque*) contain important theological affirmations. These statements of faith affirm that the Church's language about the Holy Spirit is language about God, and that the Spirit's activity is grounded in the work of both Father and Son, ergo creation and redemption. *Mystici Corporis*, in its declaration of the close connection of the Holy Spirit with the Church (its "soul"), and the Scots Confession, in its stress on sanctification and regeneration as grounded in the Holy Spirit, are vital emphases. But what is particularly important for today—as I believe the Jim Barton story accentuates—is the additional reality and experience of being "filled with the Holy Spirit."

It is becoming increasingly apparent, especially through the contemporary charismatic renewal, that many are experiencing in a fresh way "the reality of the life and gifts of the Spirit." This is not related so much to the Church's ministry of Word and Sacrament or to the actuality of sanctification and regeneration, as it is to the experience of being pervaded—"filled"—by the presence and power of the Holy Spirit. This action of the Holy Spirit presupposes the Incarnation and its salvific effects, and is essentially—as the Eastern church recognizes—a Pentecostal event, namely "a new gift of God to a humanity prepared now to receive it" (*supra*). Jim Barton was a child of the Church, baptized and nourished in her bosom, and whatever his misadventures, he had received from her "sanctifying grace." Accordingly, his was a "humanity prepared" to receive this new gift of God—a gift of such plenitude as to bring forth fresh expressions of praise, joy, healing, and love as well as increasing maturity and authority. This gift of the Spirit came for the asking and through the ministry of the believing community: it was the realized experience of the fullness of God's Holy Spirit.

Finally, this story illustrates the need for Western and Eastern development to come together for a more comprehensive understanding of the Holy Spirit. The Eastern church is always in danger of overlooking the christological and salvific background for the gift of the Spirit, whereas the Western church often fails to comprehend the significance of the gift of the Spirit (Pentecost) as an act of God beyond salvation history in which there is the gift of new presence and power. In the charismatic movement of today there is a fruitful conjunction of West and East, and an enrichment that transcends both traditions. The Jim Bartons of our time accordingly represent a recovery of the ancient experience of the reality of the life and gifts of the Holy Spirit which, not fully represented in East or West, is now occurring with extraordinary force throughout the Churchand world.

Selected Bibliography

Hendrikus Berkhof, *The Doctrine of the Holy Spirit* (Richmond: John Knox Press, 1964). See especially chapter IV, the section dealing with "the filling by the Holy Spirit," pp. 85–93.

George Hendry, *The Holy Spirit in Christian Theology* (Rev. ed.; Philadelphia: The Westminster Press, 1965). Especially helpful is chapter VI entitled "The Holy Spirit the Giver of Life and Unity."

J. Rodman Williams, *The Era of the Spirit* (Plainfield, N.J.: Logos International, 1971). This book of mine deals in part I with the contemporary charismatic renewal and some of its theological implications. Part II explores relevant views on the Holy Spirit found in the writings of Barth, Brunner, Tillich, and Bultmann.

7

"The Holy Catholic Church, The Communion of Saints"

Theological Introduction

THOMAS D. PARKER

The Church is the first-mentioned element of those belonging to the "economy" (arrangement) of salvation mentioned in the Creed. It is central for the New Testament understanding of Jesus and his significance for humankind. According to the Gospel of St. Matthew, Jesus intends to build his Church so that the very gates of hell cannot stop it (chapter 16). St. Paul agrees with this in his teaching that the Church is the "Body of Christ," the first fruits of the new age (1 Cor. 12). In the Johannine tradition, those are blessed indeed "who have not seen yet have believed" through the apostolic witness, become friends with Jesus, and live in unity with him and the Father through the Spirit (John 14–17:26). The pastoral and catholic epistles share this view and add various kinds of practical instruction and interpretation of Christian life together.

It is interesting, therefore, that theological statements about the Church remain pretty much undeveloped until after the Reformation made an issue out of them. Many elements of a doctrine of the Church were matters of intense theological scrutiny, of course, especially the primacy of Rome and the position of the hierarchy, the necessity of the Church for salvation, and the doctrine of sacraments. Yet these do not constitute a developed doctrine of the Church. Most theologians and confessional documents are content to repeat the attributes of the Church, with or without interpretation: one, holy, catholic, and apostolic. The marks of the true Church were seen to be its unity and universality and its sacramental life.

The theological development of the doctrine of the Church which has culminated in the first full-scale conciliar statement on the Church (Vatican II) begins with the Augsburg Confession of 1530. According to its chapter 7, the one, holy, Christian Church consists of "the assembly of all believers among whom the Gospel is preached in its purity and the holy sacraments are administered according to the Gospel." This church will endure in its mission and is one in its gospel ministry. This view was taken up, with modifications, by many branches of Protestant Christianity. The church is the *Gemeinde* (public community) of Christian people (Luther), the company of the faithful (Calvin). Its marks are pure preaching of the Word and rightly ordered sacramental life. In some circles this included church discipline according to God's law. Such a functional understanding of the Church raises questions about the relation of the institutional organization and the spiritual essence of the Church, and so opens up discussion for disputed points.

In response, the Council of Trent (1564) identified the one Church with the "holy Roman church," and made acknowledgement of the disputed doctrines (justification, the Mass, purgatory, Mary), as taught by the council, a part of Christian faith and a determination of Church membership. The unity of the Church as a divine society is insured by its embrace of tradition, its doctrinal statements, and its (Roman) government.

A very different understanding of the Church developed in the commmunities of the Anabaptist and Free Church traditions. The Church is the company of Christians who have made a personal confession of faith sealed in baptism, with Christ as its head, and organized into local communities with a simple government consisting of elders (ministers) and deacons chosen by the people. In the development of the Free Church idea, the voluntary and democratic character of the gathered community became increasingly significant, and had an influence on other major Christian groups as well as those stemming from the so-called "radical" reformation.

In succeeding development, the prevailing views were enriched by a rediscovery of the mystical and spiritual dimension of the Church especially as influenced by St. Paul's image of the "Body of Christ." The organic analogy was taken up by theologians across traditional lines and has born fruit as similar and yet diverse as the second Vatican Council, the Calvinist Confession of 1967 and many statements of ecumenical bodies and creeds of the younger churches.

The notion of the Church as the "People of God" has become central in recent discussions largely because of its capacity to do justice both to the social-institutional and personal-communal dimensions of the Church. This people has a common priesthood and shares Christ's prophetic office, but each in their different way as a part of the whole company. As a people has its principle of common life and institutions, so the Church has its life in the Spirit and its governmental structure.

The phrase "communion of saints" expands the attributes of universality and unity of the Church. It is based on the New Testament concept of *koinonia*, the public sharing of faith, the sacraments, and the gifts of the Spirit in the body of Christ. Those who are living, will live and those no longer living are joined in one communion of saints; the Church militant, suffering, and triumphant.

In some Christian churches, this is a basis for prayers with the saints and for "veneration" of the saints. Some members of the body have received outstanding gifts for strengthening the whole body; they are God's instruments for encouraging and helping others. The Second Council of Nicea (787) carefully distinguished the true worship of God from the reverence and respect we pay to each other as saints and to the "Saints" whose ministry is extraordinary.

In other Christian churches, the communion of saints refers primarily to the form of relation enjoyed by those who are members of the body of Christ. The Gallican Confession (1559) says,

> We believe that no one ought to seclude himself and be contented to be alone; but that all jointly should keep and maintain the union of the Church, and submit to the public teaching, and to the yoke of Jesus Christ. . . .

The life of prayer and work is a life together with all the faithful in behalf of the whole Church. Church order takes place within the one, holy catholic and apostolic Church as a way of arranging for an orderly life in which "the whole body, joined and knit together . . . makes bodily growth and upbuilds itself in love" (Eph. 4:16).

Proclaim the Good News

Elder John Bowles sat in the church pew with his hands clasped very tightly in his lap. He whispered hoarsely to his wife Susan, "The pastor has absolutely no right to use the Sacrament of the Lord's Supper for his own purposes or to assure me of Christ's forgiveness for something that wasn't wrong in the first place! I have never refused the Sacrament in my life, but I don't see how I can take it under these conditions."

Pastor Bob Cornwall had just completed a communion sermon on Christ's forgiveness. He then moved to the serving of the elements by calling on the community of the church to accept God's forgiveness for the guilt they feel toward one another and toward God when they have not been able to do his will. Cornwall instructed the congregation that it was only with awareness of God's forgiveness that they should accept the body and blood of God's son.

John Bowles' mind raced back to the events of the Sunday before. Pastor Cornwall had preached a very strong sermon on the mission of the Church and on how members of Ridge Park Presbyterian Church must respond to Christ's call to "Go forth to every part of the world and proclaim the Good News." The theme of the sermon was that "the call of faith is to share the bread of life," with the conclusion that "either one shared his faith or it died."

This case was prepared by Prof. Robert A. Evans of McCormick Theological Seminary and Alice Frazer Evans as a basis for class discussion rather than to illustrate either effective or ineffective handling of the situation.

Alice Frazer Evans was educated at Agnes Scott College, the University of Edinburgh and the University of Wisconsin. She was made a Fellow of the CSI, for which she has written numerous cases. She is the coauthor of *Christianity*, a textbook for teaching religion at the high school level, and is a ruling elder in the Presbyterian Church.

As a background to his message the pastor reminded the congregation that for the past four months the church had been involved in "Operation Outreach." This was an evangelism program established as a priority by the Session, the governing body of the church, comprised of the pastor and twelve elders elected by the congregation. John Bowles remembered last Sunday that he, too, had thought through the work of the new Session committee set up to develop the Outreach program. He respected the leaders who had become involved in this program and appreciated what they were doing, but felt that the strong community-oriented projects in the church were more fitting to his own personal style of service.

John saw this emphasis on evangelism as a definite shift in the direction of the Ridge Park Church which was noted throughout the community for its long-standing involvement in social action programs. Many of the church's members were leaders in various community organizations and a substantial number in the congregation were engaged in tutorial programs in two inner-city schools and in an emergency food supply program related directly to the church. The church building was open for various political candidates prior to elections, and to gay and lesbian groups who often had difficulty finding a place to meet. John and Susan Bowles had initially been attracted to Ridge Park because of its style of open service to the community.

Pastor Bob Cornwall, who had first served for a year as an assistant and, following the death of the senior minister, as the pastor of the church for nearly three years, had been an eager supporter of the social action projects of the church. However, he had also sought to support the Session practice of designating annual priorities for ministry and mission. This past January the Session had responded to the enthusiastic request of about six members that the goal for the year be evangelism.

The goal was adopted at the annual congregational meeting the end of January. Following this, a committee of Session had been working very hard on special classes and weekly evening meetings, studying how the church could reach more people in their inner–city community. There had been announcements each Sunday by the committee members about their meetings. These meetings were concluded by teams of church members going calling on residents of the neighborhood who had visited the church in the past. The general response of the congregation to the work of this committee, in their judgment, had been poor. Only a handful of the 200 members of the congregation were actively involved in the program.

With this in mind Pastor Cornwall decided to take the work of the Outreach Committee more directly to the congregation than he had in the past. Following his sermon on the mission of the Church, he reminded the congregation of the notices on "calling" that particular Sunday which had been in the newsletter and in the bulletin for the past two weeks. When the service was over that morning everyone was expected to gather at the back of the sanctuary and go out in teams of two or three to call on residents in the community, distributing brochures on the work of the church. In his benediction Bob Cornwall had prayed that each of the Christians present would take Christ's commission seriously. He concluded by saying there was "no excuse for anyone able-bodied enough to be in church this morning not to go calling after the service." About 10 percent of the congregation, including some visitors, responded to the pastor's request.

During the Session meeting the following Wednesday, five of the twelve elders expressed their anger at the way Cornwall had conducted the Sunday service. John Bowles turned to Pastor Cornwall. "There are legitimate reasons why some members of this congregation are unwilling to go calling in the community. I'm a Presbyterian, not Pentecostal; my faith is too precious and private a matter to be foisted on unsuspecting and perhaps unwilling strangers. But my real unhappiness with Sunday's sermon and closing prayer is the clear impression you gave that there is something wrong with the faith of those who didn't go calling in the community. I, for one, had other very definite plans for Sunday afternoon, but even if I hadn't, it should have been perfectly all right for me to decide that I didn't want to go calling. We shouldn't be asked to spread the Word out of guilt, but out of joy. You made everyone who was unable or unwilling to go out feel guilty about not going."

Bob Cornwall responded slowly, "That's not my projection of guilt. It's yours. Four months ago Session voted evangelism as a mission priority and the primary goal of our church year. As your pastor I am taking that goal seriously. Some of you need to think about why you were so disturbed with that call to go and visit in the community and about why you felt guilty when you didn't go. I'm not suggesting for a minute that you have to stand on a soapbox and proclaim the gospel in order to be a part of the Christian community. But as Christians we must have a willingness to put some actions behind our convictions. An integral part of our ministry to one another is to share God's love and the knowledge of that love with others. However, I am equally convinced that in Christ's love we are forgiven even when we are unable or unwilling to see his will in our lives."

With that note Bob Cornwall called for the next committee report. The subject of evangelism was not discussed again that evening. The next time John Bowles heard about the issue was in church this Sunday morning. John felt that Pastor Cornwall was clearly referring in his comments on forgiveness to the criticism he had received not only from members of the Session but from other members of the congregation who had been offended by the style of last Sunday's service.

John looked up as Bob Cornwall began to distribute the elements to the assisting elders. The pastor was the only one present allowed to administer the Sacrament to the congregation. John felt that Cornwall was using his authority to interpret the spirit with which a Christian could accept the Sacrament. John Bowles was firmly convinced that the experience of worshiping together and sharing the Sacrament of the Lord's Supper was basic to his own spiritual health and to the wholeness of the congregation. If he accepted the Eucharist under Cornwall's stipulation of "forgiveness of guilt," he would be agreeing with the pastor's view that his guilt feelings about calling were tied to an unwillingness to do God's will—in this case specifically related to going calling in the community. He had no doubt that he needed God's forgiveness for his stubbornness, his "hardness of heart." But he felt that if he accepted the Sacrament under the conditions he saw Cornwall putting down, he would be acknowledging that he needed forgiveness on this specific issue . . . that he had done something "wrong" in not feeling that he could or should go calling in the community.

The elder handed the plate of wafers to John with the words, "This is Christ's body, broken for you."

Theological Briefs

ROBERT A. EVANS

"Broken." That is exactly what is happening to the unity of Christ's body in the Ridge Park Church. For John Bowles the service of worship on this morning is not a "Eucharist," a "thanksgiving," in which this bread, as the symbol of Christ's body, is broken *for* him and thus consummates the promise of the Johannine Gospel for more abundant life. Rather, the fabric of life for the community of faithful is being broken *by* John Bowles, Bob Cornwall and their fellow saints. Ironically, the community is being torn apart over the very vehicle, the Eucharist, which, as an instrument of grace, is intended to draw the members together as sisters and brothers in Christ. What Bob Cornwall offers and John Bowles prepares to receive embodies an image of the Church which yields not the bread of life but the symbol of death for the Church as community.

Elder Bowles and Pastor Cornwall

John may be so disturbed because he perceives more at stake here than a misunderstanding with the pastor who administers the Sacrament or a dispute over the meaning and method of evangelism. How could this particular Eucharist be an event that would facilitate and nurture Christian community, "individuals becoming members one of another?" (Rom. 12:5). For John to suppress his anger and accept the bread and wine, under what he perceives as Cornwall's "conditions," could be to affirm the Church as oppressive structure rather than as liberating community which is beyond-structure (or meta-structural). John's reception of the elements would then symbolize the essence of the Church as institution over against Church as community. The Church is surely *both*; the crucial issue for the nature of the Church is how community and institution are related.

However, if Elder Bowles is angry and confused, then Pastor Cornwall is surely hurt and frustrated. The Session has established evangelism as a priority. Although the mission focus stands in contrast to his own and the congregation's previous emphasis on social involvement, Cornwall has attempted to implement this priority through a well-developed educational program. More important, he sees the demand to share the Good News of the gospel as firmly rooted in the biblical tradition. In Cornwall's Reformed tradition the Church is marked by: the preaching of the Word, accompanied by the Sacrament (a seal of God's promise of the Good News), and by "discipline" (a "regularity of conduct" which gives evidence that the Word has been heard). Embodied in the Eucharist, preceded by confession, is the promise of God's gracious forgiveness when one fails either to hear or respond to God's will as interpreted by the Word.

Then what is all the shouting about? Bob Cornwall must feel betrayed by his elders for failing to support a style of ministry based on an agreed-upon mission task and grounded in the biblical and Reformed traditions. In their thoughts and actions, both John Bowles and Bob Cornwall seem to indicate that their sense of the "Church as community" is being violated. Rather than being liberated and humanized by their life together, they are experiencing alienation from one another and thus from their Lord whose body and blood is being offered in this celebration.

The participants in this drama hold, I believe, a basic misconception of the image and purpose of the Church. The traditional marks of the Church, whether Roman (one, holy, catholic, and apostolic) or Reformed (word, sacrament, and discipline), are inadequate to reveal the nature and mission of the Church unless illuminated and filled by an image of the Church that informs and activates the people of God. Neither John Bowles nor Bob Cornwall appear to be guided here by an understanding of the Holy Spirit working in and through the Church as community, yet this is the essential foundation of the communion of saints portrayed in the biblical record.

Power of an Image

Hans Küng reminds us, "All too easily the Church can become a prisoner of the image it has made for itself at one particular period in history" (*The Church* [New York: Sheed & Ward, 1967] p. 4). It is my judgment that the pastor and people alike in Ridge Park have become imprisoned by debilitating interpretations of a classic image of the Church as a community. This is dramatized biblically in the symbols of the "communion of saints" or what Paul Minear has called the master New Testament image of the Church, "the body of Christ." Yet at Ridge Park the interpretation seems to entail a fundamental understanding of "community" as being determined by geography and structure. An understanding of the community primarily as structure forces one to interpret the nature and purpose of the Church in terms of functions, roles, and accomplishments. Thus a Bob Cornwall or a John Bowles evaluates the significance of his community of faith on the basis of its production for, and impact on, the wider society in which the Church exists. Talk about specific tasks, sometimes disguised under mission goals, plunges the Church into goal-setting, not as the natural consequence of life together but as that which controls the rhythm of corporate existence as members of Christ's body. Task orientation can lead to a division of domains, of Presbyterian versus Pentecostal, or Catholic versus Protestant. Our locale, physically or conceptually, comes to control the criteria upon which we evaluate our life together.

Community defined in terms of domain and task allows "mission accomplished" to become the justification of the Church's common life. Thus a "mission priority" could justify suppressing the plurality and diversity of the communion of saints in order to achieve that mission. Bob Cornwall sees the priority of evangelism in terms of a program in which most, if not all, members of the community *must* engage if they are to be faithful to the Church. This is a subtle image trap that may lead Bob Cornwall to manipulate the life of the community "for the sake of the structure" and employ even the Sacrament as pressure toward accepting the task. The same image deception may lead John Bowles to reject the interpretation of the evangelism priority altogether for a task orientation of his own and thus deny himself the life-giving bread and wine of the communal life of faith. In both cases the authority of the Church founded on the persuasive power of the Holy Spirit has been exchanged for the authority of a coercive structure. The theological implication of this emphasis on domain and task is that a Christian comes to believe "in the Church" and its structures rather than believing "in the Holy Spirit working in the Church," constantly relativizing and transfiguring those very structures and tasks.

The Church as Communitas

There is an alternative interpretation of the image of the Church as community which may avoid the conceptual trap in which the members of Ridge Park seem to be caught. The image is biblically rooted in the picture of the early Church in Acts, where an experience of genuine community was always a gift of the Holy Spirit which, though itself beyond structure, penetrated and transformed the very life of the institution and the individuals who were becoming the communion of saints. This "sense of community" was and is the experienced encounter of intimate support *and* critique found in the fellowship of persons who have developed the art of loving and caring together so as to celebrate the gift of abundant life already in their midst. The distinctive element in the life of the Church is the experience of the Holy Spirit in our midst which creates a new quality of human relatedness known as *communitas.*

The Latin term *communitas* may best describe this "sense of community" by distinguishing this "modality of human relatedness" from an "area of common living." Drawing on a sociological and anthropological notion of *communitas*, I suggest it can be applied in a unique way to the communion of saints, the body of Christ as revealed in Acts, where the Church was not characterized by Domain and Task but by Spirit and Spontaneity.* The sole criterion for action inside and outside this Beloved Community is "that which builds up," and that which builds up is "love." *Communitas* as envisaged here can never be created—only celebrated. It is not a possession, but a gift. *Communitas* is not hierarchical, but rather egalitarian. *Communitas* is not static, but transformative. *Communitas* is the transpersonal embodiment of Christ's grace.

---

* This concept receives fuller explication in my USQR article cited in the bibliography, with special attention given to the insights of V. W. Turner and the imagery of Josiah Royce.

Encounters with the Holy Spirit recorded throughout the Book of Acts that persuaded Christians to sell their property to provide for the needy, to speak the Good News boldly, and even to lay down their life for a friend, were not limited by structure, role, and function. Quite the contrary, their sense of community, their being "in Christ" and therefore in the communion of saints as the New Testament and the Christian creeds describe it, was most powerful and penetrating precisely when the normal structure of their social relatedness came into question and was temporarily suspended. When structure is momentarily set aside, the focus, whether for an Ananias and Sapphira or for a Paul, is on the action of the Holy Spirit who transforms the very fabric of an ordered life.

The dynamics of life in the Church should not be conceived as a "war" or a "balance" between institution and community, as if one could finally displace the other or as if there were parity of power. *Communitas* has unique priority but cannot function apart from institutions and structures. Thus the reality of the Church involves an asymmetrical dialectic between institution and community, between Church as structure and the Church as uniquely beyond-structure. A distinctive dimension of the Church is this potential to be the "communion of saints" in dialectic with a structured institution but not defined or captured by it.

Communitas as beyond-structure, the moments when Christians *temporarily* abandon their structured tasks and masks, comes through the experience of being radically open to the transcendent, to God. Perhaps only at these moments can we be open and vulnerable enough to hear the Spirit speaking in and through us to one another and thus dare to reconceive the patterns of relatedness and mission we have taken for granted. The image of community as beyond-structure suggests that this sense of *communitas*, contrary to our normal expectation, does not emerge in the regular routine of a role, place, and task, but rather at the edge of structure, in periods of "liminality" (passing through a threshold) *between* structures, roles, and functions.

Communitas as a quality of transpersonal interaction characterized by love and critique may emerge gift-life at many moments in the life of the beloved community: moving worship, sacrificial service, constructive confrontation, or revelatory confession, but perhaps the greatest potential is in a ritual event such as communion at the Lord's table. Through the presence of the Spirit, the Eucharist may become the dramatization of a crucial moment of liminality, the ultimate threshold where all our roles, functions, and tasks are called radically into question by God's identification with and for us. Any significant distinction between priest and people must dissolve. God's real presence at the communion draws us into intimate communion with him and with others at the table. Most Christians have experienced, however fleetingly, the piercing encounter with the transcendent that terrifies and yet renews. Within the Eucharist the Spirit's transforming presence frees us to love and care for one another. The crux of *communitas* is: "What we are together is what we shall be for others."

Response to Bowles and Cornwall

Calling on the image of the Church as *communitas,* what suggestions could be made to Bowles, Cornwall, and the Ridge Park Church? It is imperative that they be concrete and constructive, for the immediacy of *communitas* is always interdependent with the mediacy of structure. We are released from structure into *communitas only* to return to structure revivified by the experience of *communitas*.

It seems clear to me that Elder Bowles ought *not* to accept the Sacrament at this ritual moment. However, his refusal need not be in anger or guilt, but as a movement in the process to confront Bob Cornwall and John's fellow elders with the need to examine critically their image of the Church and its implications for the Church's purpose and mission. Bowles appears as structurally closed to the power of the Spirit in his task-oriented rejection of the evangelism program as he does uncertain about how one would share what he calls his "precious and private faith." An understanding of evangelism not structurally dominated might emerge in which the "evangel" is shared as much in creative engagements such as social involvement and service as by proclaiming the Good News explicitly in written and verbal forms.

To refuse the sacrament will escalate the conflict, but this is consistent with the need in *communitas* "to speak the truth in love" and to communicate the reasons why any sharing of the Lord's table must finally foster reconciliation not alienation. Genuine *communitas* offers intimate support *combined* with intimate critique. Conflict and even some chaos often accompany the presence of the Spirit creating *communitas*. John must not seek a superficial peace, but a constructive confrontation concerning the nature of the Church.

How is Bob Cornwall to face the accusation of contriving guilt feelings among his congregation in order to promote a program of evangelism? To acknowledge and confront the problem of priorities as essentially due to ambiguity in their image of the Church may demand a "confession" on the part of Bob *and* John in the presence of the Session. This could be the first step in exploring through study, preaching, and dialogue what a pluralistic understanding of mission might involve for the quality of their life together in the Church and the society they seek to serve. Ridge Park needs to recognize and celebrate the diversity of the congregation in witness and mission.

A fundamental implication of the church as *communitas* is that a sense of community cannot be created or organized even if it may be fostered or encouraged. The image of the Church in Acts may merit renewed critical consideration by Cornwall; here members of the Church had a mission *because* they were a community. They lived and loved with, and for, others outside the Church, because they dared first, through the grace of the Spirit, to be something new with each other—concretely loving and caring. It is a misplaced emphasis to be in mission-*with*-a-community. Rather, the vision is to be a community-*in*-mission. Activities of calling, social service, or even participation in worship are valuable and responsible. But these activities, as well as Cornwall's interpretation of the gospel, must be a consequence of the experience of *communitas* and not the motivating factors of congregational life.

Paul Tillich and Hans Küng have reminded us of the transforming and illuminating power of a symbol or image. If we are to have the Church as Christ's body broken *for* us as in the Eucharist, rather than broken *by* us in our attempt to create community, then we must see the recovery of an image of the Church as *communitas* not as a new semantic task but as a revivifying discernment of the gift of genuine community already in our midst. The process of theological reflection concerning images of the Church, precisely because it determines thoughts, feelings, and actions, may pose a liminal situation for John and Bob, as well as students of their case, that may be an occasion for the experience of *communitas*.

SELECTED BIBLIOGRAPHY

Robert A. Evans, *Intelligible and Responsible Talk about God* (Leiden: E. J. Brill, 1973). An examination of the illuminating and transforming power of theological symbols.

———, "The Quest for Community," *Union Seminary Quarterly Review*, Vol. XXX no. 2–4 (Winter–Summer 1975), pp. 188–202. The image of the Church in Acts and contemporary culture compared to a new image of *communitas* as antistructure.

Joseph Haroutunian, *God With Us* (Philadelphia: The Westminster Press, 1965). A creative theology of transpersonal life with the Church seen as a covenanted community formed by communion.

Juan Luis Segundo, *The Community Called the Church* (Maryknoll, N.Y.: Orbis Books, 1974). A theology for artisans of a new humanity emerging from a Latin American context that sees the Church as a sign-community with emphasis on mission.

RICHARD P. MCBRIEN

This case raises at least three basic ecclesiological questions: (1) What is the mission of the Church? (2) What is the function of pastoral leadership and/or ordained ministry within the Church? (3) How do the sacraments, especially the Eucharist or Holy Communion, effect the forgiveness of sins?

The Mission of the Church

Before the Second Vatican Council Catholics understood the Church to be the "ordinary means of salvation" and the "Kingdom of God on earth." The Church's purpose was clear: to preach, to teach, to catechize, and to administer the sacraments—indeed to make the world become the Church. Protestants, on the other hand, tended to

---

RICHARD P. MCBRIEN is Professor of Theology at Boston College and Director of the Institute for the Study of Religious Education and Service. He was educated at St. John's Seminary and obtained his Doctorate in Theology from the Gregorian University. His publications include *Do We Need the Church?*, *Church: The Continuing Quest*, and *The Remaking of the Church*. He is a Roman Catholic priest of the Archdiocese of Hartford, Connecticut.

perceive the Church as the "congregation of saints wherein the Gospel is rightly preached and the sacraments rightly administered." Its mission was thus similarly clear: to preach the word and to celebrate the sacraments—in a sense, to make the world acknowledge the God who is to be found and experienced principally, if not exclusively, in the Church.

Under the impact of such views as those expressed in Dietrich Bonhoeffer's *Letters and Papers from Prison*, for example, the discussion on the nature and mission of the Church took a major turn in direction. The Church came to be understood more as means than as end, more as servant than as privileged center of God's saving presence and activity. The Church's mission is more than word-and-sacrament. It is committed as well to the pursuit of justice and the transformation of the world. The Church, however, is not somehow set over against the world, as "nonworld." On the contrary, the Church is that part of the world which is called to acknowledge the lordship of Jesus. The transformation of the world, therefore, implies and requires the transformation of the Church itself.

Accordingly, the Church exists to proclaim the lordship of Jesus in word and sacrament (*kerygma*), to offer itself as a sign and test-case of this proclamation (*koinonia*), and to use whatever resources it has to hasten the coming of God's Kingdom, a Kingdom of justice, love, and peace (*diakonia*). These three components of the Church's mission are not mutually opposed. Thus, *diakonia* cannot be separated from *kerygma*, nor *kerygma* from *diakonia.*

The Function of Pastoral Leadership and/or Ordained Ministry

Ministry exists always and only for the sake of mission. There is, of course, a variety of ministries (1 Cor. 12:4–11). Each serves the Church in different ways, but all are for the "building up of the Body of Christ" (Eph. 4:12). Indeed, the Second Vatican Council insisted that pastors "were not meant by Christ to shoulder alone the entire saving mission of the Church toward the world." On the contrary, it is their "noble duty" to recognize the services and charismatic gifts of all the faithful "that all according to their proper role may cooperate in this common undertaking with one heart" (*Dogmatic Constitution on the Church*, *n*. 30).

On the other hand, it would be a mistake to suppress the distinctive ministry of the ordained for the sake of exalting or preserving the various nonordained ministries. Ordination introduces one into a new, real, and specific relationship with the community of faith itself. Holy Order is intended to serve the good *order* of the Church. The ordained minister accepts responsibility for nourishing the unity of the local church which he or she has been commissioned to serve, and for motivating that church to fulfill its missionary responsibilities.

The Sacraments and the Forgiveness of Sins

When we sin, we sin not only against the majesty and sovereignty of God but against one another as well. Forgiveness, therefore, must come not only from God, but also from our brothers and sisters in the Church. Our reconciliation with the Lord is sacramentalized through our reconciliation with the Church: initially in Baptism, from time to time in Penance, and regularly in supreme sacramental celebration, the Eucharist or Lord's Supper.

But reconciliation with God and the Church cannot occur unless (a) we have, in fact, sinned against them; (b) we are aware of our sin as sin; and (c) we are truly repentant.

The sacraments, in other words, achieve their spiritual effect *ex opere operato . . . non ponentibus obicem* (Council of Trent). We enter into fuller communion with God and with one another through the power of Christ acting in and through the sacrament (*ex opere operato*, "from the work worked"), but only on condition that we "place no obstacle" (*non ponentibus obicem*), such as hardness of heart, or a stubborn refusal to repent.

No thorough analysis of the case, and no judgment for or against John Bowles' apparent decision to refuse the Sacrament, can be constructed without reference to the principles summarized in the preceding paragraphs.

There is something to be said, on the one hand, *against Pastor Cornwall:*

1. Cornwall exceeded the limits of pastoral propriety by apparently adopting a course of spiritual intimidation. To insist that there could be "no excuse" for any member of the congregation

not to go out and call upon nonmembers that same afternoon is presumptuous at best, overbearing at worst, and naive in any case.

2. If Cornwall did indeed suggest, as Bowles alleges, that there is "something wrong" with the faith of those who do not go calling in the community, then Cornwall did again exceed the limits of pastoral prudence.

3. Although the pastor did not explicitly connect his sermon remarks with the dispute over the "Outreach" campaign, a reasonable person might legitimately have drawn such an inference. Cornwall, therefore, had a pastoral obligation to make his hidden agenda public, if indeed he intended that such a connection be made.

4. Cornwall reveals a distinctively Protestant notion of forgiveness when he asserts that "in Christ's love we are forgiven even when we are unable *or unwilling* to see His will in our lives" (my emphasis). The assertion is problematical, at the very least.

The stronger case, however, rests *against John Bowles:*

1. The pastor did not explicitly connect the need "to accept God's forgiveness for (their) guilt" and the lack of cooperation of most members with the parish's "Operation Outreach."

2. Cornwall himself had been "an eager supporter of the social action projects of the church." But Cornwall also sought to be responsive to the decisions of the Session and the annual congregational meeting as well. This was a legitimate, and indeed necessary, predisposition on the part of any pastoral leader with a sense of accountability to his congregation.

3. Bowles' reason for not "calling in the community" are defective on two counts: (a) faith is not only a "private matter," and (b) one can proclaim one's faith evangelically without necessarily adopting ignoble and offensive means (the opposite is implied, for example, in Bowles' use of the term "foisted").

4. Pastor Cornwall never suggested that the congregation should spread the Word of the Lord "out of guilt," his intimidating manner notwithstanding.

5. In accordance with a fundamental principle of moral and sacramental theology, if Bowles was not convinced in conscience that he had sinned, then he was spiritually ready to receive the

Sacrament. He should have done so. His concern about the theological and pastoral implications of receiving the Sacrament from Cornwall's hands on this particular occasion is essentially a problem of his own making.

SELECTED BIBLIOGRAPHY

Avery Dulles, *Models of the Church* (New York: Doubleday, 1974). Touches upon all three areas (mission, ministry, and sacraments) in the light of differing models of the Church operative today (Church as hierarchy, herald, mystical communion, sacrament, and servant).

Hans Küng, *The Church* (New York: Sheed & Ward, 1967). The most comprehensive expression of Roman Catholic ecclesiology since Vatican II. Strong on questions of ministry (ecclesiastical office) and sacrament, but weaker on mission.

Richard McBrien, *Do We Need the Church?* (New York: Harper & Row, 1969). The mission, ministry, and sacraments of the Church cannot be understood except in relation to the Kingdom of God, to whose service the Church is called.

Karl Rahner, *The Church and the Sacraments* (New York: Herder & Herder, 1963). A serious introduction to the sacraments by the leading Roman Catholic theologian.

OWEN C. THOMAS

There are a number of decisions being faced by the people in this case. Elder John Bowles must decide whether or not to receive the Sacrament and whether his attitude toward evangelism is correct. Pastor Bob Cornwall must decide how to proceed in the face of the dissension in the congregation and whether his style of leadership is

---

OWEN C. THOMAS is Professor of Theology, Episcopal Divinity School, Cambridge, Massachusetts and a Fellow of the CSI. He studied at Hamilton College, Cornell University, Episcopal Theological School, and received his Ph.D. from Columbia University. His publications include *William Temple's Philosophy of Religion, Attitudes Toward Other Religions: Some Christian Interpretations* and *Introduction to Theology*. He is an ordained Episcopal priest.

appropriate. The Session committee on Operation Outreach faces the same decisions. The Ridge Park congregation must decide how to resolve its disagreement over the evangelism goal.

There are a number of issues arising out of these decisions: the meaning and purpose of the Sacrament of the Lord's Supper, the problem of guilt and forgiveness and Christian life (see Section 8), the questions of leadership style and lay versus ordained leadership in the Church, the problem of dissension and conflict in the Church, and the nature of the mission of the Church with special reference to the relative importance of evangelism and social action.

Let us consider how those issues and decisions are related to the nature of the Church. It is clear that Pastor Cornwall's attempt to coerce everyone to go calling and his defense of his leadership in the Session meeting have caused a good deal of anger, offense, and dissension in the congregation. This has probably dismayed many of the congregation, because they feel that this is highly inappropriate in the Church. The Church is supposed to be a fellowship of love, concern, understanding, and reconciliation, in fact, the "communion of saints." Is not the Church described in the New Testament as the body of Christ and the fellowship of the Holy Spirit? Anger and dissension in the Church seem to contradict the essential nature of the Church. Would it not make more sense to understand the true Church as described in the New Testament as the invisible Church kown only to God in distinction from the sinful strife-torn visible Church on earth?

John Bowles is angry and frustrated over what he believes is Pastor Cornwall's attempt to force him to feel guilty and accept forgiveness through receiving the Sacrament for something about which he does not feel guilt. This raises the issue of the meaning and purpose of the Sacrament of the Lord's Supper in the Church. Is it essential to the Christian life in the Church?

The dissension in the Ridge Park congregation derives largely from Pastor Cornwall's style of leadership. He is a strong leader, going out ahead of his people and pulling them firmly in what he believes is the right direction in the mission of the Church. This raises the question of whether the Church is essentially a hierarchical society in which the ordained ministers exercise a kind of authority which lay persons cannot.

Finally, the conflict in the congregation centers on the issue of whether or not all members should actively be involved in evangelistic calling. This raises the question of the purpose or reason for being of the Church. Is the Church essentially a missionary body called to proclaim to all people the gospel of God's salvation through Christ? Is the Church essentially a worshiping body called to represent the whole creation in praising God? Or is the Church essentially a servant body called to serve those who are in need of any kind?

I will outline an interpretation of the nature and purpose of the Church which is faithful to the Bible and the tradition and then indicate how this interpretation points toward a resolution of the questions which have been raised.

The Christian church is the community of people who have come to know God through Christ by the Holy Spirit, who have received God's salvation, who have confessed their faith in God through baptism, who continually enter into the presence of God through prayer, word, and sacrament, and who commit themselves to give testimony to God and to serve those who are in need. Thus the Church is God's instrument in the fulfilling of his purposes for the creation, namely, that the world may come to know and respond to its origin, meaning, and goal in God.

This means that the Church is a visible community of particular people and not an invisible community known only to God. It is a community of sinful people who are being saved, that is, who are being more fully reconciled to God and to their brothers and sisters. Therefore, from the beginning the Church has always been a community more or less disrupted by dissension and torn by strife, and thus it lives in continual contradiction to what it is called to be, namely, a community of perfect faith, hope, and love. So the Ridge Park congregation should not be surprised by its conflict but should learn from it and strive to overcome it.

The Sacrament of the Lord's Supper is the communal meal instituted by Jesus through which the Church recalls its salvation through Christ, and which celebrates both the presence of God in its midst and the communion of its members. It both symbolizes and effects the presence of God in the community and thus salvation in the community. Therefore, participation in the Sacrament is essential to the Christian life in the Church, and care must be taken that it is properly understood and freely entered into. Thus John Bowles should be able to consider his reception of the Sacrament as the sign and instrument of God's forgiveness of the sins of which he is honestly aware ("his stubbornness and hardness of heart"), and of his fellowship with Pastor Cornwall in spite of their differences. (He can also ask in prayer for insight into those sins of which he is not aware.) If he can do this, he should receive the Sacrament. If not, he should probably not receive, but he should certainly take up the issue with Pastor Cornwall.

Because the members of the Church are a community of those who participate in the varying gifts of the Holy Spirit of God, they have different functions in the Church and in society, but they have equal honor and dignity in the Church. Ordained ministers have particular functions in the Church, namely, preaching and teaching, administration of the sacraments and pastoral care, but they are not to lord it over the lay people. Ordained ministers have usually had more responsiblility for the function of oversight and government in the Church. But since each member participates in the Spirit, each has a responsibility for the decisions about the life and work of the Church. Since Operation Outreach has resulted in a serious division of the Ridge Park congregation over the responsibility for evangelism, the Session should call a special meeting of the congregation to reconsider the Session's decision about the evangelism goal. This may indicate the need for an educational program for the whole congregation on the nature of the Church. The Session must also take up with Pastor Cornwall his style of leadership and ask him to consider whether it has been improperly coercive.

The purpose of the Church is to give testimony to God and to serve those who are in need. So both evangelism and social action are necessary responsibilities of the Church and of each member. Because there is a variety of gifts, some members will be more involved in certain functions than other members. But each member will recognize his or her responsibility as a Christian for all the functions of the Church.

There seems to be some misunderstanding in these matters at Ridge Park. Operation Outreach seems to be limited to those "who had visited the church in the past." There is no reason except expediency for limiting evangelism in this way. Also the purpose of the campaign seems to be "distributing brochures on the work of the church" rather than giving testimony to God in Christ. Furthermore, Ridge Park is said to be well known for its involvement in social action programs. But most of the programs seem to be of the nature of social service, that is, directly helping those who are in need, rather than social action, that is, working to change the conditions and structures which cause people to be in need in various ways. The mission of the Church must include both of these. The exploration of this issue should be included in the educational program mentioned above.

SELECTED BIBLIOGRAPHY

Lesslie Newbigin, *The Household of God* (New York: Friendship Press, 1953). A discussion of the biblical basis of the Church in the light of its call to mission and unity by a former bishop of the Church of South India.

Owen C. Thomas, *Introduction to Theology* (Cambridge: Greeno, Hadden & Co., 1973), especially chapter 17. Lectures for an introductory seminary course treating the biblical basis and historical and contemporary issues in each doctrine.

Claude Welch, *The Reality of the Church* (New York: Charles Scribner's Sons, 1958). A study of the ontology of the Church with special emphasis on its relation to Christ and the Holy Spirit by the Dean of the Graduate Theological Union, Berkeley, California.

Colin W. Williams, *The Church* (Philadelphia: The Westminster Press, 1968). A discussion of the issues in the contemporary theology of the Church including its mission, ministry, and structures, by the Dean of Yale Divinity School.

8

"The Forgiveness of Sins'

Theological Introduction

THOMAS D. PARKER

The phrase "forgiveness of sins" is not found uniformly in all ancient creeds. Early rules of faith stressed the gift of immortality (Irenaeus) or a holy life (Tertullian). The phrase appears in the *Epistula Apostolorum* (c. 150), the Creed of Marcellus (c. 390) and in later Roman creeds. The Nicene Creed includes the phrase "one baptism for the remission of sin."

The forgiveness of sins is a major biblical teaching. A promise of new life and renewed creation is given in the face of human failure to live according to the law of God's covenant and creation. The accent is on the mercy and faithfulness of God rather than on the merits of humanity. In the Old Testament, forgiveness is an act of divine mercy; God keeps covenant with his people for their good and his glory in spite of their sin.

According to the New Testament, Jesus proclaims a gospel of forgiveness and new life for "sinners," without conditions; God forgives and heals because of his love for human beings without regard to their social or religious standing. In the language of one of Jesus' stories, God has the right to give equally to all workers in the vineyard, no matter how much or little they have worked. This unconditional acceptance of persons sets the terms for all Christian response to God. The New Testament urges Christians to live as those for whom the future is always open and full of hope; human life exists under the promise of divine forgiveness.

In the theological development of this theme, a distinction was soon made between justification and sanctification as two "moments" of human salvation. Both terms are Pauline, the first using a legal metaphor to speak of forgiveness as a divine acquittal, the second speaking of forgiveness as a divine gift of a holy life. Forgiveness sets up a new situation for the forgiven both in terms of the past and future. In some traditions, e.g., the Reformed, the metaphor of adoption was also employed to speak of the restored relation between God and human beings expressing forgiveness.

Two theological controversies in particular have helped shape subsequent creedal statements for forgiveness: (1) the Augustinian-Pelagian controversy of the fifth and sixth centuries and (2) the struggle between the Reformation and Counter-Reformation positions in the sixteenth century. The former was concerned with the divine source of forgiveness, how the grace of God was related to human response to that gift. The latter was concerned with the relations of justification, faith, and the new life. Both were controversies in the Western church.

The consensus of theological reflection following the first controversy was expressed primarily in Augustinian terms: following the sin of our first parents a "death of the soul" was passed on to all human beings so that we are incapable of change for the better apart from grace which comes to us "through the infusion of the Holy Spirit." This grace is received through baptism and a life of repentance; each of us is thereby wholly dependent on the divine mercy for faith and all good works.

The issue that came to the fore in the second controversy was the relation of grace as power and grace as pardon. For the Reformation traditions, as represented by the Augsburg Confession, we receive forgiveness and are judged righteous before God by grace when we believe and turn to God. Such faith is counted as righteousness by the grace of pardon in Jesus' name. The life of repentance follows as our thanksgiving for forgiveness; the power for the new life and such good works as belong to it is from the Spirit, however, which is the gift of God to all who through faith are justified by grace.

For the tradition of the Counter-Reformation, as represented by the decrees of the Council of Trent (1547), we receive forgiveness when we receive the gift of new life in our baptism through the power of the Spirit. Such a justifying act is preceded by faith, a resolve to receive baptism, and followed by the unjust person becoming just. Justification is an actual transformation of human life by the power of the Spirit, and so includes "sanctification" (making holy) as well. It follows that justification can be increased through good works or diminished by sin. In the latter case, those who have fallen away can be restored through penance. The intent is to make forgiveness and new life equal moments in a Christian relationship with God.

Since the Enlightenment the forgiveness of sins between persons has been given new importance alongside the fundamental forgiveness of God for persons. Taking up the phrase in the Lord's Prayer, "Forgive us our trespasses as we forgive those who trespass against us," newer creedal statements have spoken of a twofold reconciliation or union, that between God and humankind and that between and among sinners. This renews an element in Jesus' teaching on forgiveness.

The documents of Vatican II (1964–65) express a growing consensus. They speak of the union of all persons with God in the Spirit, and the unity of mankind which follows. The Church is a "sign of intimate union with God and of the unity of all mankind." It is also an instrument for achieving such union and unity. The language of forgiveness here is the language of dialogue: "By virtue of her mission to shed on the whole world the radiance of the Gospel message, to unify under one Spirit all men, whatever nation, race, or culture, the Church stands forth as a sign of that brotherliness which allows honest dialogue and invigorates it." In a world of oppressors and the oppressed, the doctrine of forgiveness is undergoing intense rethinking.

The Seminarian and the Bank Robbery

"Who will want a jailbird minister?" The question kept coming back to William Bradford as he sat in the rows of graduates of Midwest Theological Seminary.

He looked around the hall; many people had come to celebrate with him today. His family and new wife were there. He saw some people from his church and from the Chicago Boys Club for whom he had worked. However, most students who began seminary with him in the fall of 1969 were not there; they had already graduated. And some he had known would not be there because they were locked up in prison, a school that gives no degrees. Few would ever be able to understand fully what had happened to him, who he was, or why he was seeking to become a minister in a Christian denomination that was mostly white, middle–class, and suburban. And William himself wondered whether he could deal with the past and take this step forward toward ordination for the ministry.

Robbing the "Safest Bank in the World"

William Bradford grew up on the southside of Chicago, in one of the nation's first public housing projects. He came from a "sanctified family," as it is called in the black community, a family which was strong, held standards different from the streets, and was religious. William was a "good boy," recalled a church member who knew him as he was growing up. When he was older he became active in his church and took leadership in the Chicago Boys Club. It was no surprise that William decided to go to seminary to pursue a joint-

---

This case was prepared by Prof. Thomas D. Parker of McCormick Theological Seminary as a basis for class discussion rather than to illustrate either effective or ineffective handling of the situation.

degree program in social work and the ministry in the seminary and the university.

Lloyd Felton recalls William's first days at the seminary: "William was a quiet man. I was his faculty advisor, so most of our conversation was about his study program here and at the University of Illinois, and about his vocational plans. We had a mutual respect for one another."

At the orientation for incoming students a presentation was made by some members of a Puerto Rican organization involved in the occupation of Midwest's buildings the previous spring. William stood up and exchanged some words with the leader about identifying with people on the streets and fighting for justice. The organization represented one way of doing this, but William declared he would have to find his own way. It was an electric moment of engagement and disengagement. Others were dealing directly with the problems of the poor and minorities; William would walk his own path, by himself, if necessary.

Next morning news reached the seminary that William had been arrested for robbing a major downtown bank. Using a water pistol he had taken about $10,000 from a teller, held it a few seconds, and was immediately stopped by bank guards. He was being held at the county jail.

Lloyd Felton visited William in jail on behalf of the seminary. He found that William and his family had no lawyer and no plans for dealing with the consequences of his act. He had left letters for his wife and a fellow student, telling them in effect that they must go on. There was no rationale for the act given, although the letters reflected his feelings about the murder of Fred Hampton, a prominent black radical in Chicago killed in a police raid on his apartment. William had known Hampton and was frustrated and angry at being a black in white institutions while others seemed to deal directly with the problems of justice and equal opportunity. Although William gave Lloyd permission to get a good lawyer, he indicated he was not interested in escaping the consequences of his crime.

The Trial

A week before the trial William was out on bond. He attended a marathon weekend of group encounter with students from the seminary. This group of nine students became the nucleus of a support community that maintained a relation with William throughout the trial and during his imprisonment. Others from the church and his community expressed their concern by their presence at his trial, along with his wife and family.

The trial itself was cut and dried. In a pretrial conference the prosecutor had refused to drop the charges. In the trial he told the story of the events which had taken place. William pleaded "not guilty" to the charges. The defense consisted of witnesses who attested his good character and his history of working with church and community organizations. The Department of Probation recommended probation. William himself rejected suggestions that he plead temporary insanity.

The judge sentenced William to three years in prison, "to make him an example," as the lawyer later put it. Ironically, in a courtroom down the hall at the same moment, another judge, famous for being a hardliner, was sentencing a millionaire convicted of embezzling and using three million dollars; the judge apologized because he had to give "such an upstanding community leader" an eighteen-month sentence, of which he was to serve six. By contrast William finally served eighteen months of his three-year sentence, after being denied his first appeal for parole.

The Prison as School

When William went to prison, Lloyd became the official liaison between him and the schools in which he was enrolled. He visited William in prison on a regular basis and developed a twofold approach to the prison situation. "Since prison isolates people from their past and future into a wholly controlled present, I developed a list of people who would write William. I hoped this would give him a supportive community connected with his past and future. The list included his family, the nine students who were at the trial, other students and friends.

"I also kept William plugged into course work," Lloyd continued, "to keep his interest in professional stuides alive. William took courses in every department of the seminary, following his own interests. He also read in the social work field. The books and projects provided William with a world of his own in a viable present; they gave him a place of solitude and retreat as well as a perspective on what was happening around him. The work also reduced the number of credits still remaining for graduation when he was released."

While he was in prison William taught in the black studies program. This was a very important turning point in William's life, as well as a contribution to his fellow prisoners. He came into contact with "all those black preachers" who had been so important to his people during their times of struggle. He came to terms with his own relation to them and with the identity they could give him. In addition, William took the opportunity to investigate the Black Muslim movement. He liked their commitment to the whole person and to poor blacks struggling to carve out a piece of turf for themselves. Yet, when pressed to join them, he could not. "I believe in the 'spook-God,' " he said, referring to his own Christian faith in God in their terms. In his teaching William self-consciously kept to his own way, to the past he had, and to whatever future he might make for himself.

"William developed a reputation for being his own man," Lloyd recalled, "in prison yet not as a prisoner." In one dining room disturbance he remained "studiedly passive," quiet, determined, and aloof. Other prisoners would stop by to see what William was reading and either go away shaking their heads or become involved in conversation with him about things William believed. He kept up an unusually large correspondence with family and friends outside the wall. The prison officials later decided that he could only write and receive letters from ten people, so news and information from others had to be carried by Lloyd when he visited William.

"We developed a close personal friendship," Lloyd reflected later. "Something happened to both of us, a kind of silent understanding that brothers share."

The Commencement

In the spring of 1971 William was released on parole to live in a halfway house while he held a job. Lloyd became his parole advisor. He returned to school in the fall to complete his degrees in social work and in the seminary. The courses he had completed in prison were credited to him and he moved swiftly to graduation. In the winter of 1972 William remarried. The wedding was performed at the home of William's mother, with Lloyd officiating. "It felt good to be there and to share that moment with William, his family, and his bride," Lloyd said.

And now it was really beginning, William thought as he sat with the other graduates, listening to the speeches about great accomplishments and challenges. Yet nothing was sure except that he had been his own man, and that there was some kind of future for him. The questions tumbled in: Who will hire a felon as a minister? What will ordination mean for me, for my marriage, my family, or my church? Should they be asked to forgive what has happened or is it I who should forgive?

"William Bradford," the dean called out, and William walked up to receive his diploma.

Theological Briefs

Justo L. Gonzalez

The case of "The Seminarian and the Bank Robbery" offers opportunity for some significant reflection on the meaning of the Christian doctrine of the forgiveness of sins. The most significant of these reflections may well be that this particular doctrine shows, perhaps better than any other, the shortcomings of both the "conservative" and the "liberal" outlooks in which we have been nurtured. A "conservative" reflection on this case might well emphasize the fact that God forgives William's sin in robbing the bank, and that all that William has to do is to repent and believe in God's forgiveness through Christ. Such a perspective would probably add that William's act is the outcome or manifestation of a deeper and universal corruption caused by the state of sin. A "liberal" reflection might well point out that it is through Lloyd that William experiences the forgiveness of sins (and, although the case itself does not describe him as such, Lloyd would certainly fit the image of a white middle-class political and religious liberal). Such a reflection would then go on to add that it is only through us that our fellow human beings experience forgiveness of sin, and might well conclude that such forgiveness is tantamount to our acceptance of each other, and to our making due allowance for environmental hardships which lead some to break the law.

Justo Luis Gonzalez is Associate Professor of World Christianity, Candler School of Theology, Emory University. He has studied at the University of Havana, Union Theological Seminary (Matanzas, Cuba), Yale University, University of Strasbourg and received his Ph.D. from Yale University. He is the author of numerous articles and books. Among those in English are *The Development of Christianity in the Latin Caribbean* and *A History of Christian Thought*, in three volumes. He is an ordained Methodist pastor.

Clearly, the two options described above are oversimplified to the point of being mere caricatures. But they serve to point out the common shortcoming of the theological outlook to which we are most accustomed. This theological outlook, no matter whether it calls itself "liberal" or "conservative," is that of civil religion. Civil religion exists among us, not only in its most flagrant manifestations, but also and most insidiously in cases such as the one in question, where we seem to equate sin with breaking the civil law.

Let us look at William's act. He held up a bank with a water pistol. Is that a sin? Perhaps. But, is it a worse sin than that committed by an entire society whose money may be piled up in banks and in the hands of a few powerful persons, while people suffer from malnutrition, inadequate housing, and other sorts of violence? Is William's sin more in need of forgiveness than that of an entire society where the powerful embezzler of millions gets a lighter sentence than does William? Is his sin really worse than Lloyd's willingness to submit to the rules of the game, and to be a nice guy while making sure that he remains within bounds? Is his sin greater than that of the Church and the seminary which support themselves on the basis of vast endowment funds, and then have the audacity to tell William "we forgive you?"

All of this is not said in order to excuse William as some sort of thwarted Robin Hood. There is clearly sin in his actions. His sin is in his despairing faithlessness, which led him to a totally senseless and surreptitiously self-destructive act. The courts condemned him for having robbed the bank. But in theological terms his condemnation was in having held his faith in abeyance.

This means that when we look for "the forgiveness of sins" in this situation we must be clear about what "sins" it is that are being forgiven. In civil terms, the "forgiveness of sins" may be seen in the process, begun and nurtured by Lloyd, by which William is progressively brought back into conformity with the civil order. A "conservative" might say that this is the result of his having known that in Christ God loves him. A "liberal" might say that this is the result of his having experienced acceptance in his relationship with Lloyd, who probably made due allowance for the degree to which William's action was a response to environmental pressures. In a sense, they would both be right. But a more radically biblical outlook than both of these would locate the significance of the forgiveness of sins in this case, not in society's—and the Church's—ability to forgive William's criminal record, but rather in William's being empowered by God—in the community of faith—to accept forgiveness for his faithlessness, and to live in the knowledge that the evil powers which he challenged in despair with a water pistol will be overcome. This forgiveness of sins will allow him now to challenge these powers with faith rather than despair, and will force him also to seek to forgive those whom he will still have to combat as servants of those powers.

The fact that the forgiveness of sins is not to be equated with social acceptance by the Church does not mean that the Church does not have a crucial role to play in that forgiveness. The Church is the locus where that forgiveness is proclaimed, experienced, and shared. But the Church must take care not to confuse the sin for which Christ died with those acts which society tells us are sinful or criminal—the two may coincide, or they may not.

Finally, there is in the case itself another element which further clarifies the doctrine of the forgiveness of sins. That is William's struggle for self-identity. The forgiveness of sins is closely related to a sense of vocation, and that vocation in turn has a great deal to do with who one is. Redemption and the forgiveness of sins take different shapes for different people, according to who they are, and what God calls them to do. The preaching of a general state of redemption, in which all are alike, can be a denial of God's calling all different sorts of people to perform all different sorts of tasks. William is black. That is part of who he is. In his case, the forgiveness of sins manifests itself in his ability to claim who he is, and to seek God's will for him as a black person. His ability to share in the black struggle is part of the forgiveness of sins for him.

Selected Bibliography

Søren Kierkegaard, *The Sickness unto Death* (Princeton: Princeton University Press, 1954). A classical discussion of the relationship between sin, faith, and despair.

Juan Luis Segundo, *Evolution and Guilt: A Theology for Artisans of a New Humanity* (Maryknoll: Orbis Books, 1974), vol. 5. A discussion of the subject from a perspective similar to mine, but much more influenced by Teilhard de Chardin.

W. Telfer, *The Forgiveness of Sins: An Essay in the History of Christian Doctrine and Practice* (Philadelphia: Muhlenberg Press, 1960). A brief but excellent review of the various ways in which the Church has dealt with this issue through the centuries.

Stanley S. Harakas

In spite of its title, this case does not focus on the bank robbery as its salient feature. The issue of forgiveness is, rather, included within a context which has two foci: the two principal characters of the case, William Bradford and Lloyd Felton. They represent two life-styles, two approaches to the gospel message, two motifs on the issue of forgiveness.

William Bradford represents the individualistic approach to the Christian faith. His separation from the body of the denomination to which he belonged is clear: he is black, poor (public housing), and urban in a church which is white, middle–class, and suburban. Further, the fact of separatism is highlighted by the fact that he comes from a "sanctified family" which has standards "different from the streets." Unlike others, he is a "good boy," has to "find his own way," "walk his own path, by himself." After the robbery he writes to his wife and schoolmate that "they must go on" (without him). In prison he "kept his own way," he was "studiedly passive" during a communal disturbance. He was "aloof" and "his own man."

Though this individualistic stance is dominant, there is a counterpoint running through his character. He is somehow tied to his Church and racial group, also. He continued seminary studies even

Stanley S. Harakas is Professor of Christian Ethics and Dean of Holy Cross Greek Orthodox School of Theology, Brookline, Massachusetts. He received undergraduate and theological education at Holy Cross and his Th.D. from the School of Theology of Boston University. He has done postgraduate studies at the Universities of Athens and Thessalonica. He is the translator of *Partakers of Divine Nature*, and the author of *Living and Liturgy* and many scholarly articles. He is an ordained priest in the Greek Orthodox church.

while in prison. He refuses to give up his Christian faith in the face of the Black Muslim appeal. He identifies with black preachers in his black studies experience. In spite of being frustrated and angry at being a black in a white institution, he plans to be ordained in his denomination which is "mostly white, middle–class, and suburban."

William Bradford represents an approach to Christian living which has a long history in the Church. While retaining some identification with the historical and empirical Church, this type of Christian has sought to work out his own salvation (Phil. 2:12) generally as independent from the Church. The Anchorites of early monasticism, the idiorrythmic style (an individual life style within a loosely organized monastic community) popular among some contemporary Eastern monks, the "personal savior" emphasis of evangelical Protestants are some of these historical expressions. This individualistic approach also tends towards a "holier than thou" attitude. It naturally falls into the dilemma which asks whether others should seek forgiveness from him who is righteous, yet unrighteously used, or whether in fact he ought to seek forgiveness.

Bradford exemplifies an individualistic Christian life-style within the body of the Church. He sees the gospel as having primarily personal and individual impact; he tends to stand in judgment of the Church, seriously considering himself at times as properly forgiving it for what it has done. Thus he stands, in a sense, above it and superior to it.

Lloyd Felton represents the emphasis on community. He not only represented the faculty as Bradford's advisor, he went to the jail "on behalf of the seminary." It was from within the seminary that there arose a "support community." Felton was the "official liaison" between Bradford and the seminary community. Rather than dropping him as a person who might be considered unworthy, sullied, and impure because of his felonious action, the community continued to include him in its care. Felton, as an agent of continuing reconciliation, arranges for contact to be maintained through an organized program of letter writing. He sees to it that William Bradford, the convicted felon, is not cut off from the educational work of the seminary community. The school even gives Bradford "credit" for his prison work, never abandoning him. Further, Lloyd Felton represents the community in a sincere, heartfelt, and accepting fashion; he maintains "a close personal friendship," develops a sense of brotherhood with Bradford, becomes his parole advisor, performs his wedding. Truly, a remarkable pattern of outreach, support, acceptance, and forgiveness.

Felton exemplifies a communitarian Christian life-style representing a strong understanding of the Church as the body of Christ (1 Cor. 12:14–31). The gospel message is best exemplified in the unity of the faithful, as realized sacramentally and as expressed in a loving, inclusive, forgiving community. This means that imperfections, shortcomings, and contradictions of profession and life-style are not as damning as they are for the individualist who emphasizes his separation from what is "impure." Here, the sinner comes for forgiveness readily expecting to receive it.

The issue, theologically speaking, is basically a question of ecclesiology. If the Church is made up of individuals who are "saved" primarily in a one to one relationship with God, then there is place for an ambiguous, independent membership in a loose association of saved persons which is the Church. The Church then is dependent upon the views, the perceptions, the faith and holiness of life of the individuals who make it up. There is a tendency for such a stance to sit in severe judgment of an imperfect Church. The Christian, then, can forgive the Church. It is the righteous and holy individual Christian who is primary.

On the other hand, ecclesiologically speaking, if the starting point for understanding the Church is the community, then the individual Christian is a Christian precisely because of his interrelatedness. The Christian life is a corporate experience. It is made possible by communion with Christ, the Saints of old, with the community of faith and life. This is realized in the sacramental experience, in common belief and faith, in mutual love and support. Forgiveness is channeled through community. It is not merely pronounced, it is acted out in acceptance, support, and restoration to personal communion. Forgiveness is a function of Christian community.

A final point must be made, however. Bradford and Felton represent extremes. Bradford's individualism and Felton's communality are not exclusive. Elements of both are required of each. To collapse the one into the other would destroy important dimensions of Christian experience. It makes no sense at all to speak of a totally individualistic Christian. Despite his insistence on his private experience, Bradford remains within the denomination. *Unus Christianus, nullus Christianus* (a Christian alone is no Christian). However, it also does not make sense to speak of a community without considering the personal experiences of the members of the community. It is precisely in the interrelation of persons (both human and divine) that the community of the Church is composed.

The primacy of the community experience needs to be emphasized, especially as it relates to forgiveness. The Scriptures acknowledge repeatedly that forgiveness and reconciliation are from God alone. It is "the blood of Jesus (which) cleanses us from all sin" (1 John 1:7), "nor is there any condemnation to them which are in Christ Jesus" (Rom. 8:1). The forgiveness of sins as a function of the Christian community is highlighted by two only apparently contradictory groups of scriptural passages. The first group points to the sacramental forgiveness of sins by God, but through the Church. In the Sacrament of Holy Confession the Christian expresses repentance in a very concrete and specific manner and receives assurances of the forgiveness of sin through absolution. There is a long history of scholarly and polemical effort to discredit this Sacrament as an authentic expression of Christian teaching. Yet, the empowering words of the apostolic absolution of sins found in Matthew 16:19, Matthew 18:18 and John 20:30 were rapidly followed in Church practice with the confession of sins before the spiritual leadership of the Church (Ignatius, *Epistle to the Philadelphianus* VIII, 1; Tertullian, *De Paenitentia* 9, *De Pudicitia* 18; Origen, *Second Homily on Leviticus*; Cyprian, *De Lapsis* 16 and 19, *Epistles* IX:1; XI:2). But it should be pointed out that the clergy mediator of divine forgiveness is a representative of the whole community. It is not an act of clerical supremacy which, of itself, exercises the power of forgiveness. Rather, as is seen in the Eastern Christian formulations of the prayer of absolution, the priest pronounces himself first of all a fellow sinner, who nevertheless calls down the forgiveness of God on the penitent. It is a churchly act, an act of the community.

But forgiveness is also a broader community based experience. It is not confined to the Sacrament of Penance. Practically all expressions of the community life of Christians are vehicles for forgiveness. In the early Church almsgiving was a prominent means of obtaining forgiveness (Matt. 25:35–46, 6:2–4). It was also an expression of forgiveness. "The greatest form of almsgiving is forgiveness of others who have wronged one" (James G. Emerson, Jr. *The Dynamics of Forgiveness*, p. 123)

Many of the other sacramental actions of the Church include forgiveness as essential elements, including the Eucharist which is given "for the forgiveness of sins" (Matt 26:28) and unction (James 5:15). Most of the prayer and worship of the Church implies an understanding of the Church community as a forgiving and as a forgiveness-receiving body. It is in this context that we understand the scriptural exhortations for the mutual forgiveness of sins by Christians. "Brethren, if a man is overtaken in any trespass, you who are spiritual should restore him in a spirit of gentleness. Look to yourself, lest you too be tempted. Bear one another's burdens . . ." (Gal. 6:1–2); "forgive us as we forgive those who trespass against us" (Matt. 6:12, Luke 11:4); "take heed to yourselves; if your brother sins, rebuke him and if he repents, forgive him; and if he sins against you seven times in the day, and turns to you seven times, and says, 'I repent,' you must forgive him" (Luke 17:3–4); and, "confess your sins one to another that you might be healed" (James 5:16).

In fact then, Lloyd Felton's representation of the community as the locus and agency of divine forgiveness and the experiential reality of reconciliation proves to be the primary reality. It does not eliminate individual experience or solitary righteous prophetic judgment on the practices of the Christian community, nor even the need at times for the individual to forgive the community. However, the latter have little meaning if the community of faith and commitment does not precede it.

Selected Bibliography

James G. Emerson, Jr., *The Dynamics of Forgiveness* (Philadelphia: The Westminster Press, 1964). Deals with the dynamic relationship of the "context" of forgiveness (grace) and the "instrumentation" of forgiveness (the human aspect). He sees them as in a vital tension.

Frank Gavin, *Some Aspects of Contemporary Greek Orthodox Thought*, (Milwaukee: Morehouse Publishing House, 1936), especially pages

358–393. An older work which describes traditional Orthodox teaching on the Sacrament of Penance. It is still useful as a systematic exposition, but newer studies (primarily in Russian and Greek) make significant changes in theological focus.

Stanley S. Harakas, "A Theology of the Sacrament of Holy Confession," *The Greek Orthodox Theological Review* XIX no. 2 (Autumn 1974), pp. 177–201. An attempt to bring together various dimensions of Church experience and doctrine on repentance and forgiveness.

Seraphim Papacostas, *Repentance* (Athens: *ZOE*, 1958). A translation of a popular tract on the life of repentance and forgiveness in the Church.

Alexander Schmemann, *Sacraments and Orthodoxy* (New York: Herder & Herder, 1965). An integrated theological approach to the sacraments from an Orthodox liturgical perspective. A necessary supplement to Gavin.

Carl J. Peter

Is it William Bradford who should forgive, or should others be asked to forgive him? This *either-or* question calls for an answer in the form of *both-and.* That is what the forgiveness of sins confessed in Christian creeds indicates.

One becomes a Christian through baptism, which has long been understood as an initiation into a new way of life. As a second birth, baptism involves a dying to the common human selfishness that tries to reduce all meaning, truth, and value to the dimensions of one's own horizon at any given moment. A solipsism feigning self-sufficiency lies at the heart of sin. Divine forgiveness brings about a conversion, giving expression and needed support to the individual's spontaneous but repeatedly frustrated inclination to break out of this isolation. God's grace, which heals in baptism, brings about pardon

---

Carl J. Peter is Chairman of the Department of Theology and Ordinary Professor of Systematic Theology, Catholic University of America. He was educated at the Gregorian University and received his Ph.D. from the University of St. Thomas. He has published numerous articles and is the author of *Participated Eternity in the Thought of Thomas Aquinas*. He is an ordained Roman Catholic priest.

by initiating a reversal of the self-centeredness of sin and by promising victory over the obstacles blocking the development of the social inclinations found in every human being. The rite of christening thus provides a concrete illustration of grace perfecting rather than destroying human nature. That rite may be performed for an adult or for a child by a community acting in his or her name. In either case it is a sign indicating that a life closed to the greater than any human self has been opened up and that the pretension of human self-sufficiency has been countered by an acknowledgement of the God of Jesus Christ, who is ready to give new possibilities of existence at every moment of life, even the last—death.

The *forgiveness of sin*, which is thus connected with *conversion*, is likewise associated with *justification* or the kindness of God reckoning a closed human being open because of faith in Jesus Christ. These three technical terms designate a difference in the life of a person made hopeful in a special way despite the prospect of death. One way to understand that difference is to consider the responsibilities assumed in baptism. Among the foremost is responsibility for one's neighbor in whom the Christian's Lord is to be served even though often unrecognizable.

William Bradford wished to show his concern for justice directly. He wound up suffering for having tried. If obligations arise from one's being baptized and forgiven, they often require conduct accompanied by suffering not unlike crucifixion. One who seeks to promote justice for Christ's sake is often put sorely to the test. But the paralysis of doing nothing by way of concrete witness to the gospel until all the information about immoral situations is in (it never really is), is as much of a pitfall as mindless enthusiasm acting without concern for likely consequences. Whether or not he acted out of explicit Christian motivation, Bradford did not wait until any and all risk in acting was eliminated. But what does his subsequent status imply in terms of the forgiveness of sins?

Other Christians owe him something; they must try to appreciate the values he sought to foster in his own questionable way. Is their commitment to justice mere lip service? Why are they silent when courts are not as fair as even the law demands? The disparity between the penalties meted out to Bradford and the millionaire underlines the need to make sure that the old, minorities, and the defenseless are not for their lack of political-economic clout treated unfairly. Lloyd Felton and a few others tried to alleviate the isolation of imprisonment. But many did nothing at all. Bradford served half of his three-year term while the millionaire who disrupted law and order ever so much more got off after only a third of an eighteen-month sentence. Now punishment for the violation of laws aimed at preventing anarchy must be equitable. When it is not, Christians who remain silent and inert need forgiveness from those punished. Because others did not share his concern for justice, Bradford has every right to wonder whether they should not seek his forgiveness.

But what about his own condition? Justification involves being accounted and made righteous by God because of Jesus Christ. But it gives no grounds for being self-righteous. Rather it ought to be accompanied by a healthy suspicion about the purity of one's motivation. Unselfish love (*charity*), may have moved Bradford to act, but was it his primary motive? We do not know. Neither perhaps does he. His exchange with the leader of the Puerto Rican organization shows he wanted to fight for justice in his own way. So he staged a robbery—risking his own life and subjecting the innocent teller to the experience of terror. May he not have acted out this drama, at least in part, for the sake of self-vindication, to show himself a doer and not merely a sympathizer? His protest affected his own life and the lives of others. His first wife may have died or left him—we are not told. She may not have been up to the heartache his sense of outrage made almost unavoidable for her without her knowledge or consent. He needs to ask God and others to forgive the suffering he has caused by acting without adequately considering the likely consequences of what he was doing. Both Protestant and Roman Catholic theology see a little bit of the less than good in the best of the just. The first speaks of the baptized as being at once righteous and sinful; the other calls attention to a day-in-and-day-out sin that does not destroy one's life of grace. However different, both point to a truth. Forgiven by God in baptism, the Christian assumes responsibility for action which will almost surely involve him or her in the need to seek further forgiveness. The remission of sins does not exempt one from the need to pray: "Forgive us as we forgive."

Bradford may well have learned how to be of unique service to fellow Christians as a result of having taken a stand about which he now wonders with good reason. If so, that lesson may well make a *felix culpa* (happy fault), out of the whole episode, which has had a fruitfulness that was unplanned and unexpected. For many Christians, it is precisely this kind of outcome that points to the Spirit of Jesus doing great things in ways man neither controls nor even foresees.

Because of the hold his past has on his present—despite the forgiveness of sins—Bradford may or may not be a good prospect for the ministry of his church. He may or may not be able to lead and not just be led by instinctive reactions. Is he a likely candidate to witness in word, sacrament, and conduct to the Risen Christ, who at times wants things very different from those desired by many of his followers? This is all very difficult to decide. Not enough information is provided. But one thing is sure. He needs to be forgiven just as others need his forgiveness.

It is important that he be brought to accept the fraternal correction he deserves for adding to the world's suffering more than Christian witness of its nature must. For this reason, Lloyd Felton's role is not over. Bradford's doubts about his future indicate that he still needs help. He will likely act irresponsibly in making plans (above all with regard to a possible exercise of the pastoral ministry in his church), unless he is willing to view his past from the perspective of this proven Christian friend, who should not be silent out of human respect. Does nonparticipation in the prison disturbance reveal a basic change in Bradford, or could it be evidence of a conviction that others may be out of step but not he? He should not proceed further without attempting to confront the forgiving Christ in Lloyd, who should try to bring him to see that his recent past must not become a pattern for the future.

But this will not suffice. Lloyd and the group that worked with him must remind the leaders of Bradford's church that orderly institutional procedures sometimes occasion scandal and provoke dramatic reactions that are often counterproductive. This is particularly the case when such procedures seem to confront injustice inconsistently or simply on the basis of worldy-wise calculations which rest on the premise that the history of past dealings with injustice must dash hopes for unprecedented success in the present.

In this way Lloyd Felton can represent in his person something of the Church to which recourse should be had when members of the Christian family offend one another as clearly they have in the case of the seminarian and the bank robbery.

SELECTED BIBLIOGRAPHY

Edmund J. Fortman, *The Theology of Man and Grace* (Milwaukee: Bruce Publishing Company, 1966). A helpful set of readings on the theme.

Jaraslav Pelikan, *The Emergence of the Catholic Tradition* (Chicago: University of Chicago Press, 1971). Presents the development of Christian anthropology with clarity.

Carl J. Peter, "Dimensions of *Jus Divinum* in Roman Catholic Theology," *Theological Studies* 34, (1973), pp. 227–50. Deals with repentance after baptism.

Joseph Ratzinger, *Introduction to Christianity* (New York: Seabury Press, 1969). See especially pp. 255–78 for a contemporary Roman Catholic treatment.

J. DEOTIS ROBERTS, SR.

Forgiveness is a crucial experience for the Christian. Without God's acceptance of us by grace, we would not be able to bear the weight of sin and guilt. All attempts to paint a rosy hue of human nature is contradicted by the reality of human practice. Realism in the realm of human life demands a way to deal redemptively with sin and evil in our midst, even in our hearts and lives. Where there is a facing up to the fallenness of human nature, forgiveness takes on a critical role.

JAMES DEOTIS ROBERTS, SR., is Professor of Christian Theology, School of Religion, Howard University, Washington, D.C. and editor of the *Journal of Religious Thought*. He was educated at Johnson C. Smith University, Shaw University, Hartford Seminary and received his Ph.D. from the University of Edinburgh. His publications include *Liberation and Reconciliation: A Black Theology*, *Extending Redemption and Reconciliation*, and *A Black Political Theology*. He is an ordained Baptist minister.

The case of William Bradford casts significant light upon a deeper and a broader meaning to forgiveness. Its focus is on the here and now, and it has largely to do with how we express forgiveness to others. So much discussion of forgiveness centers upon the vertical plan of the relation of the human to the divine that we often omit the full impact of the requirement for forgiveness in its horizontal dimension, that is, between humans.

This type of case is generally seen as being unusual—at least in law-abiding Middle America which affirms the nation as a church. But among the marginals in our society, it is not so unusual. It reminds us that there are serious social ills which must be set right and that the American Dream is not the Kingdom of God. It never is if our society is viewed from the bottom up and not merely from the top down.

William came from a religious family and he was a decent guy. He wanted to change conditions. His desire to be a minister and a social worker indicates his sense of vocation to the disinherited. In some sense his being black meant a real solidarity with the "least of these." He wanted to get involved in the liberation struggle, but he was not clear as to how best to fight for justice. The path he took identified him instantly with the class of blacks the System knows how to deal with. He committed a felony by robbing a bank. At that point he was at the mercy of the police, the court, and the prison system. He expressed his anger at the violence and the injustices against the oppressed in our society in a manner which robbed him of all his rights—at least those few he had left. The privileged treatment of the millionaire in the story illustrates that this is a society separate and unequal.

The bright side of the case is manifest in the friendship and counsel of Lloyd who was a minister-teacher throughout this entire case. Furthermore, the entire support group radiated the spirit of real concern. Their relationship with William vindicates our faith in human possibilities when strengthened by the grace of God. In their community, William was accepted. He justified their confidence in him through his sense of vocation in prison as well as outside. All in all, William is easy to forgive. It is clear that he made one mistake out of mere confusion and that society made "an example out of him," as it often does of the black and the poor.

Some would look at this account and derive only a privatized lesson from it. The real issue raised here is not centered around forgiveness for William, but around the need to change a dehumanizing system which causes "decent" human beings to lose their cool and be brutalized. The case illustrates the fact that conditions can become so repressive that no just person should be out of jail. When an Apostle Paul or a Martin Luther King, Jr., are in jail, it is the jailer and the system he represents which are under the judgment of God.

There are several things that concern me as I view this case. First, it is a good case to illustrate forgiveness between the oppressor and the oppressed in a social context of rampant racism. Second, both Lloyd and William turned out to be so acceptable. Lloyd is a very compassionate do-gooder who befriends William. We are not told whether Lloyd is white, but my guess is that he is a white liberal. He sees his ministry on a one-to-one basis. He is charitable in almost a paternalistic sense. There is no indication that he questions the injustices inherent in the society which explains William's anger and transgression of law and order in the first instance. Neither is there any suggestion that Lloyd is aware of the need to reform the legal and penal systems. Third, there is a lack of concern for collective sin and guilt. Lloyd seems unaware that our society is divided between victims and beneficiaries and that there are times when judgment is mainly against those who create the conditions of oppression. May it not be that Lloyd represents those who need forgiveness more than William? It may be that William's heart was in the right place even if we question the wisdom of his means of setting wrongs right? Fourth, William is such a lovable person. He has always been such a nice guy. Even while in prison he did those things of which we all approve. His seminary education and his ministry fall within the context of the white middle-class suburban context. One wonders if Lloyd and the support group he has assembled, which saw William through his imprisonment, would have been as patient if he had been persistent in his anger?

Where is the cross of the Christian experience for the supporters of William? They did not challenge the oppressors, they merely aided the oppressed. They were anxious to tame black power, but they are not involved in humanizing white power. They are anxious to return a lost sheep to the fold, but they are not aware that the fold is not fit for habitation. Perhaps the best witness for Lloyd would have been in the cell with William or outside in protest against the unjust court and prison systems. This is an aspect of the experience of forgiveness. To be with the oppressed in their suffering and to oppose those who control the unjust powers in our society is at the heart of the gospel of deliverance. Even William, perhaps because of the undue influence of ministers, teachers, and churchgoers, among the privileged in our society, does not seem to understand the deep wounds of racism, even in the Body of Christ. If he did, perhaps he would have chosen to combine his ministry with legal, political, or economic reform rather than social work. Social work with its handout approach to social ills is at best a stopgap measure. Without an awareness of the systemic character of social problems, social work fits so neatly into the status quo and becomes a type of social engineering in favor of the well off. Black and poor people, already humiliated, are rendered more dependent and lose more of their dignity. Furthermore, one wonders why William does not seek his ministry within the context of the black church and community. To suggest this does not imply that he should not maintain fellowship with Lloyd and others of good will. It is to suggest that his center should be where the oppressed are.

It seems apparent to me that the Gospel of Liberation addresses the whole person and all of life. This implies that sin is collective as well as individual and that salvation is social as well as personal. In the presence of the Omnipotent and Holy God we are unworthy as individuals, but our transgressions are also built into our institutions and our cultures. Racism is an example of an oppression which is rooted in the collective unconscious power in our society. Thus sin as oppression is horizontal—it is the root-cause of widespread human misery.

Where there is a *gestalt* of evil, the overcoming must be a *gestalt* of grace and righteousness. Salvation is a deliverance to captives. Oppressed and oppressors alike are in bondage to systemic evils from which they need to be set free. It is important to discern the signs of the times and behold God's salvific purpose manifesting itself in *Kairotic* movements and events throughout history, the God of Jesus is Liberator of the oppressed. The God of the Exodus and the crucified and risen Lord is in the midst of our struggle for freedom and he bids us join him.

Once this full Gospel of Liberation dawns upon us, not only the depth and scope of the experience of forgiveness expand, but our perception of what we are to do takes on a heightened dimension. Not only do we realize that faith without works is dead, but we work at problems from a different angle. We may not merely rearrange structures, but we must raise questions regarding injustices deeply embedded in the established order. Here I am raising the issue regarding the approach of the principals, Lloyd and William, to the dehumanizing experience reflected in the case. They seem to accommodate themselves to the existing order. This role is quietistic and their method is a type of pacification. The very foundations of an unjust order need to be shaken. Thus, in addition to the succor and compassion of the gospel, they need to discover its prophetic power which disturbs as well as heals.

This implies that both Lloyd and William should have questioned the unjust decision of the court which meted out unevenhanded justice in the name of Justice which professes to be blind and impartial. It means that their energies and efforts should have been expended upon prison reform as much as upon the rehabilitation of prisoners one by one. This implies that a model of action more conflictual than comforting would be more consistent with a Gospel of Liberation. Therefore, social and political action should have supplemented the pastoral and personal concerns in the case. The experience of forgiveness would have passed through confrontation to a deeper human understanding. Here the gospel would not have to be applied like salve upon a gaping wound that requires surgery. A skillful surgeon must open the wound and remove the impurities in order that restoration and healing of an enduring nature might be effected. What the experience of forgiveness implies is not a superficial experience of reconciliation based upon cheap grace and sentimental love. The forgiveness of sins—personal and collective—implies that we have asked the hard questions and that we have faced the tough decisions. It implies that we have borne our own cross and have been raised to newness of life having known in our own lives and through our relationships a liberating experience of reconciliation.

Forgiveness is at the heart of the Christian faith. God out of unspeakable love, out of undeserved favor on man's part, has loved us and reconciled us to himself through Christ. We are to extend forgiveness to others. If we are estranged from our fellowman, we should seek forgiveness from the other before kneeling at the altar before God. And yet there is no reward in loving those who are lovable, in forgiving those who are acceptable. It is human to do this. It is when we are able to forgive those who represent the tough cases—the angry, the disturbed, the alienated—that we demonstrate that we know the Christian meaning of forgiveness. It is thus that we experience the cross in our lives and become fellow sufferers with Christ. It is thus that we assume the burden of the disciple and experience the cost of grace. Forgiveness must be cast in the collective mold of social sin and salvation as well as in the personal context. Forgiveness must be related to our efforts to humanize the structures of power. Forgiveness from God and forgiveness among men must be practiced in a situation where we witness for personal and social liberation. It is only thus that we pray faithfully: "Forgive us our transgressions as we forgive those who transgress against us."

Selected Bibliography

J. M. Bonino, *Doing Theology in a Revolutionary Situation* (Philadelphia: Fortress Press, 1975). Bonino's books provides a good understanding of the context of Latin American Liberation Theology. He is a major Protestant voice amidst a host of Roman Catholic theologians. I am deeply inspired by this movement.

James H. Cone, *God of the Oppressed* (New York: Seabury Press, 1975). This work by Cone, *God of the Oppressed,* uses autobiography and the sociology of knowledge effectively. It is the first serious attempt by Cone to respond to issues raised by fellow black theologians. It is his most mature and his best work, but it does not break much new ground. Cone is the major advocate of a well-developed program of liberation theology using the black experience as its context.

J. Deotis Roberts, Sr., *A Black Political Theology* (Philadelphia: The Westminster Press, 1974) seeks to carry the discussion forward in the direction of theological ethics. A theology of power is developed, making clear the potential role of the black churches in black liberation. It points in definitive ways to a liberating experience of reconciliation.

———, *Liberation and Reconciliation* (Philadelphia: The Westminster Press, 1971) attempts to interpret the experience of black Christians theologically. On the ethical front, the work seeks to provide a basis for both liberation from racism and a deeper Christian understanding and fellow-feeling between the races.

9

"The Resurrection of the Body and the Life Everlasting"

Theological Introduction

THOMAS D. PARKER

The Creed concludes with two phrases referring to the "last things" on the human journey to God: resurrection and eternal life. Both concepts are found in the New Testament, although given different treatment in various kinds of biblical literature. The idea of resurrection is central to the Apocalyptic expectation for the end time, drawn from Jewish sources, and promised to the Christian by the destiny of Jesus after his death: "If we have been united with him in a death like his, we shall certainly be united with him in a resurrection like his" (Rom. 6:5). The idea of eternal life is a more general expectation of an existence with God (blessed future) which is the fullfillment of human life, especially for the Christian.

Various biblical texts contain different emphases in their teaching on last things. Some suggest the fulfillment of expectations for the Kingdom in the life and destiny of Jesus (e.g. Luke 11:20), some suggest the fulfillment lies in the immediate future (e.g. Matt. 26:29), and others that the Kingdom is inaugurated in Jesus' lifetime and is present in power in the community of faith, to be fulfilled in a time sooner or later (e.g. Acts 1). However, the elements of what is hoped for usually include resurrection of the body (the whole person)and eternal life. In Pauline and Johannine thought, the Christian already shares in these now as she or he shares in the power of the Spirit, himself a gift of the "last times," and in the sacraments and the word of promise.

The theological development of the two phrases resurrection and eternal life, is marked by a developing consensus weaving these elements into a pattern. The basic theme is hope for the Christian. According to the consensus Jesus Christ, after his holy resurrection, giving us an example of our own, ascended to heaven and awaits the end of time, when he shall come with the holy angels in judgment on the living and dead, according to their good or evil deeds. The Church which Jesus purchased by his work of salvation will then share in his divine reign. Looking forward to the joys of the world to come, we are to pray and wait for the completion of the work of salvation. When it is complete, the Kingdom will be delivered to God the Father, and all things in heaven and earth will be united into a life of reunion with God. Our true beatitude lies in that final destiny.

The idea that there are two destinations, one for the righteous and one for the wicked, finds expression in numerous church documents and theological treatises. The righteous and the elect will both be rewarded according to their works, declares the Fourth Lateran Council (1215), and each will rise in their own bodies to receive the results of their works. The wicked will pass into "perpetual punishment" with the devil and the good to "eternal glory" with Christ.

In various ways, this idea has found wide consensus in further documents, Protestant and Roman Catholic. It combines the idea of a judgment according to works with a separation based on one's relation to God in Christ (the elect) and eternal punishment or bliss. The symbols of fiery torment on the one hand contrast with those of serene joy and blessedness on the other.

For the medieval theologians the highest end of humankind is reached in heaven, where the blessed "see God" in a transforming vision that allows them to share in the divine glory and perfection. They see "the divine essence with an intuitive and even face-to-face vision, without the interposition of any creature in the function of object seen." They take great joy from this, and possess the blessedness of "life and eternal rest" (Benedictus Deus, 1336).

Within this overall picture, many variations were and are possible. Some theologians envisioned a "millennium," a time of earthly bliss when God's will would truly be done on earth as it is in heaven, while others thought more in terms of an individual passage into eternal destiny beyond the grave. The elements of both expectations are found in the Christian Scriptures. With the exception of a few theologians such as Origen, Gregory of Nazianzus, and Gregory of Nyssa, mostly Eastern, a dual destiny for creatures has been the norm of thinking about last things. However, the minority position has urged that salvation for any single creature is impossible to conceive apart from the salvation of all creatures in and through the incarnate Son of God.

A persistent theological difference between Protestant and Roman Catholic traditions developed over the idea of a purgatory, a place where residual and nonmortal sins could be purged from the faithful prior to the judgment, so that they may enter into their final state of bliss at the judgment. The Council of Trent (1563) made belief in purgatory mandatory for the faithful, while creeds such as the Westminster Confession of Faith (1646) deny it as unscriptural. Both traditions assume a time between an individual's death and the final resurrection; they locate the soul, alive and awake, in a "place" from which it comes to be joined to the body in order to stand before the final judgment.

More recent theological reflection has emphasized the universal and cosmic significance of the "last things," i.e., their meaning for the world as such, for the entire race and the whole Church, as well as the individual. In such a setting the Church will attain its full perfection only in the future, at the time of the restoration of all things. Then the whole creation, which is intimately related to humankind and achieves its purpose through persons, will be perfectly reestablished in Christ. The signs of the age to come are present; the Christian is called to recognize and further them. However, until the fullness of reconciliation is realized, the "pilgrim Church" waits in a communion with the Church in heaven.

Dance of Life

Tears streamed down Tracy Graham's face as she blurted out her feelings to Dr. Adams. "I don't want to tell my sister that it's all right for her to die. But if I really love Sara, maybe that's what I have to say."

In talking with Dr. Adams, Sara's doctor, Tracy wanted to piece together the events of the past few months to try to understand Sara's choice to leave the hospital. Without the artificial cleansing of her blood through dialysis she could live only a few weeks. If she continued the treatment, there was a chance she could live for at least a few more years.

Tracy, now seventeen, and Sara, who would be sixteen next month, had always been very close. It was now almost six months to the day when Sara had begun to lose weight and get very weak. The family doctor said it was a kidney disease and had recommended Dr. Adams, a specialist. When both of Sara's kidneys failed, she was put on a dialysis machine which hooks up to the blood circulation system and cleans the blood of impurities as the kidneys would. Dr. Adams began to look for a donor to give Sara a healthy kidney.

Tracy remembered the arguments with her parents. She wanted to be the donor, but her mom, dad, and Sara, as well as Dr. Adams, said "no." A donor was at last found, the transplant made, but after ten days of waiting the signs were obvious that Sara's body would reject the new kidney. She was placed back on the dialysis machine. Tracy insisted again that she be the next donor. As there was a slightly better chance of her kidney being accepted, the girls' parents and Sara

---

This case was prepared by Prof. Robert A. Evans of McCormick Theological Seminary and Alice Frazer Evans as a basis for class discussion rather than to illustrate either effective or ineffective handling of the situation.

reluctantly agreed. Three weeks later Tracy's transplanted kidney was also rejected by Sara's body.

Tracy slipped into Sara's room. She later remembered telling Dr. Adams how still and pale Sara had looked with all of the tubes and machines around her. There was hardly a sign of the laughing, joyous girl who had told Tracy from the time she was seven that she wanted to be a dancer. Dr. Adams had called Mr. and Mrs. Graham and Tracy into Sara's room for a conference. He told the family then that some blunt realities had to be faced. "After two rejections, we should no longer consider a kidney transplant as a possibility at this time. In a few days when Sara is stronger, she will be able to go home and resume many of her normal activities. But she must return here to the hospital three days a week for six to eight hours to use the dialysis machine. If not, her own blood would poison her.

"At the present time there is no medication that can take the place of this machine. However, there is always the hope that through new medical advances we will learn how to combat the rejection of an organ transplant." Dr. Adams had told the family in confidence yesterday that Sara might live only a short time even with dialysis because of the possibility of several complications that could arise.

The Grahams began to make plans for the future. At this point the purchase of a dialysis machine was financially an impossibility for them, and in their part of the state none was available for rental. Thus because the family lived more than sixty-five miles from the hospital, Mr. Graham, who ran a small business in Oak Town, began to look for an apartment much closer to the city. Tracy knew that the medical costs for Sara had placed the family heavily in debt. The members of their village church, many of whom had been regular visitors at the hospital for the past few months, had spoken of their prayers for her, and had already held two bazaars to raise money for Sara's expenses. The money had covered only a fraction of the actual costs.

Mrs. Graham, who spent her days with Sara in the hospital, had begun to take in secretarial work in the evenings. Tracy, now in her senior year of high school, said that she really didn't want to go off to school in the fall, but would rather postpone this and get a job instead.

Sara told Tracy how aware she was of the love and support of the family and their friends. She said she was most aware of the tremendous faith they had in things working out for the best. Recently Sara had spoken to Tracy several times of their common Christian beliefs and of her assurance of a life after death. Dr. Adams had told her how lucky she was to have access to the machine. But Sara confessed to Tracy that the idea of living through the machine was very hard to take, and right now to think about life without dancing and running was almost impossible.

Sara was quite thin and took many days to recover from her second surgery. She had gotten acquainted with Mike, a boy on the same floor, and had told Tracey about him. "He's just a little guy. He's really twelve, but he looks about nine. He's waiting for a kidney donor, but unless one shows up pretty soon, he'll need the machine to make it. I even explained to him what the machine does. But I overheard two of the nurses talking. Right now there's no space available to schedule Mike for dialysis. Do you know that only one out of ten people who need this machine gets a chance, and our hospital has one of the only machines like this in our section of the state?"

That was over a week ago. Then just this morning, Sara had turned to Tracy and in a clear, firm voice said, "Trace, I can't stand the thought of living the rest of my life tied to this machine. It's not living for me. I want to go home now—and not come back to the hospital. I've already told Mom and Dad. They are very sad, but I think they understand. But most important to me is that *you* understand and will support my decision."

Theological Briefs

Carl E. Braaten

What did Sara find in her Christian faith that made her free to die? How could she look forward to the future with the assurance of eternal life rather than the fear of death? Those around her—family, friends, and medical specialists—looked on Sara's predicament as a problem to be solved. They were willing to make extreme sacrifices to do their part. Not unappreciative of these efforts, Sara was able to transcend the level of ambiguity at which they coped with her "case." She found in her Christian faith a transcendent hope expressed by the Apostles' Creed as the "resurrection of the body and life everlasting."

A theological brief will follow Sara's faith beyond ambiguity to the level of transcendent hope. We could get bogged down in the ambiguities of the case, which call for ethical, legal, and even political responses. Each of these is appropriate in its own right. We could ask: Is it right for the family to let Sara die when medical technology could keep her alive indefinitely perhaps? Should Sara be asked to live an artificial life at all costs? Should the life of the living be diminished by the rule of technological power? Why are there so few dialysis machines in a country that makes so many bombs? Should the individual family be forced to bear the high cost of treatment, driving it heavily in debt, rather than the society in general? If there are not enough machines to go around, how shall we decide who gets to use one? According to one's ability to pay? But ours is a theological brief, and that means to reflect on what Sara found in her Christian faith relevant to her situation.

Carl E. Braaten is Professor of Systematic Theology at the Lutheran School of Theology in Chicago. He was educated at St. Olaf College, Luther Theological Seminary and received his Th.D. from Harvard Divinity School. His published works include *History and Hermeneutics*, *The Future of God*, and *The Whole Counsel of God*. He is an ordained Lutheran minister.

Like so many Christians Sara might have held to a vague belief in life after death. She might have learned something about the immortality of the soul in Sunday School. But if she reflects on the Christian faith, she will find something there about resurrection, nothing about immortality; something about the body, nothing about the soul. And that is significant. It is universally human to hope for life after death. The Greek philosophers taught that the soul is immortal. At death it is liberated from a mortal body to return to the realm of the eternal. This Greek idea of the immortality of the soul became mixed in with the Christian doctrine of resurrection and was passed on to the masses in some hybrid version as the shape of the Christian hope.

In the Christian view the person as a whole, body and soul, is subject to the rule of death. No part of the person is inherently immortal. "The soul that sins shall die" (Ezek. 18:20). So Sara could not have found her courage, freedom, and assurance from inside herself, no matter how deeply she might penetrate to the inner core of her being. There is nothing there that lies beyond the reach of the power of death.

So what did Sara find in her faith? She found the hope for resurrection and life eternal. But this is no mere abstract doctrine or creedal formula. It is part of a story whose main subject is Jesus of Nazareth, whom God raised from the dead on Easter Sunday. Christian hope in face of death is based on the gospel of the resurrection, because in this event God has made a new beginning of life that lies beyond the destiny of death.

We are not able to give an empirical description of the resurrection of Jesus. The New Testament tells us a story in symbolic form. Our knowledge of the resurrection is conveyed through symbols and in no other way. We cannot trade in the symbol of the resurrection for a literal historical account or an abstract metaphysical concept. But we do acknowledge that our faith would be empty and our hope groundless if the symbol did not point to the living Christ who, because he remains in death no more, can be our own source of freedom and joy in face of the most certain fact of our having to die. If we speak of the resurrection as a symbol, it is important for the Christian faith that we keep the existential meaning and the historical event of the resurrection in that unity of presentation which invariably characterizes the New Testament witnesses. "If Christ has not been raised, then our preaching is in vain and your faith is in vain" (1 Cor. 15:14). This position runs directly counter to the modern school of interpretation (Rudolf Bultmann and some of his pupils) which dogmatically asserts that "the resurrection itself is not an event of past history" and that "an historical fact which involves a resurrection from the dead is utterly inconceivable" (Rudolf Bultmann, "New Testament and Mythology," *Kerygma and Myth* [London: S.P.C.K., 1954], pp. 42 and 39). If these assertions are true, there would simply be no good news for Sara in the message of the resurrection, for in taking away the solid ground of hope in the living risen Christ, she would be thrown back on the sinking sand of her own dying self, to fashion as best she could a hope in face of death.

However, Sara can find good news in the story of the resurrection, in spite of her sickness unto death, because it tells of the victory of the living God over the last enemy of life—death itself. Her own enemy has become God's enemy, and the deadliness of death has been put to death, giving rise to hope for eternal life with God in Christ. This is the core of Christian eschatology, the doctrine of the last things, as it concentrates on the personal question of life and death. The eschatological future does not merely point to some time or other in the future when the world will come to an end. There is a reference to a real future of the world in which the time dimension is not lost, but that eschatological future is present already in all who share the life of the Spirit in the body of Christ.

Sara's faith is a sign that the power of eternal life is already present and effectual in the midst of her dying. As a believer she does not have to wait until she is dead before she can enjoy the qualities of eternal life, such as love, joy, peace, and freedom. These are the animating impulses of her spirit, even in face of the terrifying threat of death. In spite of the fact that death is at work in her body, and will soon swallow it up, she can hope for an eternal future that will bring to perfection what the Spirit has already begun on the near side of her dying. This means that death, after all, does not have the last word on the life of a person, but only the next to the last. The last word is that life is offered beyond death a fulfilling future in the eternal glory of God.

The only kind of knowledge we have of the "resurrection and eternal life" is one that is mediated through the symbols of hope.

Actually, we have to admit that we do not "know" anything about the future as such, or what lies beyond death. Frequently it happens in theology that eschatological statements from the Bible are converted into literal descriptions of things that lie in the future, and usually in some other world beyond this one. Because of the abuse of biblical eschatology, many theologians have dropped the theme of eschatology altogether and thereby permit the images of hope to become fossils of the past. We cannot accept the symbols of hope literally, and we perish without the vision they mediate. There is a middle way, and that is to interpret the eschatological symbols of the Bible as expressions of hope for personal, social, and cosmic fulfillment, grounded in the story of Jesus' resurrection from the dead.

The gospel of the resurrection generates a total hope, not merely for the immortality of the soul, but also for the resurrection of the body and thus for the whole person. Furthermore, a total hope that is moved by the boundless love of God refuses to set limits. No part of the creation lies outside the scope of hope. In the case of Sara, she could leave her friends, because she could anticipate an eternal rendezvous of all united by the love of God, though now painfully separated by death. There will be a resurrection of all the dead and a restitution of the whole creation now "groaning and travailing" in its separation from God. There could be no present celebration of eschatological peace and joy, if the hope of eternal life would extend only to a small handful of Christians.

We do not know anything about Sara's picture of the final future of mankind. But we would at least hold out for her the possibility of rejoicing in a total hope, not only for herself as an individual, but for the totality of mankind and the world. There is a universalism of hope, not an esoteric gnosis, nourished by the immeasurable love of Christ and an absolute faith in the power of his Father "who gives life to the dead and calls into existence the things that do not exist" (Rom. 4:17). This universal hope relativizes the finality of all dualistic images that split the cosmos into two eternally opposite destinies, either heaven or hell. There is neither hope nor consolation in the tradition that begins at creation with the unity of the world and ends in redemption with a cosmic duality unreconciled by the power of love in Christ.

SELECTED BIBLIOGRAPHY

Walter Künneth, *The Theology of Resurrection* (St. Louis: Concordia Publishing House, 1965). This book remains the most complete theology of the resurrection. It treats the resurrection as the essential problem of Christology and the key to the whole of systematic theology.

Jürgen Moltmann, *The Theology of Hope* (New York: Harper & Row, 1967). The resurrection is interpreted as the fulfillment of the history of promise and thus the ground of hope in the power of God to bring life to the dead.

Wolfhart Pannenberg, *Jesus—God and Man* (Philadelphia: The Westminster Press, 1968). Boldly relates the resurrection to anthropological ideas, to the methods of historical-critical reason, and to the classical Christian confession of the divinity of Christ.

Krister Stendahl, ed., *Immortality and Resurrection* (New York: The Macmillan Co., 1965). Contains essays by Oscar Cullmann, Harry A. Wolfson, Werner Jaeger, and Henry J. Cadbury. It is helpful in contrasting the biblical ideas of resurrection and the hellenistic notion of immortality, as well as showing various attempts at synthesizing the two in Christian theology.

CARL F. H. HENRY

Sara's prospect of imminent death brings to light her dismal and garbled view of human destiny. Not having gone to university she was probably spared the prevalent naturalistic philosophy that human beings are chance emergents in a purposeless cosmos, that all values are subjective projections, and that each of us moves daily toward the grave as the final end. Yet she could have charted much of her own experience to support just such an outlook: an incurable kidney dis-

---

CARL F. H. HENRY is Lecturer-at-Large for World Vision International at the Asian Center for Theological Studies and Mission in Seoul, Korea and is Visiting Lecturer at Trinity Evangelical Divinity School. He was educated at Wheaton College, received a Th.D. from Northern Baptist Theological Seminary and a Ph.D. from Boston University. He is the author of *Christian Personal Ethics*, *God, Revelation and Authority*, volumes 1 and 2, and is editor of *Baker's Dictionary of Christian Ethics*. He is the founding editor of *Christianity Today* and an ordained Baptist minister.

ease at age sixteen, shattered career and marital desires; rejection of two kidney transplants doomed her to dependence on dialysis for survival and family and friends to financial chaos. Moreover, much of what her associates said might also encourage the view that human existence is, after all, a gamble in a universe disinterested in personal values; while some win, others must inevitably lose the struggle for survival. Dr. Adams spoke of "how lucky" she was to be the one in ten to have access to a dialysis machine, and of the perpetual hope that medical science would one day overcome kidney rejection. Meanwhile to Tracy and the others he privately reported the strong possibility of death-dealing complications.

The Christian hope breaks through Sara's anxiety only intermittently and uncertainly. It is a biblically vouchsafed truth that God not only has made us for himself and for a destiny in eternity, but that he is even now sovereignly present and providentially active in all experiences. Sara's trust in the Redeemer should and could illumine her plight with the confidence that he who has pledged the highest good to all who receive his word and grace will not desert her.

One must not minimize, assuredly, the superlative display of sympathy and self-sacrifice for the helpless, as demonstrated by the family's uncomplaining response to deep financial needs, which counters the notion that all human values channel into self-interest. By holding two fund-raising bazaars village church members and friends likewise put hands to their prayers. This one mention of prayer is the only suggestion, however, that other than financial or scientific help is available for Sara. Sara does, indeed, speak openly of the "tremendous faith" of family and friends "in things working out for the best." But this sentiment is hardly identical with the New Testament certitude that "God works all things together for good to them that love him, to them that are called according to his purpose" (Rom. 8:28). Sara had, to be sure, spoken to Tracy of "their common Christian beliefs and of her assurance of a life after death," but without further elucidation this sentiment seems a slim line on which to suspend confident hope in the invisible world. Nonetheless, Sara's convictions kept her from crying out, as many do, "God, if there be a God, why did this happen *to me*?" In fact, assurance of a future life prompted this teenage girl to value personal destiny beyond death above ongoing captivity to a dialysis machine.

We are left to infer that the village church somehow initiated Sara's spiritual confidence; nothing is said about her parents' beliefs, nothing explicitly Christian characterizes Tracy's recorded conversation, nothing is mentioned about personal relationships with the Lord. Jesus Christ is not once mentioned in regard to life and destiny, nor is any decisive appeal made to the Scriptures.

It is clear that a phantom-faith, a dilution of the powerful biblical revelation, is what holds Sara from despair and ennobles her reflections; at the same time this minimal awareness cheats her of the full content, prospect, and joy of Christian realities. While suicide never enters her mind, and she decries perpetuating a low grade of physical life, she nonetheless expresses no certainty that God numbers her days. To be sure, to lay down one's life for another—even if only in the sense that Mike would now have access to a dialysis machine—represents a high level of value commitments, however far short it falls of Christ's vicarious sufferings for sinners (Rom. 5:6–11). But Jesus, it should be noted, also endured the Cross "for the sake of *the joy that lay ahead* of him" (Heb. 12:2).

Hope—even of an afterlife—is not really an adequate referent for a complete theological perspective; Christian beliefs need much more than common acceptance or mental agreement to ground them persuasively. Even if Sara's hard turn of fortune did not exclude her from God's general providence and purpose, how much more it would mean to know herself bracketed by God's love in the midst of misfortune and at the borders of death. The Christian good news is that despite our sinfulness God proffers personal redemption through the death and bodily resurrection of Christ and newness of life by the Holy Spirit.

There is no acknowledgment that even at sixteen Sara, like all of us, had defaulted in love to God and neighbor; her almost lifelong ambition to be a dancer suggests little more than a self-gratifying goal. While the Gospels depict the dancing of Herodius' daughter as so bewitching that Herod gladly paid for it with the head of John the Baptist (Mark 6:22), they tell us also that music and dancing greeted the return of the prodigal son (Luke 15:25). Sara apparently had not resolved the question of what she longed to dance (or live) *for*. Is there any evidence that her life had been spiritually renewed—that she knows life that is truly life—life that flows from the Risen Lord?

Has she experienced a place in the Kingdom of God even now; does she know that eternity comprehends the whole person, that the afterlife has both bodily and psychical implications? Is any window of gratitude open to the spiritual world?

God had, in fact, given Sara not only vigorous youthful years with many opportunities for spiritual grace and growth, of which she apparently took only minimal advantage, but had also entrusted her with sight and hearing, keen mind and undeformed body to use to his glory and in service to others. Does Sara really know what life and death are? For all death's powerful menace to mankind, it is not a second god, far less does it lord it over God; God is supreme over death and superior to all created beings and things. And if Tracy loved Sara truly and fully, could what she would "have to say" be reduced simply to "it's all right for her to die"?

The discussion of life in this case proceeds almost entirely in terms of physical health or temporal prolongation, and not at all in terms of its moral and spiritual quality. To be sure, physical quality is an important aspect of life, as we are reminded frequently by medical discussions of deformed fetuses and of terminal patients, and by Sara's comment that "living the rest of my life tied to this machine" is "not living for me." But being a successful dancer instead of being tied to a machine can also be a living death. And being tied to a dialysis machine might in some cases—should God will—be an incomparable pulpit from which to witness to the world about the issues of life and death. Has Sara really been delivered from a physical or materialistic misunderstanding of life?

This question is reinforced by the fact that the alternative posed by Sara deals only with something future. She misunderstands the Kingdom of God and salvation only in terms of the life to come.

The eschatological climax of life is, of course, a glorious part of the Christian revelation. That the summit of human felicity occurs in a blessed afterlife (Phil. 1:23) and not in our immediate existence (least of all through a reorganization of our present physical and material prospects) is just as essential a Christian doctrine as that the fullness of personal life now depends upon a saving relationship with Christ, a relationship without which one invites the eternal wrath of a holy God. The Bible, moreover, does not speak of the afterlife merely in terms of spirit or soul-survival, as did Greek philosophy with its notion that matter and body are evil; Scripture emphasizes God's creative purpose in nature and man, focuses on the divine incarnation of the Logos in a body—witness the God-man, Jesus Christ—and hails the resurrection of the Crucified Jesus from the grave as fulfillment of the Old Testament prophecies (1 Cor. 15:3–4).

Beginning with the Gospels the Bible speaks openly about the future resurrection of the dead. The New Testament epistles do not present hope as some open-ended sequel to the present but as a positive outcome guaranteed by existing realities and as already governing present expectations. Since the Creator's will and purpose sustain nature and history, to object to an afterlife on the basis of the ultimacy of natural processes is mere conjecture, as is also the objection to Jesus' resurrection on the ground of the supposed absolute regularity of nature; the evidence for Jesus' historical resurrection from the dead—predicted and taught by the inspired writers—is rationally persuasive. According to the New Testament, moreover, the Risen Jesus is the first-fruits of a universal human resurrection (1 Cor. 15:20). The resurrection signals the renewal of not just a part of humanity but of the whole humanity, of persons as they exist in this life. Hence the future life is bound up not with liberation from a body but with God's creative purpose and Christ's redemptive triumph over sin and sickness. It involves corporeal existence in a resurrection body—a somewhat altered body not identical yet not discontinuous with this present body, beyond vulnerability to sickness and death (Luke 21:38), freed from all the necessary cares and unnecessary burdens of this present life, and serving as a perfect instrument for spiritual fulfillment.

Had Sara known the Scriptures she would have welcomed more profoundly the alternative to "going home," that is, of entering the eternal abiding-places of which Jesus spoke ("If it were not so, I would have told you," cf. John 14:1–3). For already in the present her life would have found its true center in the risen and indwelling Christ (John 14:23). Jesus said: "Unless a man has been born over again he cannot see the Kingdom of God" (John 3:3), and he was speaking not of a deathbed future experience but of *today*. "Anyone who heeds what I say and trusts in him who sent me has eternal life, and shall not come up for judgment, but has already passed from death to life" (John 5:24). The apostle Paul wrote that the Kingdom of God is "love, joy and peace in the Holy Spirit" (Rom. 14:16). Eternal life is lived already in the present time, if Christ is central, and lived as a life that ongoingly receives its character from God and in turn dedicates itself to God's praise and service. The believer's life depends upon the reality of Jesus' death and resurrection. The Christian believer transcends spiritual death even before physical death, because of the crucifixion of the old nature and the birth of a new nature by the Spirit of God.

Those who cling to a sinful nature lose the full life God intended at creation, for at best they mistake real life only with normal heart function, respiration and so on. Sin and sickness quickly demonstrate that death and not physical wholeness governs man's fallen existence. Everything embraced within the orbit of this earthly life, said Jesus, must be hated for his sake (Matt. 10:37); Paul did not hold his "own life dear" (Acts 20:24) and the Book of Revelation speaks warningly of those who love their life unto death (Rev. 12:11). By readiness to lose one's physical life one is freed from desiring to preserve and prolong it as the essence of life.

The Christian revelation focuses not simply on the disaster of mankind gripped by sin, sickness, and death, but also on the tragedy of fallen humanity's rejection of light and new life—that is, of salvation and of a place in God's Kingdom *today*. Full life as the Creator made and intended it involves the unity and totality of man as a psychosomatic being and keeps in view accountability to God in the last judgment. The Word of God pierces to one's innermost physical and spiritual being (Heb. 4:12) and points him or her to fullness and wholeness of personhood. A resurrection body—never in need of food or dialysis—awaits us on the other side of physical death, first in some intermediate interim form (2 Cor. 5) and then in a final form correlated with Christ's coming and future judgment (John 5:29, 1 Cor. 15:23 ff.). But spiritual life instead of spiritual death can become a very real possession even now. Physical death is not simply a transition to the coming resurrection; it is that transition by which spiritual death becomes eternal (irreversible) death. But eternal life already here and now—a quality of life "fit for eternity"—is what Christianity offers through Jesus Christ, Savior and Lord. The possibility and nature of our present being lie ultimately no more in our personal power than do the possibility and nature of our future being;

they rest on God's sovereign determination to call what is new into being (Gen. 1, Rom. 4:17). Our physical death does not terminate God's interest in us; it is, in fact, his creative and redemptive power that make possible both our meaningful todays and our worthwhile tomorrows.

Facing financially bankrupting dialysis in the absence of any precedent for medical recovery, Sara has a personal right to opt out of medication. Can she do so in good conscience, however, unless she has come to grips with God's proffered grace? By personally appropriating the larger Christian realities of eternal life she can share with Tracy, the Grahams, Dr. Adams and the hospital staff, the church and community the assurance that Christ has given her a peace unattainable through worldly tranquilizers.

Selected Bibliography

Carl F. H. Henry, *Christian Personal Ethics* (Grand Rapids: Wm. B. Eerdmans Co., 1957). The distinctive revelational-biblical basis of the Christian lifeview.

———, *God, Revelation and Authority* (Waco, Texas: Word Books, 1976), vols. 1 and 2. General theological foundations for Christian outlook and death and life.

C. S. Lewis, *The Problem of Pain* (London: Fontana, 1957). The significance of pain and suffering in the Christian outlook.

Rosemary R. Ruether

This case focuses on the poignant drama of a young girl in the critical decision between death and quality of life. It is a decision that modern technology will more and more force into our hands. Death

---

Rosemary Radford Ruether is Georgia Harkness Professor at Garrett-Evangelical Theological Seminary. She studied at Scripps College and received her Ph.D. at Clairmont Graduate School. Her publications include *The Radical Kingdom, Faith and Fraticide*, and *New Women New Earth: Sexist Ideologies and Human Liberation.*

ceases to be an event entirely outside our hands and becomes something about which we must make a decision. In so doing we are forced to face in a new way the ancient questions about the permanent meaningfulness of life.

This question about the meaning of death catches the Christian tradition in a certain embarrassment. Until recenlty the Christian tradition had assumed that its message was, above all, an assurance of the conquest of death. "Death, where is thy sting?" cries St. Paul (1 Cor. 15:55). Traditional Christianity taught its members that they should always be prepared for death. This present world should be regarded as a "vale of tears." The highest Christian calling was to achieve a "blessed death" reconciled with God, thereby assuring a glorious transit to one's "true heavenly home." Many Christians even today regard churchgoing as a kind of insurance policy on a good position in heaven after death.

Liberal Christianity has grown embarrassed with this popular view of Christianity as the "medicine of immortality," not only because of the turn to this worldliness that began with the Renaissance and has increasingly affected the theological perspective, but also because biblical scholarship has strongly questioned whether this emphasis on personal immortality is, in fact, the primary content and roots of the biblical message of messianic hope.

We are dealing here with a mammoth shift of consciousness in the last few centuries, and not just a faddish restlessness. Christianity was born into and cultivated exclusively for sixteen centuries the world alienation characteristic of the philosophies of late antiquity. This world was regarded as essentially meaningless, a place of "testing" for the "soul," a sojourn of the pilgrim who is estranged from the higher world. Heaven was more real than earth. Beginning with the Renaissance, this world and its life began to be no longer regarded as an exile for a "soul" whose true home lay in the immortal sphere beyond the stars. Rather this earth and its life is our true life and home. It is the true arena of human fulfillment. Human fulfillment is not just personal self-development. It is a collective enterprise to build a new heaven and earth here in history. Traditional churches which still cultivate primarily the religion of personal salvation regard this shift as a great loss of "spirituality," a turn to materialism and "worldliness." But for Christians who have participated in this shift of consciousness, basic themes of biblical hope, which had been buried and unrecognizable in their restatement in the religion of personal immortality, began to reveal themselves once again.

Most major theologians from the beginnings of liberalism in the nineteenth century, and including the Neo-Orthodox writers of the middle of the twentieth century, have taken for granted this shift of consciousness. Preoccupation with assuring one's personal immortality came to be seen almost as a perversion of the Christian message. From Schleiermacher to Tillich one speaks of the communion of the finite with the infinite, the temporal with the eternal, not in terms of a literal eschatology of the soul after death, but as a quality of life in relationship to the eternal here and now. Kant and Hegel, the Social Gospel, and contemporary theologies of liberation focus on the collective struggle to conquer the forces of evil within history and to build a new world more in harmony with the ideals expressed by the biblical vision of the Kingdom of God. It is this larger horizon on the meaningfulness of the whole human project in history that is the context for the question about the meaningfulness of the individual human life. Our destiny is linked corporately with humanity, with the earth. These emphases allow us to reencounter the biblical framework for hope, which does not start with the individual, but with the community and with the created world.

In this comment on the case we have been given for the creedal doctrine of eschatology, we must ask about the selection of the story itself. This case is not our only theological problem for comment. More primarily there is the "case" of the selectors of these cases. Can we assume that this selection is neutral and open to all possibilities? Or do we not have to ask whether the selection of cases has not already predetermined the theology? By asking us to expose the whole meaning of biblical eschatology in a story that focuses entirely on the private and individual drama of death, one eliminates from view the corporate, social, and historical context whereby these larger themes of the meaning of creation can be discussed as the framework for individual life. The individual appears as an isolated "case" to make her decision, without a context in a community of faith, a cosmic project of life. To confine one's comment on biblical eschatology to the terms presented to us by this story is virtually to predetermine a theology of personal immortality rather than a theology of biblical hope. Therefore I propose to comment, less on the content of the story, than on the presuppositions for selecting stories to illustrate the theme of eschatology. How has this gap between the story of personal life and death and the story of historical community hope arisen in our history? This is our experience, our collective "case history."

The concern with personal immortality emerged as a part of biblical hope only at the end of the canonical Old Testament writings. This was a time when Persian and Greek influence penetrated the Jewish world. The Old Testament did not have a distinct idea of a personal immortality (apart from the shadowy idea of survival in Sheol) until the idea of the resurrection of the dead emerges in Daniel (12:2–3). Originally the Old Testament idea of future promise was historical and communal. It looked for a future blessedness, materially as well as ethically, for the nation, not the survival of the individual beyond the grave. Finitude was accepted as natural. The evils which are to be overcome are those of apostasy and unrighteousness which create misery and injustice in society. Apostasy breaks the covenant not only with God, but, at the same time, the covenant of society and of nature. Future hope is for the fulfillment of creation in a future era of righteousness and peace, rather than for a transcendence of the created limits of existence.

The prophets, to be sure, use highly exalted language about this future era. But we should be hesitant to accept the Bultmannian allegorical interpretation of biblical hope that speaks of every form of relation to transcendence as *eschatological*. We should use this term in a more precise way to mean doctrines of transcendence of death and transformation into a new immortal life, either for the individual or for the cosmos as a whole. In this sense the "new heaven and the new earth" in Isaiah is not truly eschatological. It is an exalted language for a vision of future blessedness within finite creation.

> No more shall be heard the sound of weeping,
> the cry of distress.
> No more shall there be in it an infant
> that lives but a few days,
> Or an old man that does not fill out his days (Isaiah 65: 19, 20).

The tragic insufficiency of life, the withering of the barely formed personhood of a sixteen-year-old girl, this is part of that "cry of distress" that would be healed. But one hopes for the fullness of the created rhythm of natural life, not for its transcendence beyond these finite limits.

When the concept of the resurrection of the dead emerged in biblical thought, the framework for this was the demand for the final vindication of divine justice, not the conquest of mortality. This is why there can be a vagueness in many of the apocalypses about whether all will rise or only those in special need of divine vindication. Daniel 12:2 says only that "many shall rise," while 1 Enoch 22 envisions only the rising of the unrequited righteous and sinners. The elect are not said to be immortal, but only to "live a long life on earth" (1 En. 25:6). Only gradually does an entirely different worldview penetrate Jewish thought, a worldview that regards this finite framework of life as itself inadequate and evil. A dualism between the mortal (however prolonged) and the immortal is introduced. It then comes to be necessary to see this present mortal cosmos itself as coming to an end, to be replaced by a different, immortal cosmos, as the abode of immortal risen ones. The historical messianic future is separated out as a kind of preamble. But the two continue to be mixed together. In Revelation 21:4 the resurrection takes place before the millennium and the saints reign with Christ for a thousand years. This is then followed by the "immortal cosmos" created after the "first heaven and earth pass away." The contradictions in Christian messianism and eschatology (as well as a root of the misunderstandings between Christianity and Judaism) rest in this building of eschatology upon a framework that originally had to do with the future historical fulfillment of the nation and the earth.

The rejection of not merely sin and stunted nature, but mortality itself, as an evil to be overcome, introduced a dualistic worldview. Materiality, mutability, death come to be seen as unnatural or belonging to an inferior sphere. Humanity is no longer at home on the earth or in its own body. At the heart of the inconsistencies of Christian theology is this unresolved conflict between a this-worldly creationalism and an anti-worldly eschatologism. Although Christian theology rejected a gnostic cosmology, its spirituality became essentially gnostic by the fourth century. Since the Renaissance, Western thought has moved back toward the this-worldly body-and-life-affirming side of biblical thought that located human hope in the finite fulfillment of creation, not in its negation. But our individualism still makes every particular death an abyss that places an incomprehensible question mark over this élan of life.

In Vine Deloria's book *God is Red* we are confronted with the more consistent spirit-nature unity of a religion which has not experienced this eschatological split. Humanity roots itself in the ecology of society and nature. It is the species, not the individual, that survives. Death is not feared because finitude is accepted. The individual returns to the bones of the ancestors to be reborn. We rise again in the future members of the community. The decay of the body is not the fearful, carnal house horror of the Western rejection of mortality. It is rather a graceful return of earth to earth to reenter the cycles of nature, to rise again in the new grain of the fields.

How might these larger perspectives on life, social perspectives and cosmic perspectives, give a different framework for facing the question of the meaning of life and the waste of death for Sara and for her family? When the outrages of prolonging our physical frame begin to contradict the meaningfulness of personal life itself, when our social ties with our family and society begin to be contradicted by the effort to prolong the life of one dying human being, do we really find the peace to accept our own death by rediscovering the idea of personal immortality? Or does that peace which comes to one, even one very young, who decides that they are indeed "ready to die," come rather from a deeper awakening of the older "Indian wisdom?" Is the triumph of spirit over death a matter of a literal prolongation of the conscious self beyond the grave? Or is it rather the ability to deal with death as a conscious, and therefore finally a *human*, act? When death itself becomes a reflective act, an act of conscious self-completion, our fears and the tears of those around us are stilled by an encounter with a deeper unity.

Christians do not know, and should not pretend to know, how God will bring to fulfillment the legacy of broken life and fragmented histories. Here and now the most we know is this: that at the moment when even the prematurely dying lay hold of their lives as conscious decision, then the resurrection of the dead breaks into history.

Selected Bibliography

R. H. Charles, *Hebrew, Jewish and Christian Eschatology* (London: Adam and Charles Black, 1913). This large volume by the editor of the Intertestamental apocalypses is still the classic treatment of the development of doctrines of eschatology in the context of messianic hope.

Vine Deloria, *God is Red* (New York: Grosset and Dunlap, 1973) chapter 10. This spokesman for the American Indian Movement provides in his book a major assault on the Christian emphasis on personal immortality, especially in relation to the understanding of Nature, that is worth considering.

Rosemary Ruether "Paradoxes of Human Hope: The Messianic Horizon of Church and Society," *Theological Studies*, June 1972, pp. 235 ff. This essay is the conclusion of an unpublished manuscript on the development of messianism and Christology in its Hebrew and Greek roots, touched upon in this brief.

Paul Tillich, *Systematic Theology* (Chicago: University of Chicago Press, 1963), vol. III, part V. Tillich's treatment of eschatology represents the culmination of one type of tradition which shifts the emphasis to the relation of the self to the eternal here and now.

Appendix: Teaching and Learning by the Case Method Approach to Theology

ROBERT A. EVANS

Since the case method approach to theology is at a relatively early stage of development, it may be helpful to conclude this work with some suggestions for teaching and learning by the case method in hopes of maximizing the use of this educational instrument. These recommendations are based on extensive case-oriented teaching experiences over the last four years in seminary and college classrooms, in adult education programs, workshops and retreats for churches of most denominations, and consultations or conferences with professors of theology, campus ministers, parish pastors, and laypersons of all ages and persuasions. The ideas are drawn from articles, verbally shared insights, and "operating principles" of Fellows of the Case Study Institute. There is no "teaching orthodoxy" for the method; however, there are some hints on style that appear to be constructive for teachers and students exploring its potential. Although special responsibility falls to the teacher as a resource in any method, the comments may be equally helpful for students since they will not only be the principal participants in the learning encounter but perhaps case teachers themselves in a classroom setting in the parish.

It is appropriate to cite immediately some of the written resources upon which these brief comments are based, both to acknowledge debts and to urge the reader to explore these more extensive discussions of teaching, learning from, and also writing cases. Thanks to the Staff and Fellows of CSI Summer Workshops, there are now over a hundred cases which are classified as "Church Related Cases." These cases are available virtually at cost and are listed in a bibliography provided by the agency which distributes the cases: The Intercollegiate Case Clearing House (ICCH), Soldiers Field, Boston, Mass. 02163.

The ICCH Bibliography on "Church Related Cases" provides a brief description of each case plus relevant data on author, location, time, and issues considered. Although no briefs are available for these cases, they may provide additional or alternative resources for class discussion or for a particular theme or issue not considered in this book. Other cases might also be used as an instrument of evaluation in which a student is expected to prepare his or her own brief.

Under the auspices of the CSI one book of cases which contains a selected bibliography has recently been published: Keith R. Bridston, Fred K. Foulkes, Ann D. Meyers, and Louis Weeks, eds., *Case Book on Church and Society* (Nashville: Abingdon Press, 1974). Another book of cases edited by three scholars of church history, Jack Rogers, Ross MacKenzie, and Louis Weeks, *Case Studies in Christ and Salvation*, is to be published by The Westminster Press in the near future. Although these books do not include briefs, they contain some cases of considerably greater length than those in this volume. This allows for a more complex case which is richer in data. The relatively short cases selected for the present work are not necssarily normative or even representative of cases copyrighted by the CSI. Teachers and students may wish to explore the variety of cases available. Also a series of articles concerned with "Case Study in Theological Education," including an annotated bibliography, is available in the journal *Theological Education* X, no. 3 (Spring 1974).

Resources on the case method which may be particularly valuable for teachers and students are "Writing and Teaching Cases" by Ann D. Meyers and Louis Weeks which can be ordered from ICCH, no. 9-375-830 and is also included in *Case Book on Church and Society*, pp. 209–219. "How to Study a Case" prepared by M. B. Handspicker is available from ICCH, no. 9-376-661.

Role of the Instructor

A case is a focused segment of actual human experience that does not have a predetermined conclusion or "solution." The problems of this life situation for a person or a parish do not, in the opinion of the editors or the case authors, have only one applicable solution or single theologically appropriate response. However, some responses are usually more adequate than others. The excitement and power of cases as learning tools is in allowing and assisting students to discover for themselves not only what decision the person in the case might responsibly make, but what decision the student would make in a similar situation and why.

The analogy between a case and a mystery story was suggested in the Introduction. A mystery has clues to be discovered and assembled in order to discover the solution. The case, similarly, has clues which, evaluated by the students' criteria and values, pose various "solutions" or alternative types of response. The case teacher in this situation is not usually seen as a dispenser of information or knowledge. Rather, he or she is a co–learner along with the students in analyzing the case and proposing responsible and creative alternatives of understanding and action. The first function of the case teacher is to foster a meaningful dialogue among the students, to highlight verbally or on the blackboard the issues and insights they mutually discover, and finally to assist by employing his or her own resources in the summary and clarification of the insights which arise from the discussion of the case. This is the role of the facilitator in the learning process. The responsibility for clear goals and objectives for a given class session, of course, rests with the instructor. The case teacher does not relinquish appropriate authority for guiding the discussion in this approach; rather, the instructor's resources and skills are reflected in the quality and rhythm of the discussion.

If the instructor allows the class to speculate far beyond the data in the case or get caught up in arguing about a minor issue, this may add to the excitement but impede real progress. One role of the teacher may be periodically to remind the class to be responsible to the material in the case, even if their conclusions quite properly move beyond the situation in the case. Some instructors find that simply to ask, "What evidence do you have that your suggestion might work?" keeps everyone honest. The student is then free to call on the case or personal experience to interpret his or her view.

Some case teachers report that a useful means of guiding a discussion is to record on the blackboard or on newsprint the essence of what a student has contributed to the conversation. The role of interpreting and organizing a participant's remarks and showing the relation to other points is crucial for the skilled instructor. One case-teaching style involves probing the student to clarify what was said or alternatively for the instructor to rephrase it and then check out the rewording with the student. The participatory style of the case method can be unusually effective in drawing out a personal response from students. Experience indicates the case teacher needs to be constantly alert for vulnerable forms of self-disclosure not foreseen by the participant.

Preparation for Class Discussion

Students and teacher alike have parallel responsibility to master the case facts and comprehend the situation. Suggestions for this process involve reading the printed case several times, making outlines of characters, chronology, and basic issues, preparing written summaries of options, or by contrasting theological assumptions or conclusions in the accompanying briefs. This latter suggestion might be taken only *after* a student has thought through his or her own response to the case. The instructor has the further responsibility to project imaginatively where the class discussion may go and how to get the most out of this opportunity for learning. Many instructors utilizing case discussion declare that competent preparation of a case is crucial and, if done thoroughly, may often be more demanding than preparing for a lecture.

Fellows of the CSI usually prepare a teaching note or class plan which lists: the central issues, the principal characters and their feelings in each drama, the major events and dates in the case, and the theological resources available to the characters as well as to the students. Thinking through the various paths the case principals might take, not to supply an answer, but to enable better learning in the form of clear questions or additional data, tends to sharpen the discussion. The suggested teaching note is seen by many only as an aid to the teacher's own creative imagination based on classroom experience with each case. Illustrative teaching notes are available on some cases and may be ordered from ICCH. At the conclusion of the case discussion many case teachers have acquired the discipline of adding to their teaching notes new ideas and insights suggested by students. The acknowledgement of this process with students undergirds the reciprocal nature of this educational method.

Teaching the Case

There are different styles of initiating a case. Some instructors recommend beginning with a survey-type question: "What is the situation in the case? What does the problem seem to be?" Such a question provides a wide range of entry points into the dialogue. The second step is to ask for a deeper analysis of the problem or situation. On other occasions the instructor may wish to ask for a conclusion immediately: "What would you do if you were Senator Berg, and why?" The reasons and rationale for the decision emerge during the discussion. Conflict of opinion and controversy is characteristic of and constructive in a lively case discussion. However, some CSI instructors have a working rule when teaching a case: "On any issue there will always be a majority of *two*—the teacher and a student under attack." Honest conflict is a great learning tool *if* the reasons for the difference of opinion are made clear. The case teacher may often wish to highlight the conflict by putting respondents in direct dialogue with one another.

Especially as a session nears its conclusion the instructor may encourage the class to build on the suggestions of one another, sketch concrete alternative solutions, and then critically compare these alternatives and their consequences. One value of using the case method with some regularity is that students and teacher develop skills of analysis and presentation. As students discover the benefits of interdependent dialogue their learning will be multiplied. The benefit and quality of class discussion increases, experience indicates, as all participants become comfortable with the method.

Additional teaching tools which have been employed by other case teachers are listed here to suggest the variety of ways in which cases can be taught:

1. *Role Play*. An exciting way to heighten existential involvement with a case and to introduce an affective dimension is to ask students imaginatively to assume the roles of the persons in the case for a specified period in the discussion. In a group role play or simulation

experience the instructor might, for instance, invite the entire class or study group to be the Session of the Ridge Park Presbterian Church as they discuss with Pastor Cornwall the meaning of evangelism. A dialogue between Sara and Tracy Graham on the meaning of life after death and how to handle the sense of loss and grief often has powerful ramifications for further discussion. In this controlled use of role play the experience of many CSI teachers is that rather than asking for volunteers it is better to seek permission from participants who give evidence in the discussion that they understand the issues and can identify with the characters in the case. This permission is carried through in the "de–roling" process following a five-minute role play where the participants' personal integrity is guarded by checking with them first: "How did *you* feel about the conversation? Were you comfortable with what you said?" When they have shared, the instructor may turn to the other members of the class to discover what they learned from the role play or how they might have played the role differently.

2. *Voting.* The dialogue may sometimes be focused or brought alive by the call for a vote on a controversial issue, e.g. "How many think Jim Barton was healed through his relationship to the charismatic community?" "Who thinks Don Richardson should continue his ministry among the Sawi?" Most instructors record the vote on the board and when persons are reluctant to take a position, a category of "undecided" provides a possible opportunity to test the impact of discussion by taking a second vote later. The dynamics of case teaching reveal that a decision point may be clarified by pushing persons to decide and to defend their choice. Obviously, even a choice not to decide in a case like "The Dance of Life" has serious consequences for Sara. Many instructors also use the vote to probe for implicit reasons and assumptions that stand behind a given decision. A second vote and a discussion that unpacks why any switches were made may illustrate how the class has really informed and persuaded one another as a community of interpretation.

Concluding the Case

In concluding a case or providing a "wrap-up" some case instructors find it constructive on occasion to ask students what they have learned from the case and from one another and then list these learnings as a communal summary. However, on other occasions the instructor may appropriately have important insights or an integrative way of understanding the case or issue that he or she has a responsibility to share. The pattern of identifying these contributions as the concerns of the instructor and thus distinguishing them from any suggestion that this is *the* solution, most case teachers find is an important element in the learning experience. Any impression or expectation that the class will consistently be "trumped" by the instructor tends to negate the learning process by diminishing the students' developing confidence and skill in theological reflection. Some instructors introduce their own summary with a style which says, "This way of thinking about the case interests me and so I share it with you. Try it on and see if it fits the case. If not, discard it."

Satisfaction in the case method approach emerges when the method begins to meet the goals of both teacher and student as a learning process. The editors are hopeful that your skill and sensitivity as instructor and student of the case method will increase with practice. Further information about instruction in case teaching can be obtained by writing to the Association of Theological Schools, P.O. Box 396, Vandalia, Ohio 45377, which sponsors the work of the Case Study Institute.

59812222R00159

Made in the USA
Lexington, KY
16 January 2017